INTENT UPON READING

To a child who is intent upon reading,

all books are children's books.

E. V. LUCAS

Intent upon Reading

A CRITICAL APPRAISAL OF MODERN
FICTION FOR CHILDREN

Margery Fisher

watts
international

FRANKLIN WATTS, INC.
575 Lexington Avenue, New York 22

Oxford Companion to child. Lit-

TO JOHN MASEFIELD

First published 1961
by Brockhampton Press Ltd, Market Place, Leicester

First American Publication 1962
by Franklin Watts, Inc.

Library of Congress Catalog Card Number: 62-10374

Copyright © 1961 by Margery Fisher

Typographical designer: Gerald Wilkinson

Contents

Foreword

The miller's daughter in the fairy-tale, counting grains of sand, had no more difficult task than that of a critic discussing the whole body of children's fiction. I have made my task easier by concentrating on the last thirty years, up to December 1960. It is impossible, of course, to draw a firm line at 1930. Where it has suited my purpose I have written about books published before this date, but there are some classic works which I shall be found to have dismissed summarily or omitted altogether. I have tried to illustrate general points rather than to write a definitive survey; and I have mentioned no books which I have not read.

There have been only two brief periods in my life when I was not reading some books for children – the first eighteen months, before I began to look at books, and my four university years, when time had to be kept for other kinds of reading. The first of my six children began to be aware of books twenty-one years ago. Between them and at different times they have shown an astonishing variety of tastes. I have pursued books which I have felt they might like and have read every book that they have read. Our collection has grown to such an extent that we can supply children also from our village with reading matter and we keep open house for any who like to come and browse and borrow. And for the last ten years I have been sole reviewer of children's books for a national monthly magazine.

My enjoyment of children's books has changed in character, but not diminished, now that I must read as an adult. Reading, to a child, is an occupation engaging his immediate attention and confirming his own experience in a memorable way: detachment is out of the question. I approach a child's bookshelf, now, with a sharpened critical sense and with a parent's selectiveness. So my opinions are of two kinds. Certain stories which were formative in my childhood (among them, *The Water-Babies*, Masefield's *A Book of Discoveries*, and *The Story of a Red Deer*) can never again be merely books to read; they are so full of associations that, re-reading them,

I can fancy myself a child again and can see them as a child would. I cannot read the stories of today like this, however much I enjoy them, but when I talk to children I can see in them the same experience. To keep in touch with the likes and dislikes of the young is essential for any critic of their literature.

There are classified reading lists at the end of each chapter. Dates in brackets refer to original publication. Those books marked with an asterisk are mentioned in the text: the rest are enthusiastically recommended. In most cases I have not mentioned ages for which books might be suitable. This is a tricky business, and the choice (surprising though it may often be) is best left to the child concerned.

The drawings have been chosen because they illustrate points I have made in the text. They are reproduced here by permission of the publishers in whose books they appear.

I acknowledge gratefully the help of the Superintendent and staff of the British Museum Reading Room, the Librarian of the American Information Service in London, the Book Information Bureau of the National Book League and Miss Eileen Colwell of the Hendon Children's Library; and especially my thanks are due to Miss B. M. Makepeace and the staff of the Northampton County Library for their unfailing patience and co-operation over a long period. I record, too, my gratitude to Olive Jones and Antony Kamm, who were concerned in turn with the editing of this book, for their practical and sympathetic help through all its stages. Finally, I would like to thank my son Crispin for hours of impatient typing.

MARGERY FISHER

Ashton, 1961

Chapter 1 | *The Way Back*

Is it good? Will it sell? What is it about? Will little Johnny like it or is it more suitable for Jane? There is less and less time to ask all these necessary questions as the output of children's books grows with every year that passes. Thirty years ago it was possible for a literary critic to look at those books written specially for children, and those which children could read, and see them as a whole. Today it is hard to keep abreast of new publications, let alone keep a sense of proportion about them. There is little time to look back at the classics, to recommend them to children who, following the habit of their elders, take the easy way out and ask for the latest story by So-and-so. This time and space have to be found. Some thread must be held out to the young reader as he wanders in the maze of volumes of today and yesterday. Some advice must be offered to him, if only because his reading is so much more thorough, so much more definite in its impact, than the reading of an adult.

Whether their books have been many or few, children have always read intensely. Seventy-two years ago an American critic wrote:

> . . . somewhere about the house, curled up, may be, in a nursery window, or hidden in a freezing attic, a child is poring over The Three Musketeers, lost to any consciousness of his surroundings, incapable of analyzing his emotions, breathless with mingled fear and exultation over his heroes' varying fortunes, and drinking in a host of vivid impressions that are absolutely ineffaceable from his mind. We cannot read in that fashion any longer, but we only wish we could.
> Agnes Repplier. *What Children Read*, in BOOKS AND MEN (Houghton Mifflin, Boston, 1888) pp. 64-5.

We must help the child to choose his books so that the ineffaceable impressions will be worth while; and this means that we must regard children's books, primarily, not as toys or merchandise, but as a form of literature.

In the last fifty years and more, many critics have reviewed the history of children's books and have discussed the psychology of children's reading. Literary principles (formulas and intentions, style and technique) have nearly always been incidental. And although some of the best evaluation of children's literature comes to us in this way, as it does in Harvey Darton's balanced comments in his definitive work, CHILDREN'S BOOKS IN ENGLAND, this is not really enough. We need constantly to revise and restate the standards of this supremely important branch of literature; constantly, because of the overwhelming number of books published each year.

The best full literary discussions of children's books are already out of date. Geoffrey Trease's surefooted and vigorous TALES OUT OF SCHOOL was published in 1949, and E. S. Turner's BOYS WILL BE BOYS, with its shrewd comments on school stories and periodicals, in 1948. Dorothy Neal White's ABOUT BOOKS FOR CHILDREN came out in 1946 in England (and is rather particularly concerned with American books, many of them not available here); her delightful BOOKS BEFORE FIVE is dated 1954. Roger Lancelyn Green's TELLERS OF TALES only takes us up to 1953, and his many stimulating articles are scattered in periodicals, some of them not easy to find. Frank Eyre's TWENTIETH CENTURY CHILDREN'S BOOKS stops at the previous year, and in its limited space this excellent pamphlet can only briefly survey the crowded shelves of the 'thirties and 'forties. In 1960 the Bodley Head launched a series of monographs on children's writers, and those which have so far appeared have filled a very real gap. Shrewd in literary comment and interesting in their biographical and bibliographical detail, these little volumes are essential for anyone who is studying a particular author, or, indeed, for any student of literature for children.

Reviews and book lists, certainly, make it their business to keep up to date. Book lists are not expected to deviate into literary criticism, but the very fact that they are selective gives them this status. Kathleen Lines's FOUR TO FOURTEEN, a magnificently catholic classified list, which now takes us up to 1956, has undoubtedly done much to help parents find the best books for children, and both the Library Association and the National Book League publish very useful lists from time to time in pamphlet form. Two periodicals, the *School Librarian* and the *Junior Bookshelf*, keep abreast of children's books in reviews which are long enough for useful general points to be made, and this is the case also with the special supplements issued by *The Times Literary Supplement* two or three times a year. These supplements, and the far too sporadic reviews in daily and weekly newspapers, deserve a better fate than to be used for lighting fires; for although reviewers are lamentably restricted in space, they can (and the best of them do) fit in the happiest and most stimulating ideas about the books they are discussing.

I join the ranks of this growing regiment of critics and reviewers with a lively sense of my debt to them. Without their work I should not have known where to begin.

These preliminary remarks may seem to herald a solemn book. I hope it will not be so. In the long run, the real motive for criticism should be the exchanging of favourites, the recommendation 'Try this, it's good.' Rash as it would be to suppose that this is the motive of all literary criticism, in fact I believe it almost always is in the case of writing about children's books. For a good book for children is not, and never has been, the sole property of children. C. S. Lewis has remarked that he is 'almost inclined to set it up as a canon that a children's story which is enjoyed only by children is a bad children's book.' There is a moral for critics here, as well as a prescription for good writing.

Enjoyed. That is the word to note in Lewis's remark. When we write about children's books we are in a special position. We bring an experience of reading to bear on books which are not intended primarily for us, in which we share by invitation. We should not make public pronouncements about such books if we do not like them or if we do not like the kind of book which they are perhaps failing to be. If we have forgotten the delight of sailing sticks down a gutter, we cannot really get far with chronicles of a four-year-old's day. If we think of horses simply as large and alarming, we should leave pony books alone. Enjoyment must come first. And then, we must try to remember what it is like to read like a child, with that pure, headlong, unguarded enthusiasm Agnes Repplier described.

And, remembering this, we must look for the virtues that a child looks for in his books—energy, sincerity, imagination. All this must be reconciled with the duty of a literary critic to state standards and measure books against them. The average child does not think, when he is reading a story, how good the style is or how well drawn the characters; but we know he will get more lasting pleasure from reading Walter de la Mare or Arthur Ransome than more sensational, superficial writers. We have to recommend from an adult standpoint: at the same time, we have to read with what knowledge we have of the tastes of childhood.

Obviously, any criticism of children's books is going to be prejudiced, not only by personal taste but also by the passage of time. I could not write in the same spirit about THE WATER-BABIES and AT THE BACK OF THE NORTH WIND. Kingsley's story was one of the formative books of my childhood. I must have read it thirty times between the ages of six and ten. When I read it now I am aware of elements which made no impression on me then—like the satire of contemporary ideas and events or the pattern of religious thought. But I can remember, too, my simple enjoyment of the descriptions of place and people, of those glorious lists of polysyllables. I can still read the book as a child would read it. Because I did not read any of George Macdonald's books when I was young, I have to try to find out at second-hand how he affects a child, and my children can only give me a partial answer. So, like all critical books, this will be a mixture of guesswork, analysis, partiality and fact, spiced, I hope, with continuous enjoyment.

I shall be dealing entirely with children's fiction. Factual books, which become more numerous and more competent every day, demand a book on their own. I shall leave out, too, any particular consideration of volumes of verse for children. In writing about children's stories one is, very often, writing about poetry; imagination takes its own shape, especially in children's books. Probably it is arbitrary to make a distinction between fact and fiction, but it makes more sense, at any rate, than a distinction between prose and poetry when we are discussing, for instance, a fantasy or a fairy-tale.

A curious form of snobbery is growing up today, the idea that the child who reads non-fiction is somehow more meritorious, more worthy of respect than the child who reads fiction. The librarian who really feels this is so is, I suppose, thinking only of the *best* non-fiction and the *worst* fiction. I can only hope so. All the same, it is a dangerous view, let it mean what it may. Sometimes a child wants to read a book with a factual slant, a textbook on electricity or trains or carpentry or cooking, because he wants to collect facts for a particular purpose. Another time, he wants to read a story, to discover not facts first of all but ideas, suggestions, pictures, imitations and versions of the facts he knows. He is not *better* at one time than at another; he is different. The child who looks at a photograph of a chair is learning something; the same child, looking at Edward Lear's picture of the chair and table walking together, is also learning something. The child who looks at a map of the Amazon basin, and the child who reads Ronald Syme's RIVER OF NO RETURN— why should one be thought of as more virtuous than the other? The wise librarian and teacher is making this distinction one of convenience only, but there still seems to be some need to affirm the value of imaginative fiction, and that I shall try to do.

Why is the child held fast in his window-seat, rapt into another world? Which books will hold him like that? Which books will merely occupy his time? In his early years a child is willing to accept any world the writer creates, not with conscious, conscientious belief in its truth, but by participation. The critic, as I have said, must try to achieve something of this whole-heartedness, while not losing his literary sense. But what about the writer?

A reviewer, perhaps suffering from a weekend surfeit of junior novels, wrote sadly:

> Writers should every now and then be rigidly kept from writing for a year. If at the end of that time they have a nervous breakdown from frustration, they should be allowed to write. If, on the other hand, they are quite fit and happy, they should be put on to office work, knitting, gardening, or some other pleasant occupation, permanently and full-time. This would be fairer to children.
> 'Something of Value'. *The Times Literary Supplement*, Children's Books Section, 4 December 1959, p. ix.

Let us assume, however much we may agree with this complaint, that the writer wants to write, and is not merely using a piece of experience because he believes it is saleable in story form. Why does he choose to write for children, and what is he setting out to do?

First, obviously, he is setting out to create a world to suit a child, whether that child is two or ten or fifteen—a world scaled down in an appropriate way from the adult world. He is using a set of facts and ideas in a certain way. Graham Greene, when he wrote THE LITTLE STEAM ROLLER, was using the concept of smugglers at an airport which, if treated in another way, could have gone into one of his adult Entertainments. Alison Uttley, when she wrote A TRAVELLER IN TIME, was using facts which would have been unaltered in themselves if they had been used in an adult historical novel, instead of in a story centred on a schoolgirl and the perceptions of a schoolgirl. Invented creatures and invented landscapes—Tolkien's Ents and Hobbits, the Snark, Palmer Brown's land beyond the pawpaw trees—work their way up from adult dreams and preoccupations and memories.

All these things are ready to be adapted to the world of a child, and they can be adapted simply by an intellectual effort; but anyone who enters the child's world, whose dreams and wishes in some measure become merged into a child's dreams and wishes, will produce a better book than the writer who writes, as it were, from the top of his head. One will write a story about a rabbit who runs away and gets into mischief: the other will write PETER RABBIT.

The author must be involved. He must somehow enter into the world of his book or it will never come to life. He must either go back to childhood, consciously or unconsciously, or he must share the childhood of young people round him. When he creates his imaginary world he must start with his own knowledge and work outwards. If he is involved like this it is almost axiomatic that he will not be writing to order but because he wants to, because (as C. S. Lewis puts it) a children's story is the best art-form for something he wants to say, 'just as a composer might write a Dead March not because there was a public funeral in view but because certain musical ideas that had occurred to him went best into that form.'*

The author's return to the world of a child is governed by adult compulsion, sometimes simple, sometimes alarmingly complex. Sometimes it is a compulsion just to tell stories. When Patricia Lynch was a child she was privileged to listen to Mrs Hennessy, one of the last of the travelling story-tellers. Her response was immediate and

* Three Ways of Writing for Children. I. The Proper Meeting between Man and Child: C. S. Lewis. (In *Fifty-Two*, A Journal of books and authors from Geoffrey Bles. Autumn 1959, no. 4, p. 5.)

complete. Her love of stories grew along with her love of telling them. The old woman's technique, her lilting vernacular, her easy relations with her listeners, her compelling formulas and repetitions, all sank into the child's mind and returned to her when she began to write herself. There is hard work behind Patricia Lynch's stories but there is also an innate, joyous love of story-telling. To take a different kind of case, when Mary Treadgold wrote that splendid pony story, WE COULDN'T LEAVE DINAH, her adult skill was fused with emotions revived from childhood. She wrote, she tells us, 'in a passion of recollection', after she had heard the news of the invasion of the Channel Islands. She wrote, too, remembering how, when she was fourteen, she had longed to be different, 'extrovert, with clear-cut and developed values, plenty of courage, and good at games—I having been the kind of child who had and was none of these things.'* This reconsideration of childhood was, presumably, the least conscious element in her writing, but it is what makes the story so good.

Sometimes the return to childhood is not really a return. Kenneth Grahame, for example, had in some ways never left the pastures and paths of childhood, and although this added to the perplexities of his adult life, it meant that THE WIND IN THE WILLOWS, behind its sociological comment, its satire, its allegory, its private jokes and portraits, is one of the freshest and most appealing books that ever engaged the attention of a child.

The 'escape' into humour of Lewis Carroll and Edward Lear, whatever it revealed of their temperamental needs, does not undo the fact that they strike straight at the hearts of adults as well as of children; it explains it. Biographical criticism can, of course, lead a long way from the texts in question; can even, sometimes, spoil a childhood favourite if we read it with a morbid preoccupation with its deepest origins. Harvey Darton has said the last word on this in his wise remarks about ALICE IN WONDERLAND:

There is no need here to articulate, as it were a skeleton, the alleged dual personality of Dodgson. It can be done, with a reasonable amount of insight, by anyone who is able to guess at the mind of a bachelor specialist in a precise subject, living in a period of accepted inhibitions, who suddenly, for a few glorious

* In CHOSEN FOR CHILDREN (Library Association, 1957), p. 28.

moments, sees quite clearly and lovingly all that mixture of credulity, acumen and innocence which we call a child, and becomes ageless himself.

F. J. Harvey Darton. CHILDREN'S BOOKS IN ENGLAND (Cambridge University Press, 1958 edition) p. 267.

There is no need to be alarmed or affronted by the idea that some of the best children's books provided escape or compensation for their authors. It is interesting to know why an author has tracked back to his childhood, but it is more important to examine how he does it and what use he makes of his journey.

The impulse that makes him write for children is, almost literally, a journey, for it will be more often associated with places than with people. For children, people take their place along with kettles and kittens, in a wide landscape that has its own order, and memory holds the key to this special order. Imagination and memory together pick out objects, people, atmosphere and impulses, on a principle that no grown-up can consciously work by. John Masefield has said that he wrote THE MIDNIGHT FOLK 'from memories of childhood, and from scenes and images that had been in my mind for a long time, and imaginings about places that had been important to me as a child, and are important to me still.' Before these memories were sorted and chosen for the story, they had their own order, their own relevance to a child's life. Very often the memory of a place is the motive force for a story in which it seems to take second place; but as you read and reread the story, the setting seems to spread and swallow the whole. It is so with THE MIDNIGHT FOLK, and with A TRAVELLER IN TIME, where the house, Thackers, based on a house Alison Uttley knew and loved as a child, dominates the story. Philippa Pearce, when she was lying awake in a hospital bed night after hot night, longing for coolness and water, began deliberately to imagine herself, step by step, back at the river of her childhood. So MINNOW ON THE SAY began, and, behind the lively characters, the ingenious plot and the rounded picture of the activities of two small boys, the Say flows on, through the imagination, never forced into the foreground, but always present. Her second book, TOM'S MIDNIGHT GARDEN, grew round a house she had known as a child, and I remember her remark that a friend had commented on the size of the house in the story, saying it must have been a mansion. It was, in fact, a house of ordinary size, but the writer, completely one with her story, had drawn it with a child's memory.

For Edward Ardizzone, too, the backgrounds of his stories, in words and pictures, are the backgrounds of his own life:

> Tim's house by the sea is a house we stayed in as very young married people at Walmer, near Deal. The docks and the ships and the sailor men—I knew them all as a very small boy in Ipswich before the war when I and my cousin Arthur played truant and spent our days mucking about among the ships and barges. We were always allowed on board, to poke our noses into the engine room and mess about all day long.
> Edward Ardizzone, speaking at the National Book League, 18 February 1960, on Book Illustration (in *Books*, no. 329, May–June 1960, pp. 94–5).

These backgrounds are visualized with the enjoyment of recaptured youth and the enjoyment of communication as well, for the stories of Tim and Lucy and Ginger were written for his own children, as the Babar books were written for the young de Brunhoff, as Alice grew out of a story told to three small girls, as Rat and Mole and Toad and Badger were the characters in bedtime tales for Alastair Grahame, as the stories of Teddy Robinson were told to a little girl about her own bear. Innumerable stories, particularly for small children, have as their beginning an easy, pleasurable alliance of adult and child. If narrator and listener are in sympathy, and if the narrator is not trying to demonstrate any imagined superiority, the book that comes from this kind of partnership will have some good about it even if it is not skilfully written, for it will have the qualities of sincerity and truth.

Of course there will be some adult comment even in stories which began at bedtime. The adult writer cannot shed all his prejudices and become, literally, a child again. His training and skill will have some value, and above all in giving a purpose to his story. It is the fashion nowadays to decry the story with a moral, but no story can be written without one, though it may not take the sermon form familiar to the child of the last century. The nursery virtues are to be found in Alison Uttley's tales of Tim Rabbit as they were found in the stories of Mrs Molesworth. The adventure story of today proclaims courage and honesty and self-reliance in a different tone of voice but no less unmistakably than it did a century ago. Among other things, the writer for children is an interpreter of life, especially of contemporary life, and in this sense the child expects that writer to inform him, to make categorical statements to him which he is not old enough to make for himself.

We may conclude, then, that a child's story must, ideally, be written from the heart and from at least some memory of and contact with childhood. It must appeal directly to the imagination of the reader, must create a unique world into which the child will go willingly and actively. It must, necessarily, contain some proportion of adult comment, but this must be delivered as from one intelligent individual to another, not in a spirit of condescension. And it must be written, within the demands of the particular story, as well as possible.

Reading List

(Books mentioned in the text are marked * throughout the lists)

1.*General works on children's books and children's reading*

*Bodley Head Monographs. Bell, Anthea. E. NESBIT. Clark, Leonard. WALTER DE LA MARE. Crouch, Marcus. BEATRIX POTTER. Green, Roger Lancelyn. J. M. BARRIE, LEWIS CARROLL. Meek, Margaret. GEOFFREY TREASE. Shelley, Hugh. ARTHUR RANSOME. Sutcliff, Rosemary. RUDYARD KIPLING. *Bodley Head* 1960.

*Crouch, Marcus, *ed.* CHOSEN FOR CHILDREN. *Library Association* 1957.

*Darton, F. J. Harvey. CHILDREN'S BOOKS IN ENGLAND: five centuries of social life. *C.U.P.* (1932) 1958.

*Eyre, Frank. TWENTIETH CENTURY CHILDREN'S BOOKS. *Longmans* 1952.

*Green, Roger Lancelyn. TELLERS OF TALES. *Ward* (1946) 1953.

Junior Bookshelf (Tower Wood, Windermere, Westmorland: annual subscription 17s. 6d.).

*Library Association (Chaucer House, Malet Place, London, W.C.1). Printed book-lists are issued from this association from time to time.

*Lines, Kathleen. FOUR TO FOURTEEN. *C.U.P.* for N.B.L. (1950) 1956.

*Lynch, Patricia. A STORY TELLER'S CHILDHOOD. *Dent* 1947.

*Meigs, Cornelia, and others. A CRITICAL HISTORY OF CHILDREN'S LITERATURE. *Macmillan of New York* 1954.

*National Book League (7 Albemarle Street, Piccadilly, London, W.1). Annual lists of children's books from 1957, occasional special lists, and articles in their monthly magazine, *Books*.

*Repplier, Agnes. *What Children Read*, in BOOKS AND MEN. *Houghton Mifflin*, Boston 1888.

School Librarian (Journal of School Library Association, 29 Gordon Square, London, W.C.1). Some articles of general interest.

*Trease, Geoffrey. TALES OUT OF SCHOOL. *Heinemann* 1949.

*Turner, E. S. BOYS WILL BE BOYS. *Michael Joseph* 1948.

*White, Dorothy Neal. ABOUT BOOKS FOR CHILDREN. *O.U.P.* 1949.

*White, Dorothy Neal. BOOKS BEFORE FIVE. *O.U.P.* 1954 (first published by N.Z. Council for Educational Research).

2.*Story-books mentioned in the text*

*Grahame, Kenneth. THE WIND IN THE WILLOWS (see Chap.4).

*Greene, Grahame. THE LITTLE STEAM-ROLLER (see Chap.2).

*Kingsley, Charles. THE WATER-BABIES (see Chap.6).

*Macdonald, George. AT THE BACK OF THE NORTH WIND (see Chap.5).

*Masefield, John. THE MIDNIGHT FOLK (see Chap.6).

*Pearce, A. Philippa. MINNOW ON THE SAY (see Chap.14).

*Pearce, A. Philippa. TOM'S MIDNIGHT GARDEN (see Chap.7).

*Syme, Ronald. RIVER OF NO RETURN (see Chap.12).

*Treadgold, Mary. WE COULDN'T LEAVE DINAH (see Chap.10).

*Uttley, Alison. A TRAVELLER IN TIME (see Chap.7).

Chapter 2 | *Pictures in the Nursery Fire*

The style of a child's story matters no less at the picture-book stage than it does later. Children first become acquainted with books by looking *and* listening; at this stage it is looking first, for most of them, but what goes in one ear does *not* come out of the other. It stays embedded in the memory. A child's taste in words, no less than in the visual arts, gets its start here, for better or for worse.

For these first years, though, the pictures must carry the story as much as the words do. Sometimes they will be predominant, the words merely acting as links. In William Nicholson's CLEVER BILL, for example, each picture is accompanied by three or four words at most; they are no more than captions. It is the pictures that tell you, with dash and colour, how the little soldier, left behind in the packing, runs across country to rejoin his mistress at the dockside. This is how a painter tells a story, and the artist/author Françoise is working in something of the same way. If a mother reads Françoise's neat little anecdotes about Jeanne-Marie to a three-year-old, she will find the stories perfectly shaped to suit him, but if the child is left alone with one of these books he will be able to follow what happens by the pictures. The scenes by the Seine, at a country fair and in the meadow are illustrated in simple blocks of colour. Booths, sheep, passers-by, trees and the little girl herself stand out against a background merely suggested. Gay and firm, the pictures lead the child into a whole world of miniature incidents and dramas to which the words supply an accompaniment.

Verbal description must be cut drastically in books for small children, for words tire them more quickly than pictures do. The wise writer for this age (Beatrix Potter is one shining example) reserves adjectives, as it were, for the illustrations, where innumerable small points, some of them sophisticated, can be stressed.

Phyllis Krasilovsky, in THE COW WHO FELL IN THE CANAL, tells in a series of simple statements how Hendrika floated down to a small town and was taken home by lorry. It is a starting-point, this text. The full story is told in Peter Spier's pictures, and the atmosphere of a Dutch town is established in a way which would have been impossible in words. There is, besides, the artist's comment, his attitude to this lively and improbable story. This comes out as clearly in his pictures as the author's does in the cheerful style of her prose. A commonplace tale can be touched to new life by this personal idiosyncrasy—and, for small children's stories, most often in pictures. I remember for instance the folk tale of the Turnip, as it is illustrated by Lewitt-Him in the volume of verse-tales, LOCO-MOTIVE, with its enormous, jovial humour expressed in washes of succulent colour, and the feeling of mystery which shines through Ray Bradbury's SWITCH ON THE NIGHT. This fable uses the most commonplace incidents of a child's life, and Madeline Gekiere's pictures enliven it with their deliberately simplified colour, including the device of the coloured page, and their use of abstract design.

Personal feelings communicate themselves so readily in pictures like these. To go back to a very different kind of illustration, take Kate Greenaway's books for children. The verses are laboured and sometimes absurd, but in her pictures she has recorded all the enjoyment, the gaiety and the busyness of small children. She communicates at once the sympathy of a grown-up watching children, and the child enchanted by her play. A good illustrator can always annotate the world of childhood for parents as well as for children. Adrienne Adams's drawings for Rumer Godden's IMPUNITY JANE express beautifully a child's absorption in small things. Jean de Brunhoff and his nephew have shown another mood in their pictures of Babar's three children, sliding down the banisters, dressing up in Indian costume, racketing about like any human children. Sympathy and imagination together have made miniature worlds which need pictures. It is through pictures most of all that small children will see their own inclinations and actions as if in a mirror; words would have killed these moods stone-dead.

What small children are looking for, of course, is a description of the world as they see it. The heroes of their picture-books may be trains or elephants or they may be children like themselves. The action may be familiar or fantastic. It is usually, in fact, a combination of the two. The appeal of Diana Ross's stories about the little red engine lies in the welding together of everyday and far away. The child follows with delight, in words and pictures, when the engine goes out into the world, adventuring as boldly as the child does in his fancy, challenging larger and more powerful engines, venturing to London, to India, even to the Moon, but always coming back to Taddlecombe, to his friends, little dog Hurry and the gamekeeper's cat. Very little of the background of the stories, the shifting of scene, can really be expressed in words; they are there to deal, simply, with the story; nor can the endearing personality of the engine be shown except in pictures, and this Lewitt-Him and Leslie Wood have done with superb success.

Diana Ross's chief contribution to these stories is the device of repetition which she has made peculiarly her own. Her stories, like so many others for this stage of childhood, are incantations, lulling a child to sleep and filling his mind with images and ideas which recur for his delight. Best of all Diana Ross's stories in collaboration with Leslie Wood is WHOO WHOO THE WIND BLEW, a cumulative tale in which we follow the fate of various garments as the wind snatches them away one by one from their disgruntled owners. The procession of odd individuals grows longer and longer. Rich old grandmother, corporation dustman, famous singer and the rest, they all follow the growing skein of errant clothes in picture after picture, and the fun gets faster and better as the words build up to a ridiculous climax.

Repetition, the multiplication of objects—this can produce pleasing patterns to the eye as well as pleasing groups of words. Wanda Gag's nursery tale, MILLIONS OF CATS, is a good example of this. As the old man selects cat after cat, accumulating a concourse of animals, the repeated phrase 'hundreds of cats, thousands of cats, millions and billions and trillions of cats' is pointed by the author's amusing designs.

Wanda Gág's work has always the quality of folk tale. It is at once fantastic and homely. Part of the charm of this tale lies in the oddity of the country through which the old man journeys, and part of it lies in the conclusion, when the battle is over and the lamplight shines on the happy old couple with their own cat, the most beautiful cat in the world because he is their own. The reassurance of domestic security, so vital for small children, comes across better in the

Drawing by Peter Spier for Phyllis Krasilovsky's THE COW WHO FELL IN THE CANAL (World's Work)

Below: Drawing by Reiner Zimnik for his DRUMMERS OF DREAMS (Faber). A design which depends on repetition pictures than in the words; any expression of this lamplit mood would be heavy and sentimental in words.

Children need not always see themselves in their own world. They need not always look at scenes where children are children. Against the safe background of nursery tea, the infants of Kate Greenaway dress up and copy the manners and modes of their elders. In the picture-books which Caldecott made for the nursery, the world is a robust adult world of hunting parsons and coy maidens, where children tag along and have a wonderful time; but in SING A SONG FOR SIXPENCE the world is handed over to the young. Here is a boy king, his crown set down on the table, earnestly counting his money beneath pictures of nursery heroes, while his sister rules demurely in a delightful nursery filled with toys. It is all a glorious game of make-believe.

Nothing pleases children more, of course, than to be made free of the adult world through picture-books. In Jean de Brunhoff's stories, Babar the elephant is, clearly, a small boy, privileged by a double magic to lead a human and an adult life. The text offers merely a plain statement of what the elephants do, but in the pictures the whole delightful invasion of the adult world is made clear. Celeste dipping her croissant into her coffee, as the pair breakfast in bed; Babar being fitted for a suit (and, like any child, riding up and down in the store lift); Celeste in her nurse's costume, tending the wounded elephants under instruction from the useful old lady; Babar and Celeste, wrecked on a desert island, setting up camp:

> Ils ont dressé leur tente, puis, assis sur de grosses pierres, ils mangent avec appétit une excellente soupe au riz cuite à point et bien sucrée. 'On n'est pas si mal sur cette île,' dit Babar.
> Jean de Brunhoff. LE VOYAGE DE BABAR (Jardin des Modes, 1932) p. 9.

The elephants imitating a small boy and girl imitating a bourgeois couple—it is an irresistible sequence. It is the same with Ardizzone's glorious picture-books about Tim and his friends. Here is the world he knew as a child, illuminated by his sympathy as a parent. Here all the dearest wishes of childhood come true. Charlotte learns to make pastry, Lucy has a real party frock, and Tim is the prototype of all small boys, squaring up in the post-office to send a telegram, spying on the mutineers, shouldering his worldly goods in a handkerchief, always resourceful, always cheerful, always with a tip-tilted look of concentration and curiosity. Now and then in Ardizzone's books we hear the authentic voice of authority: 'Well dash my wig. Boys, boys and a dog in the cab of my engine. Can't have them here. Impossible. Against Company regulations. Go away at once.' So the engine-driver, in NICHOLAS AND THE FAST-MOVING DIESEL. But the two boys do drive the train, and, like the succession of mayors and sea-captains in the *Tim* books, the railway officials give way to youth and pin medals on their chests.

Now this is not only a joke. The child is pleased to see another child doing grown-up things, and the effect is one of comedy rather than of humour. This comedy will lie, for the child, mainly in the pictures, so that a simple, short text is all that is necessary. For this reason I think Kathleen Hale's books about Orlando the marmalade cat fall just short of the top rank, though from the decorative point of view they are superb. She puts too much into words. She spoils her good jokes (built on the incongruous meeting of two worlds) by forcing them into words. The free, spontaneous, gorgeous detail of her lithographs does not need elaboration in the text, but it sometimes gets it. Not always. One of her best stories, ORLANDO'S INVISIBLE PYJAMAS, turns round the unfortunate baldness of the marmalade cat's hindquarters as a result of an accident with some paraffin. Grace knits him a replica of his own coat, so that he can face the world without embarrassment. And he does, until he meets a dog and tries to put his fur up. In the text, this is stated simply. It is elaborated in the pictures—first, of a dog rocking with derisive laughter at Orlando's smooth back, then of the same dog turning tail when he sees that the cat's fur has grown and that he is really in earnest. This is fine technique, for the joke is essentially a pictorial one. Elsewhere, Kathleen Hale adds unnecessarily to the pictures. In ORLANDO KEEPS A DOG, the wonderful double-spread (pp. 24–5) of Grace and her poodle hurtling across a snowbound landscape is redrawn in words:

They raced over ploughed fields that looked like white corduroy; past trees wearing mittens and jerseys of ivy; they followed the tracks of the rabbit round a snow-covered haystack, that reminded Bill of an iced cake. They were startled by what they thought was a strange beast with antlers, swishing his tail and stamping, but it was only Orlando's friend Vulcan, the horse, who was scratching his head against a fallen branch.

Kathleen Hale. ORLANDO KEEPS A DOG (Country Life, 1931) p. 24.

The comic items here, especially the trees with jerseys, misfire in words but are triumphantly amusing in line and colour, and there is, besides, the beauty of design, of the detailed foreground and the lovely distant view of a little town encircled by the river. The point does not need driving home in words as well as pictures. Children are more likely to appreciate the full horror of Mr Cattermole's supper, for instance ('a horrid mess of raw onions, peppermint-creams and fish') when they see it, in colour, and surrounded by other surrealist evidences of the recluse's housekeeping.

The earlier books about Orlando are much simpler. The artist enjoys herself making designs and lets the pictures carry most of the story. We know far more about Grace in those early stories, by seeing her take a carpet-sweeper into a pigsty or dip Tinkle carefully into a river pool, than we do later, when there are more verbal comments on her maternal devotion, her efficiency and her gentleness. There are, in fact, too many words in these later books, and these words express too much, so that we have a text suitable for an eight-year-old linked with pictures which are just right for children of three and four. Not that older children do not get a lot of pleasure out of Orlando; but the perfect Orlando age, I think, is four.

At the same time, picture-books must have a text, and this text must sound right. They will be read aloud, and therefore they will depend above all on good, easy, musical sentence-rhythms. The simplest sentence can have a good shape. One of the best books I know for small children is Alastair Reid's I WILL TELL YOU OF A TOWN, a poet's impression of a fishing town from early morning till sunset, presented in prose embellished by verse and by delicate line-drawings, all three mediums knit into a beautiful whole. There is nothing complicated in the language of a passage like this:

The day is ticking away, and the old clock, which has watched over the town for centuries, is counting the children on their shouting way to school. Six little fishing children from the corner cottage, five from the red house by the fire station, four from the farm, three from the white lighthouse, twins from the gardener's hut, and one alone, little Billy from the bakery, waving to his mother with a red woollen cap.

Alastair Reid. I WILL TELL YOU OF A TOWN (Hutchinson, 1959) p. 15.

Or of this falling close:

Swish, swish. The waves are hushing on the beach. Sleep, sleep. The dogs are dreaming of bones. The boats in the harbour stir slowly round and bump softly together as the tide turns. The seagulls fold their careful wings, and the chickens cluck softly in the still farmyard. Only the light in the lighthouse is still awake, blinking a welcome or a warning to any ships at sea, across the rocks and the chasing tides.

Ibid., p. 36.

This is the prose of a writer who hears the rhythms of human speech. Nobody telling a story, if he has any talent at all, keeps his voice at the same level, his words at the same length or his sentences in the same shape; and the writers whose work will live are those who have the story-telling gift, the true narrative rhythm. One of the most attractive tales to read to small children is E. M. Hatt's THE CAT WITH A GUINEA TO SPEND, a cumulative tale. An old lady decides to give a party for her twelve great-grandchildren (the roll-call of their names rings through the story). She sends her cat, Nod-by-the-fire, to do the shopping, with certain conditions and warnings; each of these is taken up and developed, and they are neatly woven into the quiet end after the party. The book is a delight for its originality and sparkle, for Leslie Wood's striking pictures, and for the crisp, rich style. Here is the story-teller enjoying words:

As Noddy passed by the rattling, creaking mill, out popped a dusty mill mouse and made him a mocking grimace. 'Poor Noddy!' she taunted him, 'aren't you a foolish cat to be off to town on a fine Spring day, when you might be chasing field mice among the meadow-sweet and mill mice among the meal-sacks!' And Noddy shook his head most remarkably quickly to and fro, which meant 'Of course I'm not!'

E. M. Hatt. THE CAT WITH A GUINEA TO SPEND (Faber, 1947). n.p.

Simplicity does not mean short, blunt sentences, and it does not mean short, blunt words. The opening of PETER RABBIT is simple; not basic. In her books, if Beatrix Potter wanted to use a long or an unfamiliar word, she did. Enid Blyton and others think that children are taxed too much if they are confronted by so much as a polysyllable, but generations of them, as young as three, have enjoyed without too much intellectual effort the end of Tom Kitten's adventure—'My friends will arrive in a minute and you are not fit to be seen; I am affronted,' said Mrs Tabitha Twitchit'; or Jemima Puddleduck's search for a 'convenient dry nesting-place' or Sally Henny-Penny's 'remarkable assortment of bargains.' It is learning without tears, if you like. It is also an enormous pleasure, the sharp shock of a new, exciting word; a pleasure for the listening child, and a pleasure for the adventurous reader getting at it phonetically and making a guess at its meaning.

There are authors who have deliberately catered for this particular taste. Leslie Brooke, for instance, in those ingenious rhymed tales, JOHNNY CROW'S GARDEN and JOHNNY CROW'S PARTY, and Ludwig Bemelmans in his comical verses about Madeline, which depend for their point on the apt placing of unusual words. But this must be as it comes. Every author must be free to write as he pleases, not tied down by fear that a child might not be able to understand what he writes, nor by any snobbish feeling that he has to show off. He only needs to remember that children are bold and experimental, that they like a mixture (in words and in pictures) of the rational and the irrational, the simple and the crowded, the known and the unknown.

In all these books, pictures and words are interdependent and of equal importance. But it is not long before the child who has been used to books begins to listen more than to look. Now he needs stories, still illustrated, but with the text putting in a stronger claim to his interest. This is the time (perhaps when a child is four) for the nursery chronicle, the picture in words of the child's life; an extension of picture-books, because it is still a simple survey of the life he knows. When he reads, or listens to, the stories about Minikin or Milly-Molly-Mandy, he is reliving his own life, enjoying the expected.

A simple survey, this is what children enjoy, but not an over-simplified one. It may sound easy to write a tale about a perfectly

"Once upon a time there were two huge great fairies"

I tell you a story? Once upon a time there were two huge great fairies——"

"Mary-Mary!" said Miriam. "Go away at once. You shouldn't have been listening."

"—and their names both began with an M——" went on Mary-Mary.

"Oh, do go away!" said Miriam and Meg.

"—they were called Margarine and Marmalade——" said Mary-Mary.

"Shall we push her out?" said Martyn.

"Take me away!" said Mary-Mary in Moppet's voice. "I don't believe in fairies—I only believe in mice."

Mary-Mary crawled out from under the table, saying to Moppet, "Very well, I'll take you away and tell you a mouse story." And she went into the kitchen where Mother was busy cooking the dinner.

Mary-Mary sat under the draining-board and told

⇝ 55 ⇜

page from MARY-MARY (Harrap) by Joan G. Robinson (illustrated by the author) ordinary day in the life of a perfectly ordinary child: anyone who has tried it knows it is extremely, painfully difficult. It is one thing to recall to yourself the pleasures of playing pirates or looking for hidden treasure, quite another to reconstruct, honestly, and without being arch or patronizing, the special joy, to a four-year-old, of feeding a stray kitten or walking in the rain. Few writers have done this without taking a deep breath and adopting an attitude, and this of course at once separates them from the child reader. One of the sterling exceptions is Jane Gross, who in an unassuming volume of tales, HARRIET AND SMITH, succeeded in presenting the daily adventures of a small girl and her cat with almost photographic fidelity and with no trace of affectation. Harriet talks to Smith as if he were another child; Smith behaves as he pleases, now like a cat, now like an odd but pleasant companion. The relationship between the two gives a new twist to stories which are very ordinary as far as their subject is concerned.

It takes courage to play the theme of early childhood absolutely straight, and it takes ingenuity to vary the pattern of tiny domestic adventures. Joan G. Robinson, in her tales of Mary-Mary, gets attention at once because of her heroine, one of the most amusing naughty girls I know in fiction. Diana Ross, in WILLIAM AND THE LORRY and NURSERY TALES, uses repetition and verbal pattern brilliantly. Doris Rust, in numerous stories for small children, constantly changes the emphasis in what are quite ordinary incidents. So, in ALL SORTS OF DAYS, the story of a rainy day is centred on the umbrellas in the stand, their personalities and their fate; it is through their talk that you see what is going on in the home. A foggy day is described through the comments of a ship's tug on the river, a train, a green car and so on. A sunny day has frogs for its chief characters, and a windy day the wind himself. All the stories reflect the ordinary everyday life that a child knows and loves to have repeated.

But it must be repeated honestly and with sympathy. It is no use talking down to children, in books, and it is no better to treat them with ostentatious respect. They must be addressed *as children*—as beings with their own values, walking beside us, not in front or behind. I cannot imagine a child of seven, or even of five, being satisfied with the tone of H. B. Creswell in MARYTARY, as he tells how a clever dog discovered two lost children:

Off he ran into the wood, and at first he did not find any smell worth telling about. Then he came to a quite nice smell, and he followed it, and it was a pretty white cat, but it ran up a tree. And next he met a lovely smell, all furry like Mummy's stole, but more; and he followed the smell along the ground and it was a beautiful bunny rabbit with black ears, but it ran into a hole in the bank. Next of all he smelt a most delicious scrumptious smell, nicer than anything; and what do you think it was? It was the fish bones that Johnny had thrown down, frizzling in the fire, far, far away. So the old dog followed where the smell came from till he reached the river. Then he put up his nose, sniffed, said 'Bow wow,' jumped in and swam over to the island. Wasn't it clever of him? H. B. Creswell. MARYTARY (Oxford University Press [1928] 1950) pp. 12–13.

But I can imagine a child of that age responding to this:

The door of Mr Parfitt's cottage was opened by a young girl in a red frock. Tony was relieved. Everything about Mr Parfitt's cottage had looked and smelt so very odd, that he would not have been greatly surprised if the door had been opened by the cat, with a white apron round its tabby waist. Olive Dehn. THE PIKE DREAM (Hamish Hamilton, Reindeer Books, 1958) p. 29.

The date of publication of these two books is important. Olive Dehn's is thirty years later than H. B. Creswell's, and in those thirty years our ideas about seven-year-olds have changed a good deal. All the same, there is still much sorting to do among contemporary stories before we can find books for this age where the author really shares the recollected pleasures and pains of childhood. We must throw aside puppies and kittens in favour of cats with dash and character. We must put aside trivial catalogues of nursery events and look for family chronicles with humour and imaginative energy. Above all, we must criticize out of existence books that adopt a monosyllabic style and an infantile manner. It is no use thinking of a young listener as infantile. It is true that he is still clinging to his own world, still seeing pictures in the nursery fire; the books he enjoys and needs keep him close to his own world, where lie affection and security. But, to him, that familiar world is always new and exciting, and the writer can keep it so.

Drawing by Edward Ardizzone for his TIM AND CHARLOTTE (O.U.P.)

Reading List

(Unless otherwise stated, the books in this section are illustrated by their authors)

*Ardizzone, Edward. LITTLE TIM AND THE BRAVE SEA CAPTAIN (1936), redrawn and with additional text 1955, LUCY BROWN AND MR GRIMES 1937, TIM AND LUCY GO TO SEA (1938), redrawn and with additional text 1958, TIM AND CHARLOTTE 1951, TIM TO THE RESCUE 1949, TIM IN DANGER 1953, TIM ALL ALONE 1956. *O.U.P.*

*Ardizzone, Edward. NICHOLAS AND THE FAST MOVING DIESEL (1948) 1959, JOHNNY THE CLOCKMAKER. 1960 *O.U.P.*

Ardizzone, Edward. PAUL, THE HERO OF THE FIRE. *Penguin* 1948.

Bannerman, Helen. LITTLE BLACK SAMBO. *Chatto* (1899) continuously in print. Best of all repetitive tales for the very young; other tales of Black Quasha, Black Quibba etc. are also popular.

*Bemelmans, Ludwig. MADELINE (1939 U.S.A.) 1954, MADELINE'S RESCUE (1953 U.S.A.) 1954. MADELINE AND THE BAD HAT (1957 U.S.A.) 1958. *Deutsch.*

Berg, Leila. LITTLE PETE STORIES. *Penguin* (Puffin Story Books) (1952) 1959. Illustrated by Henrietta Garland. Subtle humour, sure understanding of a four-year-old's pleasure in puddles, drains, his shadow, etc.

Bettina. PAOLO AND PANETTO. *O.U.P.* 1960. Exquisite tale of rich boy, poor girl and faun playing in a dream world: superb illustrations by the author.

*Bradbury, Ray. SWITCH ON THE NIGHT (1955 U.S.A.). Hart-Davis 1955. Illustrated by Madeline Gekiere.

*Brisley, Joyce Lankester. MILLY-MOLLY-MANDY STORIES. *Harrap* 1928, and many other titles, recently from other hands.

*Brooke, Leslie. JOHNNY CROW'S GARDEN 1903, JOHNNY CROW'S PARTY 1907, JOHNNY CROW'S NEW GARDEN 1935. *Warne.*

*Brunhoff, Jean de. THE STORY OF BABAR THE LITTLE ELEPHANT (1931 France) 1934, BABAR'S TRAVELS (1932 France) 1935, BABAR THE KING (1933 France) 1936, BABAR'S FRIEND ZEPHIR (1936 France) 1937, BABAR AT HOME (1938 France) 1938, BABAR AND FATHER CHRISTMAS (first published in France 1941) 1940. *Methuen.*

*Brunhoff, Laurent de. BABAR AND THAT RASCAL ARTHUR (1947 France) 1948, PICNIC AT BABAR'S (1947 France) 1950, BABAR'S VISIT TO BIRD ISLAND (1951 France) 1952. *Methuen.*

Burton, Virginia Lee. THE LITTLE HOUSE (1942 U.S.A.). *Faber* 1947. How the city grew round a country house: lovely pictorial procession of the seasons.

*Caldecott, Randolph. PICTURES AND SONGS. *Warne*, from 1878.

Chönz, Selina. A BELL FOR URSLI (1946 Zürich) 1950, FLORINA AND THE WILD BIRD (1952 Zürich) 1952. *O.U.P.* Translated by Anne and Ian Serraillier. Illustrated by Alois Carigiet. Verse tales from Switzerland with rich illustrations.

*Creswell, H. B. MARYTARY. *O.U.P.* (1928) 1950.

*Dehn, Olive. THE PIKE DREAM. *Hamish Hamilton* (Reindeer Books) 1958. Illustrated by Sonia Markham.

Drummond, V. H. MRS EASTER'S PARASOL 1944, MISS ANNA TRULY 1945, THE CHARMING TAXI-CAB 1947, MR FINCH'S PET SHOP 1953, MRS EASTER AND THE STORKS 1957. *Faber.* Gay, humorous fantasies, as pointed in words as in the author's pictures.

Flack, Marjorie. THE STORY ABOUT PING (1933 U.S.A.). *Bodley Head* (1935) 1956. Enchanting story of a duckling on the Yangtse: superb coloured pictures by Kurt Wiese.

*Françoise. JEANNE-MARIE COUNTS HER SHEEP 1955. JEANNE-MARIE IN GAY PARIS 1957, SPRINGTIME FOR JEANNE-MARIE 1958, JEANNE-MARIE AT THE FAIR 1959. *Brockhampton.*

*Gàg, Wanda. MILLIONS OF CATS. *Faber* 1929.

*Godden, Rumer. IMPUNITY JANE. *Macmillan* 1955. Illustrated by Adrienne Adams.

*Greenaway, Kate. UNDER THE WINDOW (1879) 1956, MARIGOLD GARDEN (1885) 1959. *Warne.*

Greene, Graham. THE LITTLE TRAIN 1946, THE LITTLE FIRE-ENGINE 1950, THE LITTLE HORSE-BUS 1952, THE LITTLE STEAM-ROLLER 1953. *Parrish.* Illustrated by Dorothy Craigie. Crooks and spirited vehicles in lively tales.

*Gross, Jane. HARRIET AND SMITH. *Hulton* 1958. Illustrated by Paddie Spratley.

*Hale, Kathleen. ORLANDO THE MARMALADE CAT: A CAMPING HOLIDAY 1938, ORLANDO THE MARMALADE CAT BUYS A FARM 1942, ORLANDO THE MARMALADE CAT: A TRIP ABROAD 1949, ORLANDO THE MARMALADE CAT: A SEASIDE HOLIDAY 1952, ORLANDO THE MARMALADE CAT: HIS SILVER WEDDING 1944, ORLANDO BECOMES A DOCTOR 1944, ORLANDO KEEPS A DOG 1949. *Country Life.*

Hale, Kathleen. ORLANDO THE JUDGE 1950, ORLANDO'S ZOO 1954, ORLANDO'S MAGIC CARPET 1958, THE FRISKY HOUSEWIFE 1959. *Murray* (Harlequin Books).

Hale, Kathleen. ORLANDO'S HOME LIFE 1942, ORLANDO'S EVENING OUT 1941, ORLANDO'S INVISIBLE PYJAMAS 1947. *Penguin.*

*Hatt, E. M. THE CAT WITH A GUINEA TO SPEND. *Faber* 1947.

*Hillyard, Mary D. MINIKIN'S VISIT 1953, MINIKIN'S NEW HOME 1954, MINIKIN AND HER FRIENDS 1955, TIMOTHY, MINIKIN AND ALL 1956, A TREAT FOR MINIKIN 1958. *Dent.* Illustrated by A. H. Watson.

Jones, Harold. THE VISIT TO THE FARM 1941, THE ENCHANTED NIGHT 1947. *Faber.* Charming, rather mannered tales of small girls.

Kaye, Geraldine. THE BOY WHO WANTED TO GO FISHING. *Methuen* 1960. Simple tales of two small children in Malaya, sliding from everyday to glimpses of the supernatural. Exquisite drawings by Peggy Fortnum.

Kellway, Mary. HAPPY DAYS. *Hutchinson* 1959. Illustrated by Sheila Rose. Red-letter days of a five-year-old who lives by the sea.

*Krasilovsky, Phyllis. THE COW WHO FELL IN THE CANAL (1957 U.S.A.). *World's Work* 1958. Illustrated by Peter Spier.

*Lewitt-Him. LOCOMOTIVE. *Minerva Publishing Co.* 1939. Adapted from the Polish by Bernard Gutteridge and W. J. Pearce.

Lewitt-Him. THE FOOTBALL'S REVOLT (1939). *Sylvan Press, Nicholson and Watson* 1944. Humour, fantasy, odd bright pictures.

Lewitt-Him. FIVE SILLY CATS. *Minerva Publishing Co.* 1944. Cumulative tale for the very young.

McCloskey, Robert. MAKE WAY FOR DUCKLINGS. *Viking*, New York 1941. Family of ducks reared in Boston city: enchanting and amusing pictures.

*Nicholson, Sir William. CLEVER BILL (1926). *Faber* 1958.

*Potter, Beatrix. THE TALE OF PETER RABBIT. *Privately printed* 1900. *Warne* 1902, continuously in print; as are the many other titles.

*Reid, Alastair. I WILL TELL YOU OF A TOWN. *Hutchinson* 1959. Illustrated by W. Lorraine.

*Robinson, Joan G. MARY-MARY 1957, MORE MARY-MARY 1958, MADAME MARY-MARY 1960. *Harrap.*

*Ross, Diana. THE LITTLE RED ENGINE GETS A NAME. *Faber* 1942. Illustrated by Lewitt-Him.

*Ross, Diana. THE STORY OF THE LITTLE RED ENGINE 1945, THE LITTLE RED ENGINE GOES TO MARKET 1946, THE LITTLE RED ENGINE GOES TO TOWN 1952, THE LITTLE RED ENGINE GOES TRAVELLING 1955, THE LITTLE RED ENGINE AND THE ROCKET 1956, THE LITTLE RED ENGINE GOES HOME 1958. *Faber.* Illustrated by Leslie Wood.

*Ross, Diana. NURSERY TALES 1944, WILLIAM AND THE LORRY 1956. *Faber.* Illustrated by Irene Hawkins.

*Ross, Diana. WHOO WHOO THE WIND BLEW. *Faber* 1946. Illustrated by Leslie Wood.

*Rust, Doris. A WEEK OF STORIES 1953, A STORY A DAY 1954, ALL SORTS OF DAYS 1955. *Faber.* Illustrated by Shirley Hughes.

Sisson, Rosemary Anne. MR NOBODY. *Macmillan* 1956. Illustrated by Rosamond Stokes. Cumulative and repetitive tales with a slight flavour of fantasy.

*Zimnik, Reiner. THE PROUD WHITE CIRCUS HORSE (1956 Zürich) 1958, translated by E. M. Hatt. JONAH THE FISHERMAN (1954 Germany) 1957, DRUMMERS OF DREAMS (1958 Germany) 1960, translated by Richard and Clara Winston. *Faber.* Stories with a moral, decorated with the author's sharp, fascinating drawings.

Chapter 3 | *There and Back by Tricycle*

So far the young reader has had it all his own way. He has been the hero of his own bedside story, time and again, and he is still the hero even when the story takes an improving turn. Nursery morals make themselves felt gently through many picture-book characters, from Kate Greenaway's well-behaved exemplars to that industrious and domesticated pair, Babar and Celeste; and, more flatteringly, through the mischievous and ingenious monkey, Zozo, in Harry Rey's stories, as he calls up the fire-station, falls into a pudding mixture and knocks himself out with ether at the hospital. The charm of Zozo is not that he is a naughty boy, but that he is a naughty monkey. Sin and retribution are felt indirectly and the lesson is put a stage further away from the child, who is free to enjoy the fun. Toys, in particular, are useful scapegoats as well as attractive subjects for a story.

The classic example, Carlo Collodi's PINOCCHIO, with its irresistible jumble of virtuous improving fairies and mischievous boys, is still on the fringe of the overtly moral period; it first appeared in England in 1892; but the story has never lost its appeal for children, though they are now less accustomed to straight moralizing, because the author writes with such joviality and lets his sympathy for Pinocchio come out so clearly through the moral. This nursery classic makes a curious contrast with a counterpart of the present day, MONKEY BEHAVE by Margaret Behrens, a lively tale with a toy monkey standing all through between a boy and his mischief. Here the moral is introduced in a very different fashion. Behind the book is all the weight of Freudian psychology; the child must be persuaded, studied, cajoled. A vade-mecum for modern parents, this is also a most amusing story, and few children will realize, when they first read it, that, like Pinocchio, it is an oblique study of a boy growing up and learning to live with his fellows.

Stories about toys give children a wonderful chance to be naughty by proxy. They also give them a delightful miniature picture of a domestic world. The little girl who first listened to the tales of Teddy Robinson, and the countless little girls who have followed her, see their own world dramatized. Teddy Robinson does everything that young Deborah does (and the author's delightful drawings make you believe this). As she imitates her elders, camping, cooking, shopping, visiting, so her toy, with the bumbling humour of all teddy bears, imitates her. Whether read aloud to a three-year-old or read word by laborious word by a forward five, stories like these provide safety and excitement at the same time.

Helen Clare gives children a different kind of pleasure in her stories of the five dolls, for young Elizabeth Small is able to shrink and take part in the minute contrivances of her own dolls' house. When she enters that tiny portal she ceases to be a child. She becomes instead a visitor, behaving with decorum and politeness. She may no longer move her dolls about to suit her whim, but must accept them as they are, conceited Vanessa, kindly Jane, Jacqueline with her few words of English, and all. When the front of the dolls' house is taken off, it shows a tiny version of the adult world, and the dolls serve as models, as it were, for the child whose life is broadening before her. It is for the advantage of this view of life, I am sure, that Rumer Godden has chosen dolls as the central characters of many of her fables for children. Candy Floss, the mascot of a coconut-shy; Impunity Jane, a Victorian pocket doll with the spirit of a buccaneer; gentle Holly in the Aylesbury toyshop—they have personality as well as appearance. Above all, there is THE DOLLS' HOUSE. This is a miniature novel, a tale full of situations that come frighteningly near those of adult life. Totty, the farthing doll, in her contest with the sinister Marchpane, is as interesting to an adult reader as to a child, and for different reasons. A child watches the drama entranced, dotes on little Apple, holds his breath to see what Marchpane will think of next, despairs for feather-headed Mrs Plantagenet. The adult catches echoes of domestic discord everywhere, admires the surreptitious satire of the story, and admires, too, the impression of stiff shrewdness which the author gives to her dolls. Like the family in Edward Bawden's lithograph, THE DOLLS AT HOME, they behave exactly *like* dolls pretending to be people.

So that, while it might seem that stories about toys were bound to keep a child within the nursery walls, in fact they can very easily take him outside them. Sometimes the adult note is struck only irregularly. A. A. Milne, in his stories of Pooh, uses some of his characters for satire. Owl and Kanga and, most of all, Eeyore, belong properly with all those animals, from Æsop's dog down to George Orwell's pig, who have given a devastating imitation of human temperaments. Lightly handled (they are toys, after all), Milne's little creatures can sometimes send a shiver down your spine. At the same time, Pooh and Piglet are facets of the child, and Pooh's house brings the same domestic pleasure to a child reader as a dolls' house does. So far, so good. The snag is that Milne, though he writes easily and with charm, does not seem to me entirely at home in the child's world.

Pooh belongs to the period of nannies and nurseries, when a parent was a parent, and, however friendly father and son may be, they are in two different worlds. This is emphasized by the bedtime-story framework ('Coming to see me have my bath?' 'I might,' I said. 'I didn't hurt him when I shot him, did I?' 'Not a bit.' and so on). The narrator is always there, occupying something of the position, physical and mental, of the Tramp in Čapek's *Insect Play*, and his asides and interpolations have an air of facetiousness which is uncongenial to some children of today. The interpolations, the free use of capital letters for comic emphasis ('Would you read a Sustaining Book, such as would help and comfort a Wedged Bear in Great Tightness?'), the lapses into sentimentality, are blemishes, to my mind, on a set of tales which, for their inventive energy, their verbal wit and their sheer exuberance have earned a permanent place on children's bookshelves.

WINNIE-THE-POOH and THE HOUSE AT POOH CORNER have picked up much of the soft atmosphere of children's writings in the 'twenties. There is at least one toy story of the period which has conspicuously avoided this, a book which should never have been allowed to go out of print. POOR CECCO, by Margery Williams Bianco, which came out in 1925, is something on its own, full of character, full of incident, delivered straight from child to child, as it were, with no middleman. Cecco, the wooden dog, with his conscientious, rather laborious care for the other inmates of the toy-cupboard; lonely, home-loving Jensina; Tubby and Bulka, the two sentimental, rather witless plush dogs; the wax dolls, Gladys and

Virginia, with their snobbish idiom; and the rascally cat, Murrum; they are all as real and exciting as their adventures. The story, told in a vivid style, is perfectly adjusted to a child's world. Listen to this comment on the marriage of Tubby and Bulka:

> Scarcely was the ceremony over, and every one had crowded round to kiss the bride, than the Lion came forward, with Anna sidling along behind. They too wanted to get married, seeing how simple it all was. Harlequin was willing, but Poor Cecco put his foot down.
>
> 'Nonsense!' he declared. 'One wedding at a time! It's Tubby's turn to-day, and besides, there are no more gifts ready. Anna has spent all the summer shilly-shallying on account of that stupid green meadow of hers, and now she must just content herself with being engaged for the present!'
>
> So they were engaged, formally; Anna, after some coyness, consented to wear a grass ring round her left ankle, and she took off her bell and hung it about the Lion's neck.
>
> Margery Williams Bianco. POOR CECCO (Chatto & Windus, 1925) p. 173.

and what child could resist the picture of Jensina's house on the ash-heap:

> She was an industrious little person, one could see at once, and had not wasted her time, for when she led them presently round the side of the ash-heap there stood a cosy little house which she had built herself, out of an old soap-box, and of which she had every reason to be proud. She had spread a bit of carpet on the floor and made a sofa to sleep on, and pillows stuffed with thistle-down, and she had hung the walls with scraps of wall-paper and fine pictures of tomatoes and peach-orchards, saved from old fruit cans. She had even a little kitchen, with plates and egg-cups and a real coffee pot, and all these things she had gathered one by one on the dump-heaps and brought home. Only the coffee pot, being too large, had to stand outside, but it looked very well there, and gave an air of hospitality to the place.
>
> Ibid., p. 66.

In this story we have left the nursery for a more spacious and varied world. The small child can go on a conducted tour of many lands hand-in-hand with a travelling doll. This is no new story-telling device. It is more than a century since MEMOIRS OF A LONDON DOLL appeared (though it is still, perhaps, the best of its kind ever written). The jointed wooden doll, Maria Poppet, who leaves the establishment of Sprat the toy-maker in High Holborn, sees London in many aspects before she settles down at Ashbourn Hall; sees the inside of a pastrycook's, watches a child toiling in a milliner's, goes to the opera, sits to a celebrated portrait-painter, sees the Lord Mayor's show and a pantomime at Drury Lane—all through the eyes of a doll, which is to say, through the eyes of a child sharpened by adult experience. The pantomime is described as a child would see it, with the final significant detail:

> ... now and then through one side of the curtain we caught a glimpse of something so bright that went by, like tall flags on painted poles, and tops of spears, and parts of mantles of people's dresses; and once, underneath the bottom of the dark green curtain, we saw run along a little pair of bright silver feet.
> 'Mrs Fairstar'. THE MEMOIRS OF A LONDON DOLL (Harrap 1923. First published 1855) p. 148.

but the Lord Mayor's show is seen as if by a doll:

> ... I also saw the principal dolls of this wonderful show—I mean the Lord Mayor in his coach, with the wooden Sword-bearer and the gingerbread Mace-bearer—at least, they looked like wood and gingerbread; and, indeed, so did the Lord Mayor himself ... He gave a sigh as he passed us, and laid his hand upon his fine stomach, and then he gave a smile.
> Ibid. pp. 130-31.

The doll's point of view, egocentric and unique, gives piquancy to small adventures. There is Rachel Field's inimitable wooden doll, Hitty, through whose eyes we see a panorama of American social history. Hitty is afraid many times in the course of her travels, but even when she is washed overboard from a whaler and is in danger of being swallowed by a hungry fish, her dignity is unruffled. Conscious arrogance and unconscious humour combine to give a special flavour to this story, as to Dorothy Ann Lovell's tale of Emma the royal doll, who travels through the lanes of England in search of her high-born relatives, and, in all her curious adventures, preserves a dainty wooden dignity.

Some of these doll stories, with their emphasis on character, will appeal more to girls than to boys, but out of the toy-cupboard, too, come innumerable animated engines and aeroplanes, tractors and cars, from Hardy Gramatky's Little Toot to the Rev. W. Awdry's absurd and endearing engines (not forgetting the Fat Controller, one of the best portraits of a bureaucrat in fiction). No child who enjoys bustle and change can do better than to start solo reading on Elizabeth Chapman's series about Marmaduke the lorry and his adventures with Joe, his cheery driver, Archibald the engine, and all the men, women, animals and vehicles he hobnobs with on his trips in the hills round Manchester. Simple and direct, these stories give great pleasure for their gay common-sense, and because Marmaduke trundles through a world not so very different from the world of everyday. And a child's world. Marmaduke is as unpredictable as any small boy. We are not expected to read too much into these airy fables; like the drawings that accompany them, they are spun out of simple things.

The style of these stories was selected to suit children from four to about seven. Ursula Moray Williams had no particular age in mind when she wrote THE ADVENTURES OF THE LITTLE WOODEN HORSE—or so I suppose, for the book is wise, mature, richly written, and has the ageless appeal of fairy-tale. It has the fairy-tale point too, for the little horse, with his scratched paint and his indomitable courage in adversity, is the younger son of a Grimms' tale, even to

Drawing by Eccles Williams for Elizabeth Chapman's MARMADUKE THE LORRY (Brockhampton)

the way he ends up in a palace. This is a story that will last a child for many years. When he is five he can listen to it as an adventure story, and at ten he can reread it and hear the voice of poetry speaking, a little melancholy, a little distant. And he may notice, now, that the wooden horses' involvement with the world has been by no means simple. He has not always found people agreeable, and he has certainly not found them easy to understand.

There is so much to attend to in a story like this that you cannot assign it to any particular age, but you *can* say that it will help younger children when they are taking that last step from the nursery into the outside world. And that is what they must now do, in their reading. The nursery chronicle is no longer capacious enough to contain all they want to discover. They must get on their tricycles and venture out to see what the world is like.

To find suitable books for children of six to nine is not at all easy, and it is probably less easy now than it used to be. Forty years ago the customers for children's books belonged mainly to reading families; they were children who read early, who read easily, and who could move on pretty quickly from their primers to THE WIND IN THE WILLOWS or TOM SAWYER. Nowadays, among the countless thousands of children demanding books for first solo reading, there are many who are reading late—at six or seven instead of four or five. These children need stories that go further than the mere chronicling of junior pursuits, to tempt them on. They want a *story*. Brockhampton Press was the first publishing house to produce specially for the young reader, the slow reader or the reluctant reader, what may be called 'domestic episodes'; and other publishing houses (among them Hamish Hamilton, with Antelope and Reindeer books, Burke with Wren books, Bodley Head with Acorn books) have followed their example. Each of these domestic episodes has a short, clear-cut, single story, with a point rather than a sequence of domestic events. Each, at its best, shows an intelligent combination of the ordinary and the unordinary, a little twist of the familiar, and this is often underlined by the illustrations.

The daily round of sand-castles, dolls' tea-parties and dressing-up has been changed, and not only the scene but the whole outlook of the actors. For these domestic episodes reflect homes where nurseries and nannies have given place to a free and easy atmosphere. The change in our social life, the mix-up of classes, the new know-

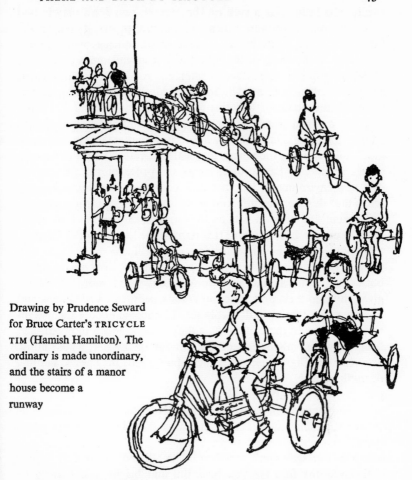

Drawing by Prudence Seward
for Bruce Carter's TRICYCLE
TIM (Hamish Hamilton). The
ordinary is made unordinary,
and the stairs of a manor
house become a
runway

ledge children are acquiring, almost without knowing it, of the work
and play of all sorts of people—these are reflected in the stories now
being offered to five-year-olds and their slightly older brothers and
sisters. Just as the social background of reading children has enormously expanded, so has the range of subjects that are used in children's stories. An illustration would be the work of Mary Cockett, who
writes for children of six and over. JAN THE MARKET BOY and
SEVEN DAYS WITH JAN might seem, at first glance, to resemble very
closely a type of family chronicle. But Jan lives in a working

family. His father has a stall on the market, and Jan's play is tied up with work all the time. When he races caterpillars, it is down the side of an empty crate he is supposed to be shifting; when he discovers the back streets of the little town, it is while he is on his way to deliver goods to his father's customers. Again, in ROLLING ON, Mary Cockett tells of a town boy who goes to stay with his grandfather in the country. But this is no ordinary visit. Grandfather lives in a caravan attached to a steam-roller, and his work takes him all over the place. Dan not only has to learn country ways, he has to meet children from the village and learn to get on with them in the village school; he has to discover all the protocol and the interest of a new environment. It is not only because of the unusual social scene that this story is different; it is also because it is the story of a child exercising his own wits on his own life, finding out how to get on with people, how to learn. It is right in the line of modern theory, this story, with its new freedom in a child's life.

Leila Berg's clever tale, THE HIDDEN ROAD, also moves firmly out of the middle-class nursery world, and (which is more important) gives children their own function among people of varied ages and opinions; for Jeremy and Nicola learn to accommodate themselves to the families in the council flats they have so much resented, and from the oldest inhabitants of this London backwater, whose house was once the Big House of the neighbourhood, they get something to think about:

'And the squirrels have gone,' wailed Nico, 'and the ducks. They've been frightened away . . . driven away. *Why* do all the best things go?'

'Oh, but they don't, my dear.' The old lady seemed surprised. 'I loved the fox. He was beautiful and bright. But I knew he killed the chickens . . . The famous old gentleman who had tea down there a hundred years ago was very clever and really very kind, but he was a very rude man who upset a lot of people, I daresay. . . . You mustn't think that everything that goes is nice, and everything new is horrid.'

'Most things,' said Jeremy suddenly, 'are a bit nice and a bit horrid.'

The old lady nodded vigorously. 'So you've found that out, have you?' she said.

'Oh, I've known that for ages,' said Jeremy, as if it wasn't important.
Leila Berg. THE HIDDEN ROAD (Hamish Hamilton, Antelope Books, 1958) pp. 99–100.

The moral purpose of the nineteenth century is oddly echoed in stories like these. The tone is different, but the moral, less directly offered, is essentially the same—that children must learn to live honestly and usefully in the world as they find it. Rosemary Garland, in particular, never lacks a social point. In THE SECRET CURTAINS, an English child and her French neighbour opposite make friends with the freemasonry of children, though they cannot speak each other's language. In DONKEY BOY, an unmanageable street-Arab finds a niche in the country. In THE COUNTRY BUS, a group of children help an elderly man down on his luck.

These theories of daily life, carefully adapted to the young, add spice and point to the stories; they certainly do not restrict them in any way. The Victorian child took it for granted that his stories would have an improving note and I think our children will end up by doing the same. Certainly the morals in their stories will be more lightly stated and stated with more humour, for when children live cheek by jowl with their parents, authority has to wear a different, less noticeable guise. A story like Pauline Clarke's THE ROBIN HOODERS strikes the typical note of today. Robert, Serena and Tom, who live in a village, decide to do good deeds; but not because they want to be good. Serena has been rereading stories of Robin Hood and they think robbing the rich to help the poor would make a good game. They are not under instructions from tracts or parents, and they have to find the path to generosity through mistakes and minor successes, until the major triumph when they discover (by accident) a treasure which helps their dear Miss Laurel to regain her manor house. In a word, they are children learning to behave suitably and with energy in a very mixed world.

The kind of book I have been discussing often has some indication of age on its dust-cover. These indications are a convenience so long as parents and librarians do not take them literally. Obviously, it is a pity to give a child a book that is too childish; a good deal less harm is done if you give one that is too old (so long as it is not absurdly out of range). Children develop in jumps and, in their reading, they need always to be a jump ahead of themselves, with books that are just too old, just too deep, so that they can be always moving on. Anyone choosing for a child must appraise, select, be guided first by the publisher's note of age, but afterwards, and much more, by a knowledge of the individual child.

Most of these books are designed for first solo reading, and their style is carefully organized to that end. It is dangerous to aim at 'simple, clear language', as the advertisement of one series states, if this is to imply any control or any restriction on the use of long words; but the danger will be avoided so long as we are concerned with authors of the calibre of Norman Dale, Meriol Trevor, Leila Berg, Olive Dehn and Barbara Euphan Todd (to mention only a few). They have taken their own line and have given children books which are within their capacity, but which, because of individual style, will not hold them back. Children who read early will soon gobble up these domestic episodes and will look for tougher, richer reading. But the slow and reluctant reader will find plenty to think about, for the subjects of these stories are expandable. A feud between families in adjoining holiday caravans, the building of a council estate on a beloved playground, a move from town to country or from country to town—these are events which affect children and their parents and neighbours in different ways, and in the best domestic stories the child is well aware of many strands of meaning. The citizen of tomorrow is today being better served with his first stage in story-books than he was five years ago.

Reading List

1.*Stories of dolls and toys*

Ainsworth, Ruth. RUFTY TUFTY THE GOLLIWOG 1952, RUFTY TUFTY AT THE SEASIDE 1954, RUFTY TUFTY GOES CAMPING 1956, RUFTY TUFTY RUNS AWAY 1957, RUFTY TUFTY FLIES HIGH 1959, RUFTY TUFTY'S ISLAND 1960. *Heinemann*. Illustrated by Dorothy Craigie. Agreeable, comical tales in which a golliwog has the kind of small domestic adventures a child would enjoy.

*Awdry, Rev. W. RAILWAY SERIES. *Ward* 1945 onwards. Illustrated by John Kenney.

Bailey, Carolyn Sherwin. MISS HICKORY. *Viking*, New York 1946. Illustrated by Ruth Gannett. Spirited tale of a twig-doll with a nut head fending for herself in winter in the New Hampshire country: full of delightful detail.

*Behrens, Margaret. MONKEY BEHAVE. *Hart-Davis* 1958.

Berg, Leila. THE STORY OF THE LITTLE CAR. *Epworth Press* 1955. Illustrated by Sillince. Everyday adventures of an attractive little vehicle.

*Bianco, Margery Williams. POOR CECCO (1925 U.S.A.). *Chatto & Windus* 1925. Illustrated by Arthur Rackham.

Brisley, Joyce Lankester. ADVENTURES OF PURL AND PLAIN. *Harrap* 1941. Delightful domestic adventures of two wooden dolls. Illustrated by the author.

Carson, Hilda. PLAIN MARY JANE 1957, MARY JANE AND THE VISITORS 1959. *Harrap*. Illustrated by Astrid Walford. Adventures of a doll's house family.

*Chapman, Elizabeth. MARMADUKE THE LORRY 1953, MARMADUKE AND JOE 1954, RIDING WITH MARMADUKE 1955, ADVENTURES WITH MARMADUKE 1956, MERRY MARMADUKE 1957, MARMADUKE AND HIS FRIENDS 1958, MARMADUKE AND THE ELEPHANT 1959, MARMADUKE AND THE LAMBS 1960. *Brockhampton*. Illustrated by Eccles Williams.

*Clare, Helen. FIVE DOLLS IN A HOUSE 1953, FIVE DOLLS AND THE MONKEY 1956, FIVE DOLLS IN THE SNOW 1957, FIVE DOLLS AND THEIR FRIENDS 1959. *Bodley Head*. Illustrated by Cecil Leslie.

*Collodi, Carlo (pseud). PINOCCHIO. *Dent* (Children's Illustrated Classics) 1951 (in original English translation of M. A. Murray, first published by Fisher Unwin in 1892). Illustrated by Charles Folkard.

*'Mrs Fairstar' (Richard Hengist Horne). MEMOIRS OF A LONDON DOLL (1855) *Harrap* 1923.

*Field, Rachel. HITTY (1929 U.S.A.). *Routledge* 1950. Illustrated by Dorothy P. Lathrop.

Fletcher, David. MISS PRIMROSE. *Hutchinson* 1955. Illustrated by Rosalie Fry. Travels of a conceited doll and her reformation; unusually good characterization.

*Godden, Rumer. IMPUNITY JANE 1955, THE FAIRY DOLL 1956, THE DOLLS' HOUSE 1947, THE STORY OF HOLLY AND IVY 1958, CANDY FLOSS 1960. *Macmillan*. Illustrated by Adrienne Adams.

*Gramatky, Hardy. LITTLE TOOT (1939 U.S.A.). *World's Work* 1958. Illustrated by the author.

Judah, Aaron. TALES OF TEDDY BEAR. *Faber* 1958. Illustrated by Sheila Hawkins. A bear and his friends leading more or less human lives: most individual humour.

*Lovell, Dorothy Ann. THE STRANGE ADVENTURES OF EMMA. *Faber* 1941.
Illustrated by Irene Hawkins.

McFadyen, Ella. PEGMEN TALES. *Angus & Robertson* 1959. Selected from
PEGMEN TALES 1946, and PEGMEN GO WALKABOUT 1947. Illustrated
by Edwina Bell. Two Australian children and the home-made toys that come
to life.

*Milne, A. A. WINNIE-THE-POOH 1926, THE HOUSE AT POOH CORNER 1928.
Methuen. Illustrated by Ernest Shepard.

*Rey, H. A. ZOZO. *Folding Books* 1942. Illustrated by the author.

*Rey, H. A. ZOZO RIDES A BIKE 1954, ZOZO TAKES A JOB 1954, ZOZO GETS
A MEDAL 1958. *Chatto & Windus.* Illustrated by the author.

*Robinson, Joan G. TEDDY ROBINSON 1953, MORE ABOUT TEDDY ROBINSON
1954, TEDDY ROBINSON'S BOOK 1955, DEAR TEDDY ROBINSON 1956,
TEDDY ROBINSON HIMSELF 1957, ANOTHER TEDDY ROBINSON 1960.
Harrap. Illustrated by the author.

Symonds, John. LOTTIE. *Bodley Head* 1957. Illustrated by Edward Ardizzone.
Eighteenth-century setting, adventures of a doll and a dog. Wholly enchanting.

Tozer, Katharine. THE WANDERINGS OF MUMFIE 1935, HERE COMES MUMFIE
1936, MUMFIE THE ADMIRAL 1937, MUMFIE'S MAGIC BOX 1938, MUMFIE'S
UNCLE SAMUEL 1939, MUMFIE MARCHES ON 1942. *Murray.*
Illustrated by the author. Adventures of a toy elephant in his own magic land
and in ours: comical fantasy with poetic undercurrent.

Williams, Ursula Moray. HOBBIE. *Brockhampton* 1958. Illustrated by the author.
Spirited toy collects a gang of hobby horses and escapes to the seaside.

*Williams, Ursula Moray. THE ADVENTURES OF THE LITTLE WOODEN
HORSE (1938). *Penguin* (Puffin Story Books) 1959. Illustrated by Peggy Fortnum.

2.'*Domestic episodes*'

*Berg, Leila. THE HIDDEN ROAD. *Hamish Hamilton* (Antelope Books) 1958.
Illustrated by B. Chapman.

Berg, Leila. ANDY'S PIT PONY. *Brockhampton* 1958. Illustrated by Biro. Fact
and feeling beautifully blended.

Carter, Bruce. TRICYCLE TIM 1957, BALLOONING BOY 1960. *Hamish Hamilton*
(Antelope Books). Illustrated by Prudence Seward. Crisp tales in which small
boys find wonderful outlets for their energy and initiative.

*Clarke, Pauline. THE ROBIN HOODERS. *Faber* 1960. Illustrated by Cecil Leslie.

*Cockett, Mary. JAN THE MARKET BOY 1957, SEVEN DAYS WITH JAN 1960.
Brockhampton. Illustrated by Peggy Beetles.

*Cockett, Mary. ROLLING ON. *Methuen* 1960. Illustrated by Shirley Hughes.

Dale, Norman. JOHNNIE-BY-THE-RIVER. *Hamish Hamilton* (Antelope Books) 1957. Illustrated by Zélide Teague. Adventures of tough river-boy in fair weather and flood.

*Garland, Rosemary. A SWARM IN JUNE 1957, illustrated by Valerie Taylor. THE COUNTRY 'BUS 1958, THE LITTLE FOREST 1959, illustrated by Cecil Leslie. *Hamish Hamilton* (Antelope Books).

*Garland, Rosemary. DONKEY BOY. *Hamish Hamilton* (Reindeer Books) 1958. Illustrated by Constance Marshall.

*Garland, Rosemary. THE SECRET CURTAINS. *Harrap* 1959. Illustrated by Sheila Rose.

Hough, Charlotte. THE TRACKERS. *Hamish Hamilton* (Reindeer Books) 1960. Illustrated by the author. Adventures, exciting and sometimes absurd, of two boys and a small girl on an island in a lake.

Kennett, John. THE CRUISE OF THE COOT. *Brockhampton* 1959. Illustrated by Joan Milroy. Boating story with mildly satirical note: well written.

Kyle, Elisabeth. THE MONEY-CAT. *Hamish Hamilton* (Reindeer Books) 1958. Illustrated by Cecil Leslie. Unusual treasure-hunt in a cottage.

MacGibbon, Jean. PETER'S PRIVATE ARMY. *Hamish Hamilton* (Antelope Books) 1960. Illustrated by Janet Duchesne. A boy's adventures with toy soldiers—exceptionally real characters and conversation.

Mayne, William. THE FISHING PARTY. *Hamish Hamilton* (Antelope Books) 1960. Illustrated by Christopher Brooker. Village school on special day. Clear-cut, wonderful tale of children enjoying themselves in their own way.

Williams, Ursula Moray. THE MOONBALL. *Hamish Hamilton* (Reindeer Books) 1958. Illustrated by the author. Children find magic creature from outer space.

from THE CRUISE OF THE COOT (see above)

Chapter 4 | *Mrs Bunny and the Rabbits*

One of the pictures my children liked most when they were small was Jean de Brunhoff's impression of the monkey town in BABAR'S FRIEND ZEPHIR. Zephir the monkey is home for the holidays. Here is the station in the background, father busy with the luggage and the children skipping with excitement like any human brothers and sisters. There are the tree-houses, with monkeys leading suburban lives—reading the paper, watering flowers in a window-box, stirring soup. A fantasy, and at the same time a picture based on accurate observation. If children go to the monkey-house at the Zoo they do not expect to see a chimpanzee stirring soup, but they can often see female chimpanzees being motherly. It is quite as natural to put monkeys into houses, in a story, as it is to tell a domestic tale to children through the agency of a dolls' house, and animal stories for the younger children have, more often than not, an element of fantasy in them.

From time to time, and particularly in the late nineteen-thirties, there has been criticism of this way of interpreting nature, but this seems to have had as little effect on stories about rabbits or monkeys or horses as the several attempts to bring reason into fairy-tales. It hardly seems likely, in fact, that a child will classify beetles and butterflies inaccurately in his teens as a direct result of having been given, in childhood, pictures of butterflies dancing in evening dress or beetles wearing mackintoshes. Certainly it seems a good thing to protest (and I am sure it should be done more often) against the travesty of animals that you find in some cheaper picture books. There can be no excuse for putting funny hats on hippopotamuses or making monkeys talk in bursts of facetious slang; and it is equally necessary to take a stand against the prettifying of animals, particularly the smaller animals. There are only too many writers who think they can do as well as Beatrix Potter did by dressing up a rabbit and calling her Mrs Bunny. So long as a rabbit behaves like a rabbit, I see no reason why she should not have human attributes as well as a human name; but the very word 'bunny' has picked up a sentimental connotation since the days of Benjamin Bunny and his uncompromising papa. Inaccuracy, vulgarity, sentimentality—these are the three dragons that haunt the path of the writer of animal stories. Children can very easily be deluded by the stories they are given in their first years, and silly books about animals are among the most corrupting influences they can meet.

Good fantasy is another matter. This will attach itself more easily to some animals than to others. Cats and dogs have by centuries of domestication drifted on to the fringes of human behaviour. In family tales, indeed, they are apt to be treated as supernumerary characters, though this has to be done with some tact if it is not to be sentimental; and it is only one step to turn them into pirates, nurses or explorers in space. As for mice, they are, as Beatrix Potter has taught us, perfectly fitted for the dolls' house and the doll-size tale, in their daintiness and dressability. The many writers who use a mouse family to make a domestic tale for a small child have necessarily concentrated on this aspect, and have left out the messy, marauding side. In Eve Titus's books about Anatole there is even a wry admission of this. This strong-minded mouse becomes a cheese-taster in a factory, to emphasize to men the usefulness of his race, and the notes he pins on the various samples are in fact most useful to the manufacturers. The joke is well within a child's range, but the joke they prefer is the more simple one of mice keeping house, like so many little dolls. In stories like THE FLY-BY-NIGHTS by Averil Newell or Rosalind Vallance's tales of Tittymouse and Tattymouse, animals are so deeply immersed in human doings that illustration must come to the rescue to redress the balance. Very little exaggeration—a pair of spectacles here and a gesture of the paw there—and your mice are tiny human beings and still perfectly mouselike.

So long as a writer does not falsify natural fact, except by the initial changing of mice into humans, children may be left to enjoy innumerable ways of treating them in fiction. They will even understand something of Rumer Godden's purpose in THE MOUSEWIFE, a tender tale built round an anecdote in Dorothy Wordworth's Journal, about a friendship between a mouse and a caged dove.

The author has made of this a parable about the oppressed, but it still remains a delicate and readable story about a mouse and a dove, matched with delicate naturalistic drawings by William Pène du Bois.

Humanization can only be successful if something is preserved of the original animal. Beatrix Potter's tales depend on the fact that the animals behave like themselves masquerading as humans. They are humans only in order to appeal more directly to the children who read about them. The animal is always the starting-point; she works outwards from there. She never brings her animals into relation with each other unless this would naturally happen (as, for instance, in Jemima Puddleduck's meeting with the fox, or the same fox's contest with Tommy Brock). Alison Uttley's method is somewhat different. The friendly alliance of Little Grey Rabbit, Squirrel and Hare is not based on natural fact, nor is the character of Grey Rabbit particularly rabbitish (though Hare's irresponsibility is a legitimate extension of the behaviour of hares in spring). Yet in the Grey Rabbit stories, and in the tales of Snug and Serena, the field mice, and of Little Red Fox, the small animals of the countryside are most sympathetically humanized. Successfully, because this has been done very moderately, and because the background of the stories, in words and in pictures, is so lifelike. It is idealized, of course. Here are wild flowers in full bloom, rich autumn hedgerows, good weather. If it does snow, the mice go out with mufflers and lanterns; they do not starve. But the picture of the country is as true as we need it to be in this kind of story and it depends on a knowledge as sound as that of Beatrix Potter or Kenneth Grahame.

In Alison Uttley, too, there is the particular charm of folk lore and legend. Her animal stories are really fairy-tales. The swan, in LITTLE RED FOX AND THE MAGIC MOON, is a fairy-tale princess; the country superstitions about hedgehogs are used with gentle humour in the tales of Fuzzypeg and his milkman father. The characters of Wise Owl (in the Grey Rabbit books) and Toad (in the stories of Snug and Serena) preserve something of immemorial folk mystery. The same element is present, in a more robust form, in the rustic tales of Sam Pig and Tim Rabbit which are always popular with children. And in none of these stories is there any trace of sentimentality or flippancy. Listen to the beginning of another woodland tale, THE UPSIDE-DOWN MEDICINE by Racey Helps:

Do you like eating nuts? You do? And so do squirrels, but even squirrels can eat too many. Tippety Nippet was a squirrel and he was VERY fond of nuts; but once he ate far too many, as you shall see.

Just as Tippety Nippet was a nice sort of squirrel, so his tree-house was a nice, cosy sort of house. No doubt it would seem a little queer to you, for it had only one room. Tippety told people it had four rooms, for he called the blue-carpet part the bedroom (as it truly was, for there stood the little green bedstead), while he called the flowered-carpet part the dining-sitting-room-kitchen.

Racey Helps. THE UPSIDE-DOWN MEDICINE (Collins, 1946) p. 1.

This is a clever and amusing story, like the rest of the series about Barnaby Littlemouse and his friends; the pictures are attractive to look at, though a little too near grotesqueness for my liking; but they are marred, text and pictures, by an uneasy jocosity, and I am sure part of this is due to the fact that the author has chosen his animals arbitrarily. The stories do not rise out of the nature of rabbits, squirrels or tortoises; they are accounts of what happened to these animals because the author intended that they should.

It is, of course, unfair to compare any writer with Beatrix Potter, but for most of us she is a standard, not only for animal fantasies for the very young but also for straight animal stories. MRS TITTLE-MOUSE, after all, can be read as an ecological study of a mouse burrow, and a very accurate one it is too. The other things in the book—the glancing humour, the shrewd character-drawing, the loving but matter-of-fact precision of the domestic background— each element gains from the others. It has been said that generations of middle-class children owe their mature taste in landscape to the Peter Rabbit books, and it has been said, besides, that generations of middle-class housewives have an ambivalent attitude to mice because of them. It is always worth repeating that generations of children have, unconsciously, learned to observe carefully and accurately the world of animals through this most conscientious of observers. Beatrix Potter is the final answer to the determinedly practical reader. In late middle age she became a notable breeder of Herdwick sheep. Her specialist knowledge at county sales did not stop her from writing, in THE FAIRY CARAVAN, a piece of charming conversation among ewes on a hillside, and of expressing pictorially the woolly, anxiously maternal side of her flock. Her books teach children how to live with animals and how to know them.

This is, of course, what any good animal story will do. Beatrix Potter's indirect method of teaching is more in line with modern practice than the frankly instructive technique of some of her contemporaries. Edmund Selous's JACK'S INSECTS, an extreme example of the educational story, would seem unutterably prim and improving to children today, although the conversations between Jack and the creatures he meets have a dry humour that gave me a lot of pleasure when I was six or so. Sermonizing is not altogether a matter of date. Rutherford Montgomery and René Guillot, writing in the present day, are almost as explicit in their plea for the proper treatment of animals as Anna Sewell was when she wrote BLACK BEAUTY more than eighty years ago. Other writers widely separated in date—Kipling and Meindert De Jong, for example—bury their moral purpose more deeply.

If you have a moral, you are humanizing animals in a sense, and this is inevitable in stories for older children, just as it was in fantasies for the young. In spite of an increasing specialist vocabulary, the biologist still has to use some human terms when he describes animal behaviour. The writer who presents the life history of an animal to children, when he has described environment factually, must use his own experience and idiom to describe the imagined emotions of that animal. The most accurate and detailed account of the birth and early days of a young animal—like Niko Tinbergen's THE TALE OF JOHN STICKLE—cannot do without the ideas of home, maternal care, education. The author's illustrations, too, take us much further than the purely scientific standpoint. Each drawing is precise as to fact, but each has a strong element of design and expresses the author's aesthetic pleasure in the natural world.

Every author will make such compromise as suits him. A classic animal story, the Hon. J. W. Fortescue's* STORY OF A RED-DEER, draws the Hind as a kind of Lady of the Manor (even the belligerent Vixen addresses her with respect) and the rest of these Exmoor animals have their proper accents, from the Cockney of the half-domestic rabbits to the rich Devonshire of the old buck rabbit and the muddle-headed woodcock. The hierarchy of a nineteenth-century country parish is reproduced quite naturally and with

*Afterwards Sir John Fortescue.

Drawing by Niko Tinbergen for his THE TALE OF JOHN STICKLE (Methuen)

delightful comedy, in the conversation and relationships of the animals, and at the same time the home and adventures of an Exmoor stag are described with absolute fidelity. The beautiful ending of the story shows how the author has fused his point of view with his intuitive rendering of the feelings of the deer:

And the wild baying ceased; and he heard nothing but the chorus of the waters in his ears. Once he struggled to raise his head, and the great brown antlers came looming up for a moment through the eddies; but as he passed down to the deep, still pool beyond the fall, the water called to him so kindly that he could not but obey...

So the waters closed over the stern, sharp antlers, and he bowed his head and was at peace.

Then men came and pulled the great still body out of the water; and they took his head and hung it up in memory of so great a run and so gallant a Stag. But their triumph was only over the empty shell of him, for his spirit had gone to the still brown pool ... So there he remains; for he had fought his fight and run his course; and he asks for nothing better than to hear the river sing to him all the day long.

Hon. J. W. Fortescue. THE STORY OF A RED-DEER (Macmillan, 1919 ed.) pp. 210–12.

Sixty years later, H. Mortimer Batten drew an equally striking picture of a red deer's life, in THE SINGING FOREST. This time the scene is the Highlands of Scotland, the hero Corrie, a stag hand-reared by the laird's children and afterwards released. This is a more objective story than the older one. The deer has a personality, in a limited sense, but there is no attempt to equate him with a social type. He is observed by people, who present their picture of him, and indeed of a whole complex of natural life, as accurately as possible. And as sympathetically, for the author has in common with Sir John Fortescue the fact that he has known and loved the country he describes and has watched the animals there.

These are more than animal stories. They are poems, if you like, of country life, not as an extension of civilization, but as a world in itself, owning man merely as an inhabitant. To an imaginative child, such books are an unforgettable experience. Again, to read Henry Williamson's life stories of Tarka the otter, Salar the salmon and the rest is to be made more intensely aware of the natural world. When Williamson writes about animals he thinks of them, not as humans, but as individuals. He follows Tarka through the seasons, through dangers and delights, with an intuitive sympathy not in the least impaired by his extreme accuracy in matters of fact. He puts thoughts into the minds of his characters (and we must call them 'characters') but they are probable thoughts only. The mantle of Williamson has fallen on David Stephen, whose style, less poetic, has the same fine selective quality. A passage like this is an illustration in itself:

In the Mossrigg wheatfield, cushats and magpies staggered and side-stepped as they fed on the fast-freezing ground. The ragged trousers of the parchment-faced rooks whipped about in the wind, as they delved with much wing-flicking and tail-fanning. Pica was one of sixteen bellicose magpies dibbling in the hardening earth crust, and time and again he was almost toppled forward on to his beak when the wind tipped him under the tail. The pigeons danced in unwilling circles as cupped wings caught the

wind. Across the pasture, beyond the fence, sheep plodded in twos and threes to the shelter of the Strip, while the wind combed the wool on their spines into a variety of ephemeral partings.
David Stephen. STRING LUG THE FOX (Lutterworth, 1950) pp. 82–3.

It is an illustration of a special kind, of course; it seeks, through words, to create an intense atmosphere of cold, but not a precise picture of a place. This the reader cannot get from words; whatever picture floats into his mind will be fragmentary, vivid in one or two particulars that strike him, changing, probably, if he rereads such passages. The drawings for STRING LUG THE FOX, by Nina Scott Langley, naturalistic and detailed, do not carry the imagination forward as the words do; they add an actuality to certain scenes in the book. It would perhaps be true to say that the illustrator can do more to fix fact in the reader's mind than the writer can; pictures like these are functional, like the more decorative drawings of Maurice Wilson for another book by Stephen, THE RED STRANGER. But they are not solely functional. These two artists, and more strikingly, Charles Tunnicliffe in his drawings for TARKA THE OTTER, show their enjoyment and understanding of natural life as much as the authors do.

Stephen's stories are full of this enjoyment, this appreciation of the teeming life of the Lowland grouse-moors, the keepers and farmers and landowners who are concerned with the busy, secret ways of fox and owl and stoat. His command of detail is tremendous and his power to vary it and change the focus from man to wild creature and back again. At the end of a book like STRING LUG THE FOX we know a good deal more of the minutiæ of wild life than we knew before, but we are not conscious of having been taught. We know more, too, about the way a fox thinks—but not more than we legitimately should. Here is an account of the fox detecting a gin on one of his regular routes:

. . . he did not jump on to the boulder. He wanted first of all to investigate the matter of its changed appearance. Wading out to it, shoulder deep, he sniffed critically. Through the odour of the moss, and in spite of the scent-destroying wash of water, he recognized the smell. . . . Steel! String Lug pondered, but did not paw. He gripped the outer fuzz of the moss covering and jerked, sliding back on his haunches till he almost fell in the water. The gin lay exposed, slick on his stepping-stone, with jaws spread to catch his feet.

At that moment String Lug knew fear—real fear. It is doubtful if he realized at once that the gin had been set specially for himself, or that Pate was the man responsible. What he did appreciate was that he might well have walked right into it had he not stopped to consider the boulder's altered appearance. But when he found another gin carefully planted beside his favourite rowan tree on the ridge, he knew that it was meant for him. And that was the beginning of trap wisdom for String Lug.

Op. cit., pp. 80–81.

This is not to offer children a spoof insight into the minds of animals, but to present probabilities worked out by observation; and, above all, to present cause and effect so they tie up into a stirring story.

For the good animal story is not only about an animal. It is about a whole environment, the heritage of all young readers. The life stories of animals, of this classic kind, belong with BEVIS and B.B.'s matchless BRENDON CHASE and Masefield's fine chronicle for boys, A BOOK OF DISCOVERIES, for they represent the wish that lives in us all, young and old, beyond the pastoral convention or nationalist sentiment, to identify ourselves with the land around us.

There is the other side of the picture, too. If animals achieve characters when they are placed in the centre of their habitat, they get a reflected character when they are involved in a human story.

Chiang Yee's YEBBIN gives a picture of social life in a small town in Southern China, with its rituals of behaviour and its rigid class distinctions. Yebbin the monkey is a 'character'. He enjoys human company, he readily learns tricks, and because of his natural inquisitiveness he comes to be a deciding factor in the troubled love affair of the herb dealer's son and the daughter of the scholar next door. At the same time the animal is observed and described as an animal (more successfully in line and water-colour than in the rather diffuse and undistinguished text). BLACK BEAUTY is a piece of social history. From the reminiscences of Beauty and Ginger and Merrylegs there emerges a picture of England a century ago, in village and city. The documentation is important in linking the two themes, human relations and kindness to animals, in rather the same way as the social and poetic themes are linked in AT THE BACK OF THE NORTH WIND. Meindert De Jong's touching story, THE WHEEL ON THE SCHOOL, combines the yearly cycle of a stork with a vignette of a Dutch village; and a later story, ALONG CAME A DOG, sets a dog and a crippled hen against the background of an American smallholding. Every move the hen makes, in the yard, the chicken-house or the riverside where she hides, is meticulously described against an equally meticulous background. The tiny farmhouse drama is played out almost visibly for the reader, and behind it there is De Jong's invariable moral—'He prayeth well, who loveth well, Both man and bird and beast.' There is no fuss about this moral. In SHADRACH, a touching story of a small boy and his pet rabbit, there is not a word that does not contribute directly to the story. But the folk-lore simplicity of this, and the other stories, takes them straight to the heart, and Maurice Sendak's drawings likewise show the warmth of homely affection in its proper setting.

Stories about domestic animals necessarily follow a double pattern. The life of an animal is cut into the life of a man, and the success of each story will depend on the author's honesty and good sense when he is describing the emotions of animals. Horse stories—perennially popular with children—offer a wide choice of techniques. There is the purely factual piece, like BEN by Primrose Cumming, a panorama of the life of a cart-horse in London and the country, illustrated with photographs. There is the horse-breaking story, where men and animals share the centre of the stage. In Don Patton's BROWN JUG, for instance, with its vivid picture of Canadian horse-breakers and trappers, the bond between the horse and his half-breed rider is fairly and movingly described, with attention to both characters. There are tales where a man's adventures run side by side with those of a horse; Will James's cowboy tale, SMOKY, is a classic example, and H. M. Peel's FURY, SON OF THE WILDS, a splendid picture of Australian horsemanship, is a worthy successor. All these stories hint at the supposed feelings of the horse, and dwell on the affection that is recognized between man and beast. HORSE IN THE CLOUDS is bolder in its approach. This story about an Argentine ranch and the colt Pampa was written by Helen Griffiths when she was sixteen. Her very evident love of horses and her young spontaneous love of writing have carried her through a story which might have led many older writers to disaster. She has really suc-

Drawing by Maurice Wilson for David Stephen's THE RED STRANGER
(Lutterworth)
Below: Drawing by Astrid Walford for Rosalind Vallance's TITTYMOUSE
AND TATTYMOUSE (Harrap)

ceeded in following the thoughts in an animal's mind—for Pampa is far more important and more interesting than the English boy who finds him or the Spanish boy who breaks him in. Perhaps we can draw a moral from this free-moving story, the moral that though there are many things to avoid when you write an animal story, you probably have the best chance of avoiding them if you write from the heart more than from strict biological theory.

Mary Elwyn Patchett's Australian stories are written in this free, friendly spirit. The writer is looking back on a childhood spent with animals. The horses in TAM THE UNTAMED, the dingoes and kangaroo dogs in WILD BROTHER, are just as well described as the sheep station and the people who live and work there, and their feelings are just as believable. So it is, too, with Rutherford Montgomery's stories of Northern Canada, like CARCAJOU and MISTER JIM. Jim, the grizzly, has, from living with men, developed characters of humour and sociability which are, obviously, latent in wild grizzlies. In CARCAJOU, the character of the wolverine is observed, as it were, from further off, drawn almost like the villain in a melodrama and yet with accurate detail. These tales look back to the enchanting stories of Ernest Thompson Seton, but the climate has changed in the last thirty or forty years. Seton's bear cubs and beavers were described as if they were small boys and girls playing. Montgomery's stories are, first and foremost, stories about the wilds, and the humanization is only secondary to the factual picture.

Nowadays a serious animal story will less often use direct speech than did the stories of thirty years ago; but the Kipling type of stylized dialogue used by animals has been used brilliantly by René Guillot in his series of tales about African animals. Guillot knows Senegal and the Sudan well, and the hunter-naturalist Marlow, who plays some part in all the stories, may be taken to be a self-portrait of the author in his relation of interested patron to jungle animals. Guillot writes as accurately as a naturalist but as vividly as a poet. He deliberately enters into the minds of his characters. In OWORO, for instance, he relates the chimpanzee's pattern of thought to that of aboriginal tribes, and the story is haunted by the quest of the monkey for the secret spring, Koguli, famed in monkey tradition:

Oworo, as a child with the tribe, knew nothing of this at first but soon he began to guess the meaning of their annual migration

through the heart of Africa in obedience to a law as old as the world. But it is not the rains that lead the chimpanzee—they go quite at random, rather as black men do who hear the rumours of gold and, trusting to luck, quit their villages and go wandering in search of the wonderful river that flows with nuggets of gold. Rene Guillot. OWORO. Translated by Gwen Marsh. (Oxford University Press, 1954) Foreword, p. vi.

Animals talk in Guillot's books, they feel, they reflect. The cheetah in KPO THE LEOPARD thinks about her adoption of the leopard cub; Sama the young elephant thinks about the dangers he may meet in the jungle. They give human expression to their instinctive behaviour. Guillot is a poet, in that he believes in an affinity between man and animals, an affinity better shown in action than in philosophy; symbolized by the friendship of Sirga the lioness and the African boy Ulé. These stories are unique. Some children will find them difficult to read; the style, though verbally simple, is very compressed. A few may be impatient with the way plot and reverie are woven together. For the discriminating child, and the child who likes to send his imagination far and wide, they offer at once a firm statement about man's duty towards animals and a series of imaginative exercises which would be hard to beat in any sphere of children's writing.

Guillot has followed Kipling in giving his animals free expression for their thoughts, but Kipling keeps his animals nearer to the human world. They have personality as well as speech, in human terms. Bagheera, aristocrat of the jungle, with his pride and his ceremonious way of talking; Baloo the bear, clumsy and affectionate; Kaa the snake, a coiled Svengali; the surly, greedy, deceitful tiger, Shere Khan; these are as near to human character as they are to animal behaviour. Occasionally they carry a weight of satire; the Bandar-log do, for instance, those fickle, conceited monkey-people. It is no new thing to use animals for satire; probably they made their first appearance in literature in satirical fables, like those of Æsop, and the use of animals to point morals about human behaviour first brought them, through simplified forms of medieval bestiaries, to the attention of children in this country. Probably children take little note of the satirical twist in stories like Hugh Lofting's about Dr Dolittle; but, though these were begun, it is said, as a relief from the atmosphere of the first world war, they are, in one sense, commentaries on human beings. This makes the characters less naturalistic, of course. If you compare, say, Jemima Puddleduck with Dab-Dab, you can see at once which is the real duck, which is a fussy housewife disguised as a duck. Lofting's animals are human types in animal shape, and the humour of the books depends on the incongruity of animals behaving like humans. This satire is far less observable in Lofting's simplified drawings. Here, the animals are drawn *as* animals, though in a slightly grotesque manner, and when they perform any action which is more proper to humans, it is done stiffly, as if they are holding positions they have been taught.

So that we have here neither pure satire nor a picture of the animal world. We are tracking back to the fantasies for small children, and the books are so gay and light-hearted that it is quite possible for children to enjoy them without noticing any of the sharpness at all. When the Doctor gives Nightshade the vixen various strong-smelling essences to put on her cubs' pads, to protect them from hounds, children are amused in just the same way as they are amused by Prince Bumpo's proposal to use gum of different flavours on the postage-stamps of Jolliginki. In fact, one is a good joke; the other is an expression of strong feeling. But the feeling does not upset the easy-going pace of the story.

I am not so sure about the consistency of E. B. White's STUART LITTLE, that odd (and, to me, rather frightening) fantasy about an American wife who unexpectedly produces a mouse as her second son. Doctor Dolittle's animals are touching when they go in for human activities because they do these things as an animal would. But the enumeration of all Stuart's special arrangements, for washing, for climbing up to the basin by way of the bath-chain, for sitting at table, and so on, all emphasize the fact that he is trying, agonizedly, to act as a human being. His shrewd remarks about humans seem to me to have the same nastiness as the pert remarks of a precocious child at a tea-party. This American story is neither satire nor fantasy, but a surrealist mixture, and there is nothing of the charm of animal life to take the taste of the satire away, for Stuart's life is led entirely in a New York apartment.

The atmosphere of THE WIND IN THE WILLOWS, though this book is a far more searching satire, is wholesome and fresh, redolent of the country (even if it is idealized country), and it is the continuous picture of the river, and of the animals that live on and round and near it, that carries through the many threads of the story, conscious and unconscious, tragic and comic, revealing and secret. This is not a child's story pure and simple. Neither is GULLIVER'S TRAVELS. Neither is STUART LITTLE. Neither is ANIMAL FARM. Yet there is so much that children will find for themselves in these books that they will be read many times before they are completely understood. Grahame's story, in fact, when it was first published, baffled the attempt of various critics to pigeon-hole it. Peter Green, in his biography of Grahame, quotes Richard Middleton's review in *Vanity Fair* as one of the very few which kept a clear head:

> The book for me is notable for its intimate sympathy with Nature and for its delicate expression of emotions which I, probably in common with most people, had previously believed to be my exclusive property. When all is said the boastful, unstable Toad, the hospitable Water Rat, the shy, wise, childlike Badger, and the Mole with his pleasant habit of brave boyish impulse, are neither animals nor men, but are types of that deeper humanity which sways us all . . . And if I may venture to describe as an allegory a work which critics, who ought to have known better, have dismissed as a fairy-story, it is certain that *The Wind in the Willows* is a wise book.
> Peter Green. KENNETH GRAHAME (Murray, 1959) p. 259.

THE WIND IN THE WILLOWS is a wise book; it is a complicated book; yet it has given more pleasure to children than almost any other. Firm and strong it certainly is in its implications, but it is a long way from the derisive and shattering propaganda of Erich Kästner's THE ANIMALS' CONFERENCE or George Orwell's ANIMAL FARM, in which animals stand for so much of human error that they have almost ceased to be animals at all. Grahame's story will not push philosophy or satire at a child. It will rouse in him, at different times, pity and anger, enjoyment and laughter; it will satisfy the desire for these things as it satisfied Grahame when he wrote it; and it will leave the animal world where it was, untouched by human sentiment or speculation. The animals return to the river and the wood unchanged; but the reader, young or old, can never again feel blank or indifferent towards them.

Reading List

1.*Horse Stories*

Ball, Richard. BRONCHO. *Country Life* 1930. Illustrated by G. D. Armour. Life-story of a horse, especially in cavalry regiment in First World War.

Downie, John. GALLOPING HOOFS. *Nelson* 1936. Illustrated by the author. First-person story told by horse-breaker on cattle station in N.W. Australia.

*Griffiths, Helen. HORSE IN THE CLOUDS. *Hutchinson* 1957. Illustrated by Edward Osmond.

*James, Will R. SMOKY. *Scribner's*, New York (1926) 1929. *Penguin* (Puffin Story Books) 1941. Illustrated by the author.

Mitchell, Elyne. THE SILVER BRUMBY. *Hutchinson* 1958. Illustrated by Ralph Thompson. Life-story of a wild horse in Australia; straightforward and vivid.

*Patton, Don. BROWN JUG. *Routledge* 1936.

*Peel, Hazel M. FURY, SON OF THE WILDS. *Harrap* 1959. Illustrated by Joan Kiddell-Monroe.

*Sewell, Anna. BLACK BEAUTY (1877). *Dent* (Children's Illustrated Classics) 1948. Illustrated by Lucy Kemp-Welch. *Ward, Lock* 1954. Illustrated by Lionel Edwards.

Wayne, Mel. WILD HORSE KINGDOM. *Collins* 1960. Illustrated by Christine Price. First-person story of a young man establishing breeding-ranch in Wales: vigorous and exciting.

2.*Fantasies about cats*

Coatsworth, Elizabeth. THE CAT WHO WENT TO HEAVEN (1930 U.S.A.). *Dent* 1949. Illustrated by Lynd Ward. Fairy-tale of the Buddha, beautifully written and illustrated.

Coblentz, Catherine. THE BLUE CAT OF CASTLE TOWN (1949 U.S.A.). *Longmans* 1949. Illustrated by Janice Holland. Gentle moral tale with nineteenth-century American background.

Grigs, Mary. THE YELLOW CAT. *O.U.P.* 1936. Illustrated by John and Isobel Morton-Sale. Travels in foreign countries.

Simson, C. Fraser. CANAL CATS. *Blackie* (Frederick Books) 1955. Illustrated by Maurice Wilson. Robust domestic tales of feline house-keeping in Regent's Park.

Todd, Ruthven. SPACE CAT (1952 U.S.A.) 1955, SPACE CAT VISITS VENUS (1955 U.S.A.) 1956. *Chatto & Windus*. Illustrated by Paul Galdone. Witty stories with topical adventures.

3.*Fantasies about Mice*

Austin, Margot. PETER CHURCHMOUSE (1941 U.S.A.) (1943) 1958, GABRIEL
   CHURCHKITTEN (1942 U.S.A.) 1958, GABRIEL CHURCHKITTEN AND THE
   MOTHS (1948 U.S.A.) 1959, TRUMPET CHURCHDOG (1948 U.S.A.) 1959.
   World's Work. Illustrated by the author. Comical tales of village church
   and its unofficial visitors.

Bell, Vicars. ORLANDO AND ROSALIND. *Faber* 1960. Illustrated by Dorothea
   Patterson. Sophisticated tales of literary-minded mice at home.

*Godden, Rumer. THE MOUSEWIFE. *Macmillan* 1951. Illustrated by William
   Pène du Bois.

*Helps, Racey. THE UPSIDE-DOWN MEDICINE. *Collins* 1946, and many other
   titles in the Barnaby Little Mouse series. Illustrated by the author.

*Newell, Averil. THE FLY-BY-NIGHTS. *Black* 1947. Illustrated by Kathleen
   Hilken.

Sharp, Margery. THE RESCUERS. *Collins* 1959. Illustrated by Judith Brook.
   Adventure story appropriate to mice but with adult humour and characterization.

*Titus, Eve. ANATOLE (1956 U.S.A.) 1957, ANATOLE AND THE CAT (1957
   U.S.A.) 1958. *Bodley Head*. Illustrated by Paul Galdone.

*Uttley, Alison. SNUG AND SERENA PICK COWSLIPS. *Heinemann* 1950, and
   many other titles in the Little Brown Mouse series. Illustrated by Katharine
   Wigglesworth.

*Vallance, Rosalind. TITTYMOUSE AND TATTYMOUSE 1946, TITTY AND
   TATTY BY THE RIVER 1949, TITTY AND TATTY'S HOUSE-WARMING 1958.
   Harrap. Illustrated by Astrid Walford.

4.*The British country scene and its animals*

*'B.B.'. BRENDON CHASE. *Hollis & Carter* 1944. Illustrated by the author.

*Batten, H. Mortimer. THE SINGING FOREST. *Blackwood* 1955. *Penguin* (Puffin
   Story Books) 1958. Illustrated by Maurice Wilson.

Budden, John. CHARLIE THE FOX. *Country Life* 1932. Illustrated by G. D.
   Armour. Open-air story of the hunting field and the woods.

Ferry, R. H. WHERE THE RIVER RAN. *Hodder & Stoughton* 1960. Illustrated by
   Margaret Ransome-Block. Elegantly written story of an otter in the West
   Country, her relations with men and beasts; notable illustrations.

*Fortescue, Hon. J. W. (afterwards Sir John Fortescue). THE STORY OF A
   RED-DEER. *Macmillan* (1897) 1958.

*Jefferies, Richard. BEVIS, THE STORY OF A BOY (1882). *Cape* 1932. Illustrated
   by Ernest Shepard.

Masefield, John. A BOOK OF DISCOVERIES. *Wells Gardner* 1910. Illustrated by Gordon Browne.

*Stephen, David. STRING LUG THE FOX, illustrated by Nina Scott Langley, 1950. THE RED STRANGER, illustrated by Maurice Wilson, 1958. *Lutterworth.*

*Uttley, Alison. THE SQUIRREL, THE HARE AND THE LITTLE GREY RABBIT. *Heinemann* 1929, and numerous other titles in the Little Grey Rabbit series. Illustrated by Margaret Tempest.

*Uttley, Alison. LITTLE RED FOX AND THE WICKED UNCLE 1954, LITTLE RED FOX AND CINDERELLA 1956, LITTLE RED FOX AND THE MAGIC MOON 1958. *Heinemann.* Illustrated by Katharine Wigglesworth.

Uttley, Alison. THE ADVENTURES OF NO ORDINARY RABBIT, illustrated by Alec Buckels. *Faber* 1937, and numerous other titles in the Tim Rabbit series. (See also Chap. 6).

*Uttley, Alison. TALES OF THE FOUR PIGS, illustrated by Alec Buckels. *Faber* 1939, and other titles in the Sam Pig series. (see also Chap. 6).

*Williamson, Henry. TARKA THE OTTER. *Putnam* 1927. *Penguin* (Puffin Story Books) 1937. Illustrated by C. F. Tunnicliffe.

Williamson, Henry. THE HENRY WILLIAMSON ANIMAL SAGA. *Macdonald* 1960. Comprising TARKA THE OTTER, SALAR THE SALMON, THE EPIC OF BROCK THE BADGER, CHAKCHEK THE PEREGRINE.

5.Miscellaneous

Barker, K. F. BELLMAN: THE STORY OF A BEAGLE. *Black* 1933. Illustrated by the author. Training and experience on the Westmorland fells: sporting atmosphere.

Baudouy, Michel. OLD ONE-TOE (1957 France). *Methuen* 1960. Translated by Marie Ponsot. Illustrated by Ralph Thompson. Family of children and their relationship with a fox: beautifully written, with understanding of man and beast.

*Brunhoff, Jean de. BABAR'S FRIEND ZEPHIR. (see Chap. 2).

Fallada, Hans. THAT RASCAL FRIDOLIN (1955 Germany). *Heinemann* 1959. Illustrated by Imre Hofbauer. Humorous, natural tale of badger's maraudings.

Finger, Charles. A DOG AT HIS HEEL. *Harrap* 1937. Australian sheepdog and his work; a touching and interesting tale.

*Guillot, René. SAMA (1950 France) 1952, SIRGA (1951 France) 1953, OWORO (1951 France) 1954, KPO THE LEOPARD (1955 France) 1955. *O.U.P.* Translated by Gwen Marsh. Illustrated by Joan Kiddell-Monroe.

*Jong, Meindert De. THE WHEEL ON THE SCHOOL (1954 U.S.A.) 1956, SHADRACH (1953 U.S.A.) 1957, ALONG CAME A DOG (1958 U.S.A.) 1959. *Lutterworth.* Illustrated by Maurice Sendak.

Karazin, N. CRANES FLYING SOUTH (1936). *Longmans* (Heritage of Literature Series) 1952. Translated by M. P. Krovsky. Migration from Russia to Egypt and back: accurate details, personalized birds, jaunty humour.

*Kipling, Rudyard. THE JUNGLE BOOK (1894) 1950, THE SECOND JUNGLE BOOK (1895) 1950. *Macmillan.* Illustrated by Stuart Tresilian.

*Montgomery, Rutherford. CARCAJOU. *H. C. Arrowsmith* 1937. *Penguin* (Puffin Story Books) (1943) 1948.

*Montgomery, Rutherford. MISTER JIM. *Faber* 1952.

*Patchett, M. E. TAM THE UNTAMED. *Lutterworth* 1954. Illustrated by Joan Kiddell-Monroe.

*Patchett, M. E. WILD BROTHER. *Collins* 1954. Illustrated by John Rose.

*Potter, Beatrix. THE FAIRY CARAVAN. Privately printed 1929, *David McKay* Phil., 1929. *Warne* 1946. (See also Chap. 2).

*Selous, Edmund. JACK'S INSECTS. *Methuen* (1910) 1920. Illustrated by J. A. Shepherd.

*Tinbergen, Niko. THE TALE OF JOHN STICKLE. *Methuen* 1954. Illustrated by the author.

Wilson, Erle. COORINNA. *Deutsch* 1953. Life story of Tasmanian (marsupial) wolf, distinguished in style, and fascinating in setting.

*Yee, Chiang. YEBBIN: A GUEST FROM THE WILD. *Methuen* 1947. Illustrated by the author.

6.*Animal Satire*

*Grahame, Kenneth. THE WIND IN THE WILLOWS. *Methuen* (1905) 1931. Illustrated by Ernest Shepard.

*Kästner, Erich. THE ANIMALS' CONFERENCE (1949 Switzerland). *Collins* 1955. Translated by Zita de Schauensee. Illustrated by Walter Trier.

*Lofting, Hugh. THE STORY OF DOCTOR DOLITTLE 1922, THE VOYAGES OF DOCTOR DOLITTLE 1923, DOCTOR DOLITTLE'S POST-OFFICE 1924, DOCTOR DOLITTLE'S CIRCUS 1925, DOCTOR DOLITTLE'S ZOO 1926, DOCTOR DOLITTLE'S CARAVAN 1927, DOCTOR DOLITTLE'S GARDEN 1928, DOCTOR DOLITTLE IN THE MOON 1929, GUB GUB'S BOOK 1932, DOCTOR DOLITTLE'S RETURN 1933, DOCTOR DOLITTLE AND THE SECRET LAKE 1949, DOCTOR DOLITTLE AND THE GREEN CANARY 1951, DOCTOR DOLITTLE'S PUDDLEBY ADVENTURES 1953 (posthumously published stories collected and edited by his wife). *Cape.* Illustrated by the author.

*Orwell, George. ANIMAL FARM. *Secker & Warburg* 1954.

*White, E. B. STUART LITTLE (1945 U.S.A.). *Hamish Hamilton* 1946. Illustrated by Garth Williams.

Chapter 5 | *The Land of Faerie*

Satire is a late experience in a child's reading life. Until he is in his teens he is likely to see, in Toad and Rat and Badger and Mole, animals who divertingly behave like human beings; he will not see them as types of humanity. But when he meets cats and bears and snakes personified in fairy-tale, he will respond to their inward meaning imaginatively and at once.

The attitude of primitive man to animals was not far from that of the child who meets them in fairy-tale. He assumed human characteristics for them. He liked them, feared them, exploited and placated them, and no doubt from earliest times he clarified his own view of them by putting them into stories. When he told a story in which an animal did something *for* him or *to* him, he was getting to terms with the natural world. In the same way, he could people the natural world with imaginary beings, spirits of wood and tree and mountain, beings which were sometimes friendly (like brownies and other household spirits) or sometimes malicious and even hostile (like trolls and ogres and gnomes). If this is not the only explanation for the fairy race as we now know it, it is at least a satisfactory one.

The magical origins of fairy-tale are far away from us now. From earliest times, oral tradition has been enriched by the writing down of tales or by the telling of them by specialists, bards and itinerant poets, who added their own twists and conceits. Local and national events and characteristics, allegory and moral, domestic anecdote and detail—all these have been shaping the fairy-tale for centuries and sophisticating it. Yet no fairy-tale is worth anything without the two primitive emotions in which lie the beginnings of magic—fear and wonder. Storm and cold, fire and the loneliness of mountains, the fear of the elements is implicit in traditional fairy-tales from the Maori to the Spanish, from Russia to Africa. It is at the very root of

George Macdonald's stories, in the magnificent rushing end of THE PRINCESS AND THE GOBLINS and in Diamond's adventures with the North Wind:

> For a few moments, Diamond seemed to be borne up through the depths of an ocean of dazzling flame; the next, the winds were writhing around him like a storm of serpents. For they were in the midst of the clouds and mists, and they of course took the shapes of the wind, eddying and wreathing and whirling and shooting and dashing about like grey and black water, so that it was as if the wind itself had taken shape, and he saw the grey and black wind tossing and raving most madly all about him.
> George Macdonald. AT THE BACK OF THE NORTH WIND (Dent, Children's Illustrated Classics, 1956) p. 60.

It gives imaginative unity to J. R. R. Tolkein's impressive contemporary epic of magic:

> Suddenly a song began: a cold murmur, rising and falling. The voice seemed far away and immeasurably dreary, sometimes high in the air and thin, sometimes like a low moan from the ground. Out of the formless stream of sad but horrible sounds, strings of words would now and again shape themselves: grim, hard, cold words, heartless and miserable. The night was railing against the morning of which it was bereaved, and the cold was cursing the warmth for which it hungered.
> J. R. R. Tolkein. THE FELLOWSHIP OF THE RING (Allen & Unwin, 1954) p. 152.

Another modern writer, Angela Ainley Jeans, has built two fine stories, LISTEN TO THE WIND and THE KINGDOM OF THE WINDS, on a personification of the elements which has more than a touch of primitive grandeur.

The good illustrator of fairy-tale will try to convey this general feeling rather than struggle in vain to put down in line the intangible happenings of fairy lands. What happens in traditional fairy-tale does not take on a concrete semblance in a child's mind. As he reads, he is beset by haunting visions just out of reach. He knows what is happening, he feels the mystery and magic of it, but he does not want to see it. All the same, it can be *suggested* in illustrations. They can show us a scene that will put us in the right frame of mind for a

Drawing by Peggy Fortnum for Patricia Lynch's JINNY THE CHANGELING (Dent). The mood of one kind of fairy-tale. Below: Drawing by Joan Kiddell-Monroe for James Reeves's ENGLISH FABLES AND FAIRY STORIES (O.U.P.)

fairy story, a scene which evokes fear and wonder in us. Joan Kiddell-Monroe, in particular, has a style well suited to do this.

Fear in one story may be wonder in another: the two are never far apart. Both rise from an apprehension of the supernatural which still nourishes fairy-tale in our own day. The tiny visions of Diana Ross's Miss Pussy; the valley with its mist-enlarged, galloping horse, which the little changeling sees in Patricia Lynch's JINNY THE CHANGELING; the glimpses Eleanor Farjeon gives us, in THE SILVER CURLEW, of moonlit mystery; the haunting landscapes of Walter de la Mare's story of THE THREE ROYAL MONKEYS; these are all much nearer to primitive fairy-tales than their style might suggest.

The Land of Faerie is a place to fear and to marvel at; to see in dreams or to imagine in snatches. It is also a place that enshrines human wishes. For a fairy story is more than a description of nature. There is something happening; and it is usually something fortunate, in the long run, to compensate for the world as it really is. Fairy-tales are made out of a natural desire to change life in imagination if it cannot be changed in fact. George Macdonald's North Wind is grand and terrifying; she can also be gentle, and can even up the inequalities of life for little Diamond. Beside the terrors of snake-filled marshes and icy wastes and burning deserts, there are pictures of ideal worlds, paradises for those who are willing to search for them. They may be worlds described in very human terms, like the civilized world in a Chinese fairy's magic box, with its wide city streets and shops and 'dragons of many colours, all horned and fire-breathing'; or they may be suggestions, like the land of Nowhere in an Australian aboriginal legend, 'oceans of nothingness and soft billowing clouds, topped with pink and gold', or they may be worlds rounded out with symbolism, like Hans Andersen's description of the Garden of Eden:

The lion and the tiger darted like lithe cats through the green thicket that smelt like the blossom of the olive, and the lion and the tiger were tame; the wild wood-pigeon shining like the fairest of pearls fluttered the lion's mane with its wings, and the antelope, that elsewhere is so timid, stood still and nodded its head, as if it too would like to join in the play.

Hans Andersen. FORTY-TWO STORIES. Translated by M. R. James (Faber, 1953 ed.) pp. 134-5.

By the time fairy stories come to us they have been considerably sophisticated. The youngest son does not want compensation for his lowly place in the tribal hierarchy, he wants to win half a kingdom and marry a princess. The basic wish, though, is still, as it always was, a wish for luck. Something from outside—a little black man, a snake saved from a forest-fire, a god from a mountain-top, whatever it is—something with magical powers is going to make up to us for our lack of good fortune. Children or adults, we all need this feeling of compensation, whether we believe in it or not. When we go to see *Peter Pan* on the stage, and clap to revive Tinker Bell, we are not clapping because we believe in fairies so much as because we all have somewhere in us the desire that fairies should exist.

The young man, then, swineherd or woodcutter or farm-hand, wants to marry a princess. There are no fairy stories that I know of where a young prince wants to become a swineherd—not permanently, that is, though now and then for a joke, perhaps, or as relaxation from his lofty station. Traditional fairy-tales are the property of children and simple folk. They begin in the kitchen, and more often than not they have been told there. They are simply told and concerned with simple things. Their stage properties are chairs and chests, the spinning-wheel and the axe, spiders' webs and bejewelled toads and attentive, friendly robins. No fairy-tale will be right for children, or right for anybody for that matter, unless the magic is simple and unless it is accepted completely within the terms of the story. Self-consciousness kills a fairy-tale more quickly than a pedestrian style or a lack of imagination.

The idea of disbelief should never enter in at all. By a paradox, the magical element should be completely matter-of-fact. A domestic fable, by James Reeves, *The Old Woman and the Four Noises*, tells how an old countrywoman learned to live at peace with the inhabitants of the creaking board, the squeaking door and the rattling window-frame:

'Don't be afraid,' said the voice. 'I am an elf. You cannot see me, but I live in your front door and I bring you luck. Every time the door is opened or closed, I squeak just to remind you I am here.'

'Well, what an odd thing,' said the old woman. 'I never knew before that there was such a thing as a door-elf that squeaked,

but now I come to think about it, I see no reason why there shouldn't be. Won't you come in and make yourself at home?'
James Reeves. PIGEONS AND PRINCESSES (Heinemann, 1956) p. 29.

This story was written only a few years ago, but it has the attitude of true fairy-tale. Traditional fairy-tales are very direct; there is no fumbling or apologizing; you are in the magic world straight away:

Long, long ago, in the days when wishing was still some use, a King's son was put under a spell by a wicked old witch. As soon as he was quite in her power, she shut him up in a great iron chest. Then, by means of her magic, she set Prince, chest, and all, down in the middle of a lonely and enchanted forest.
The Great Iron Chest, in GRIMMS' FAIRY TALES, freely translated by Amabel Williams-Ellis (Blackie, 1959) p. 163.

Not all writers of modern times have been able to strike this casual note, and, obviously, it is most easily done in the retelling of old tales. Ruth Manning-Sanders is particularly happy in her opening paragraphs in PETER AND THE PISKIES, a collection of old Cornish legends and folk-tales. Here is the beginning of *Skillywidden*:

A man was cutting furze. And where the furze was growing higher than his head, he cut a way into the middle of it, so that he would have more room to swing his hook. And what should he see in the middle of that furze brake, lying on a bed of wild thyme, but a little fellow no bigger than a mouse. He was dressed in a smart green coat and sky-blue breeches, and he had little square-toed shoes on his feet with diamond buckles. He had pulled his bit of a three-cornered hat down over his eyes to shade him from the sun, and he was fast, fast asleep.
Ruth Manning-Sanders. PETER AND THE PISKIES (Oxford University Press, 1958) p. 7.

To the Cornish, fairies are natural enough. Irish writers, from Frances Browne to Patricia Lynch, have the same complete ease of manner. It is fatal to try to avoid the traditional formulas, the 'Once upon a time' which never wears out.

This is not because it is a formula that pleases children. Fairy-tales are not the sole property of children, and it is only perhaps in the last two centuries that they have come to be regarded in this way. They are a form of poetry, and belong to everyone in whom imagination is active and free. To children most of all, therefore, because they have not yet learned that the imagination has any limits. When adults claim fairy-tales for themselves, there are often odd results. Charles Perrault, at the end of the seventeenth century, offered traditional tales to the French court as a luxury entertainment, with primitive fear well hidden under the cloak of reason, with sardonic rhymed morals tacked on at the end. To sum up Red Riding Hood like this:

This story teaches that the very young,
And little girls more surely than the rest—
Sweet, dainty things, clothed in their Sunday best—
Should never trust a stranger's artful tongue.
Small wonder if these guileless young beginners
Provide the wolf with some of his best dinners.

THE FAIRY TALES OF CHARLES PERRAULT, translated by Geoffrey Brereton (Penguin, 1957) p. 25.

is to change the terror of the woods for the perils of the city. Cinderella, Beauty and the Beast, Puss in Boots, Bluebeard, these were all country tales turned by Perrault into period pieces. The two brothers who attack Bluebeard at the critical moment might come straight from Dumas; 'one a dragoon and the other a musketeer' and each benefiting from their sister to the extent of a captain's commission. Cinderella, finding husbands for her ugly sisters, is a very different person from the anonymous waif of the Grimms' version or the romantic lady in Eleanor Farjeon's nineteen-twentyish piece, THE GLASS SLIPPER. In our own day, James Thurber has offered an adult view of fairyland. The shadow of the *New Yorker* hangs over his witty pieces, like MANY MOONS, THE THIRTEEN CLOCKS and THE WHITE DEER, with their farrago of satire, legend, fancy and verbal flapdoodle. But it is still fairyland that we enter through these stories. Prince Thag, journeying in search of the enchanted deer, meets this kind of adventure:

Four redbirds in a tangle bush sang 'verti verti verti go' as Thag closed his mouth and held his breath and shut his eyes and galloped on through the stingish ringy smoke and the trickish sicky smell, and after a long moment he rode out of the growth of gnarled and toppling trees, and beheld before his eyes the shining Valley of Euphoria.

The air sparkled with the high fine sparkle of crystal which made the three men who approached Thag seem larger than they really were. The three men stood beside Thag's horse and bowed and smiled and bowed. Thag saw that each man held in his hand a mask exactly like his face, but the first mask was stern, the second mask was sad and the third mask was solemn. The first man giggled, the second man chuckled, and the third man chortled. The first man bowed and spoke. 'We wear our masks on yesterdays and on tomorrows.'

The second said, 'And since those sad days never come—'

The third man said, 'We know no sorrows.'

James Thurber. THE WHITE DEER (Hamish Hamilton, 1946) pp. 53–4.

Parody and magic adventure go side by side in passages like this.

Part at least of the humour in these tales will only be discovered by a child from the tone of voice of an adult reading them aloud, and that same child will miss some of the point of another modern writer of fairy-tales, Diana Ross. Volumes like THE BRIDAL GOWN, CHILD OF AIR and THE WILD CHERRY present tales of traditional sort with various implications. Occasionally these overweight the story, as in the very philosophical story called *Necessity the Mother of Opinion* (in CHILD OF AIR). In *The Pest Child* (from THE BRIDAL GOWN) and *The Young Man with Music in His Fingers* (from THE WILD CHERRY) and in many others, narrative and meaning are beautifully welded together. Her best work is to be found in the cycle of stories about Miss Pussy and Jackanapes. In these, like Perrault, she has brought stylish artistry to bear on very simple plots. She has given her peacable, determined little cat a domestic background—on the face of it a very definite background, a village, faintly Regency in character, where Jackanapes, the roistering monkey, unwelcome in polite society, sets himself by his tricks to disturb Miss Pussy's composure. So far, we are in almost a Beatrix Potter world. But the horizon is shifting and unclear. Transformation is the keynote of the tales—the change from grave to gay, from ordinary to magical. Miss Pussy lives on the very edge of fairyland. *The Enormous*

Apple Pie tells how she invited her nephews and nieces to a party and how Jackanapes and Snatch, his boon companion, ate the contents of the pie and filled the case with frogs. No child could resist the careful detail of the making of the pie, or the sudden magical sequel to the trick:

> For now that the frogs are all out of the pie they gather themselves in order around the largest among them, and he, with a great air, draws a fiddle from under his arm, and each of the others produces a musical instrument, till here is a complete orchestra of flutes and strings, and bowing to Miss Pussy who is dumb with amazement they strike up a pleasant tune. Motioning to Miss Pussy that she shall follow them they lead the way back into the pie.
>
> What! Follow a band of frogs into an apple pie! Why, the thing is impossible! But as Miss Pussy and her nieces and nephews crowd round to peer into the pie the opening seems to widen, and quite easily they find themselves walking in a mossy glade, so delightful and charming they think they have found the way to paradise.

Diana Ross. THE ENORMOUS APPLE PIE (Lutterworth, 1951) pp. 17–18.

The Phœnix begins in lively style, with the kittens finding treasures in Miss Pussy's garden, including a locket which she had lost and which Jackanapes covets. Suddenly the tone changes and we are in a different world:

> So with a solemnity which would do justice to Solomon in judgment he takes out his pocket-knife and prises open the locket.
>
> Oh! But the wonder of it!
>
> A bright shining light which yet does not dazzle fills the whole room; a rosy light which quivers and seems to live, and in the heart of the light which centres in the locket a Phœnix lies, golden and beautiful, and as it raises its jewelled head the light ripples as if the Phœnix stirred in a pool, and there is a smell of such sweetness as if every scented flower in a forest of spices were being stirred by a warm wind.

Ibid., pp. 91–2.

This magic world can be over the horizon, up in the sky, under ice, or in the kitchen. Diana Ross makes magic out of ordinary things— a swing, a photograph album, a pie-dish, an old shirt. Sometimes it is pure magic—as when Miss Pussy, riding high on the swing, looks for a moment into fairyland. Sometimes, as in *Mid-summer Eve*, when Jackanapes is punished by Miss Pussy's fairy friends, the effect is richly comic just because of the ordinary domestic details:

> He staggers to the kitchen to make himself some strong coffee, but when he gets the tin from the shelf, what is this? It is full of gravel and cinders. He swears savagely and reaches for the tea caddy, frowning and trying to figure out what he did with the coffee. But when he opens the tea caddy there is nothing in it at all except thousands of little spiders which run out all over the place when he drops the caddy in disgust. And yet he can swear he filled it only yesterday with a pound of tea.
> Ibid., pp. 58–9.

But then, of course, fairy-tales have always been practical as well as poetic: the magic has always started from simple beginnings. From the folk-tales of Grimm, which are so easily acclimatized in England, to J. B. Haldane's scientific fantasy, MY FRIEND MR LEAKEY, or Naomi Mitchison's GRAEME AND THE DRAGON, we have seen the combination of ageless and contemporary. Your writer of true fairy-tale has always in the background a magical land which no man ever sees and all men long for; in the foreground are the comfortable pots and pans, or whatever ordinary circumstance is to be illuminated by the sun of that magical land. And your writer of true fairy-tale will display no uneasiness when moving from one world to another. To read Patricia Lynch's stories, in fact, is to be in two worlds at once. In THE GREY GOOSE OF KILNEVIN or THE TURF-CUTTER'S DONKEY, animals speak, leprechauns move about freely at country fairs, small objects become enchanted and then, in a flash, are ordinary objects again. Inside the humble cottage everything is peaceful and secure, but, once outside, the enchantment is everywhere, sometimes dangerously alluring, sometimes treated with humorous disrespect. Celtic twilight doesn't come into this, but plenty of Celtic easiness with the fairy folk, such as one gets also in the simply-told stories of Frances Browne in GRANNIE'S WONDERFUL CHAIR, still fresh and lively after a century, or in more modern stories like Helen Simpson's volume of Irish tales, MUMBUDGET, which veers between humour and the magic of the supernatural. From an exquisite tale of a small boy learning the music of nature, with a fairy pipe, we go on to a delicate comedy of a brownie who leaves his prim London home to give a hand in an Irish household. His help is so effective that nobody can find anything 'for how could they know that the eggs had been put tidily into a bowl on the dresser, and the rice in a tin labelled RICE.' There is a story about an elemental who comes to work on a farm, a story terrifying in its intensity and pathos, and there is a rollicking bit of fun about a banshee whom William tries to re-educate:

'That's not the way my mother taught me,' said she. 'She took pride in my voice, as well she might, though I say it, for when I was younger I could best a March wind at its height. My mother taught me to render misfortune only. Who ever heard of a person would howl for joy?'
Helen Simpson. MUMBUDGET (Heinemann, 1928) p. 160.

Poetry, mysterious happenings, jokes and absurdity, they are all there, mixed with artless art by a writer who is perfectly at home in the land of the fairies.

In all these stories the domestic background serves as a starting-point. It is the same background—the hut, the cottage, the kitchen—from which men go off to find strange adventures, in GRIMMS' FAIRY TALES. Mrs Molesworth, writing half a century after English children had first wandered into that dangerous land, took fairy-tales back into a mid-Victorian middle-class nursery. Her descriptions are gentle and general, her enchantments always turn out for the best, and the most delightful of her fairies are nothing but cotton-reels transformed. *The Reel Fairies* is a fancy designed for the young. A little girl (the author in childhood) falls asleep by the fire and dreams (or is it a dream?) that she has been made Queen of the cotton-reels she has been playing with. She is enthroned in her mother's work-box, which is drawn as a carriage by her subjects. How many writers, at this point, would have loaded the story with gauze and glitter. Mrs Molesworth makes no mistake. She sees the work-box as a child would:
    . . . she settled herself in the place the fairies had kept for her, the nice little division lined with satin, in which her mamma's thimble

Drawing by Peggy Fortnum for Diana Ross's THE ENORMOUS APPLE PIE (Lutterworth) Below: Drawing by Pauline Baynes for C. S. Lewis's THE LION, THE WITCH AND THE WARDROBE (Bles)

and emery cushion always lay. It was pretty comfortable, only rather hard....
Mrs Molesworth. FAIRY STORIES (Harvill Press, 1957) p. 77.

And at the end there is a gentle hint from the mother. It was not so pleasant, was it, to be a Queen? Better to be a good child safe in the nursery.

Yes, safe. Behind all Mrs Molesworth's stories lies the idea of security, the security of a happy and comfortable home. In *Ask The Robins*, when Linde is preparing for her dangerous night journey to the robins' wood, her sister first gives her a cup of 'good hot soup' and makes her put on all her wraps. In THE CARVED LIONS, one of her best stories, the lions make no magic, and nobody expects them to; but they bring to the homesick girl, even if only in a dream, the illusion that she has seen her parents, that she is still part of a family.

Perhaps these are not fairy-tales in the strict sense of the word. The enchantment is slight, and we never have to consider how much of it is supposed to happen and how much is merely *felt* by the characters. Similarly, Mrs Ewing uses fairy lore as a beautiful background for stories which are full of family discipline and affection, coloured with a strong feeling for the rural past. Foreground and background are connected with fact. In *Amelia and the Dwarfs*, for example, we watch Amelia change from a spoilt, destructive young miss to a thoughtful little girl. Whether she really becomes the dwarfs' slave or whether it was merely a feverish dream concerns neither author nor reader. What matters is the atmosphere of danger, the feeling of lurking mischief in the little creatures, which any child will believe could have changed Amelia's behaviour.

This domestic note makes the magic very easy to accept, but although stories like this are a long way from the traditional fairy-tale, there is the faint echo of elemental music in them. The world C. S. Lewis has created, in our own day, in his cycle of fairy adventure stories about Narnia, looks at the outset as homely as the world of these Victorian tales. In the first book of his series, THE LION, THE WITCH AND THE WARDROBE, we find four children playing hide-and-seek. Lucy, hiding at the back of a wardrobe, suddenly finds herself in a winter landscape, walking towards—a lamp-post. The transition to the magic world is superbly managed in the text, and in Pauline Baynes's drawings which subtly interpret it. The first person Lucy meets is Mr Tumnus, a faun. He is carrying an umbrella and several parcels, and he gives her a good tea in his suburban tree-root dwelling. But it is not Lucy who finds out the secret of this strange land. When she gets back to her own world, her next brother, Edmund, jeers at her story, and when he in his turn wanders into Narnia he still pretends she is making it all up. He is duly punished when he becomes the protégé of the White Witch, usurper Queen of Narnia. Like Kay with the Snow Queen, he hugs his fault to him until his conscience is awakened and he joins the others to overthrow the witch and become one of the rulers of Narnia.

Events in the kingdom may seem at times rather surprising, but they have not the complete inconsequence of events in traditional fairy-tales. Everything is the result of character, whether mortal or supernatural, and this makes it perfectly possible to believe in the beasts in PRINCE CASPIAN who have lost their freedom and power of speech but who recover them when the four children help to overthrow the prince's wicked uncle; to believe in the changing of their cousin Eustace Stobbs, in THE VOYAGE OF THE DAWN TREADER, from a priggish, vegetarian schoolboy to an eager and enterprising traveller in strange lands; to believe in the extraordinary underground kingdom in THE SILVER CHAIR, where a lost prince, heir to old Caspian, is held underground in slavery to a green lady until certain conditions are fulfilled.

These conditions show the same mingling of magic and mysticism which you find in medieval poems like *Sir Gawain and the Green Knight*, and it is no accident that this story so much resembles the poem, with its magical details. C. S. Lewis is a leading exponent of medieval allegory, and if scholarship sits lightly in these stories, his allegorical purpose gives them meaning that children will not even try to grasp at a first reading.

In these tales he shows a fairy-tale picture of the redemption of man and his right to immortality. The virtues of courage, loyalty and generosity, the faults of greed, conceit and treachery, are familiar in fairy-tale. But Aslan the mysterious Lion, king over all temporal rulers of Narnia, son of the Emperor over the sea, Aslan who comes and goes without warning, who dies to save his subjects, who fills children and beasts alike with awe and love—Aslan is an emblem of Christ.

At the end of THE LAST BATTLE, Aslan explains to the children that they will not, as in the previous books, return to their own world:

'There *was* a real railway accident,' said Aslan softly. 'Your father and mother and all of you are—as you used to call it in the Shadowlands—dead. The term is over: the holidays have begun. The dream is ended: this is the morning.'

And as He spoke He no longer looked to them like a lion; but the things that began to happen after that were so great and beautiful that I cannot write them. And for us this is the end of all the stories, and we can most truly say that they all lived happily ever after. But for them it was only the beginning of the real story. All their life in this world and all their adventures in Narnia had only been the cover and the title-page; now at last they were beginning Chapter One of the Great Story which no one on earth has read: which goes on for ever: in which every chapter is better than the one before.

C. S. Lewis. THE LAST BATTLE (Bodley Head, 1956) pp. 183-4.

I respect C. S. Lewis for coming so unaffectedly to the climax which is obviously, for him, the only possible one; but from a literary point of view the transition from adventure (which has its own ideas and importance) to Christian apologetics seems too abrupt. The history of Narnia, as he presents it, is full of implicit allegory which is enough to carry worlds of meaning to any thoughtful child. The passage I have just quoted comes after a long description of the breaking up of Narnia after the last battle with the Calormenes, the forces of unbelief; it is a description of dis-creation which has the simple intensity of a poem by Blake, and is one of the finest pieces of writing in this kind of story. Like the mythological passages in George Macdonald's stories, it goes behind religious doctrine and speaks to the awe-struck ancestor who survives in all of us. The descriptions in these books tell us more than the sermonizing. They have a literary value as well, for they hold all the stories together.

C. S. Lewis makes us believe in Narnia, rich, fertile, and hospitable; in Archenland, mountainous and mysterious; in Calormen, with its walled cities, its pomegranates and perils, the Eastern feeling which comes out also in the illustrations. Not by the maps which he provides to establish the frontiers, the principal cities and rivers for the seeing eye, but in the words, the evocative names and the finely realized landscapes with which he fills the eye of the imagination, so that you go with the four children to the Stone Table, see the boy Shasta crossing the desert, see the animals dividing at the great Door. In moments of joy, of fear and of poetic vision, this is a very real country.

So is the world J. R. R. Tolkein has described in THE HOBBIT and in the trilogy, THE LORD OF THE RINGS, a world drawing inspiration from Malory and Spenser and from Beowulf most of all.

I can remember Professor Tolkein reading Beowulf aloud at Oxford, pacing up and down the lecture-room with his gown flying, giving us an inkling of what bardic poetry ought to sound like; and his fairy-tales, if you can call them that, have the same bardic quality. They read aloud extremely well. The language is alive, thrusting, moving, plunging, piercing; even at its quietest it has the tension of near-movement.

It all began with THE HOBBIT. This is a straight fairy-tale, published in 1937, about a hero who is persuaded by a wizard to try to destroy the dragon Smaug, who lies guarding his treasure inside a hill and sallies out to terrorize the nearby villages. But this is not an ordinary fairy story. First, the hero is neither a fairy nor a human. He is a Hobbit: exactly described for us, with his stature (large Hobbits can ride small ponies), his tastes (they claim to have discovered tobacco) and his domestic life. Our particular Hobbit, Bilbo Baggins, is a sort of Hornblower with fur, a peace-loving creature elevated to be hero. 'Dear me!' he exclaims, 'what a fool I was and am! . . .I have absolutely no use for dragon-guarded treasures, and the whole lot could stay here for ever, if only I could wake up and find this beastly tunnel was my own front-door at home!' Qualities which he takes for granted help him to win in the end—his courage (which is partly lack of imagination), his sense of humour and his tenacity.

On his journey Bilbo meets by an underground river an extraordinary, malicious, slimy animal called Gollum. This is in fact not his name but an onomatopœic rendering of the swallowing noise he makes. His name we learn later, in more sinister circumstances, for, nearly twenty years after the publication of THE HOBBIT, THE FELLOWSHIP OF THE RING appeared, beginning an epic tale unique in plot and in style.

THE LORD OF THE RINGS is a quest story, like THE HOBBIT. It

has the same freshness and precision, but it is a more serious affair altogether. In the previous tale, Bilbo had won by a trick from Gollum a little rough ring which that creature called his Precious. This proved to be the One Ring which unites all other Rings, at once a symbol of power and an actual object which the whole of Tolkein's magic world is seeking. Whoever holds this ring can rule all people and all places, but he will almost certainly lose his soul.

We enter this vast, incredible world on the eve of crisis. Sauron, brooding shadow of evil, wants the ring. Gandalf, that same wizard who sent Bilbo after the dragon, knows the ring must be destroyed, thrown into the Cracks of Doom in the Fire-Mountain, which is under the eye of Sauron. The ring has for many years lain hidden in Bilbo's house, but in his old age he gives it to a young relation, Frodo, and it is Frodo, in the end, who takes on the task of seeing the Ring destroyed. His companions on the journey, assembled by degrees, are two young Hobbit friends, Merry and Pippin, Samwise (Frodo's faithful servant), Gimli the dwarf and Legolas the Elf, and two men of a high heroic race, Aragorn, a prince wandering in disguise, and Boromir, a flawed, tragic knight of the Arthurian sort. THE FELLOWSHIP OF THE RING describes how the band collected and starts them on their adventures. THE TWO TOWERS follows the enterprise into side-issues, while the armies of good and evil gather for the final battle, and this is fought out in THE RETURN OF THE KING.

These books are not in the strictest sense children's books, as THE HOBBIT is. I do not mean children cannot read them. Every child should read them, somewhere between the ages of eleven and sixteen, and everyone with a feeling for poetry, of any age, should read them too. They are immensely exciting and compelling stories, but beyond the adventure there is the poetry of vast ideas, of appearances wonderfully visualized, of a country given form and contour, colour and weather, of people (elves and Ringwraiths, magicians and hobbits, tree-wights and knights) each one perfectly realized. I have never met anyone who was lukewarm about Tolkein's books. Either you will think he has made a considerable fuss about nothing, or you will accept the world he has invented and find it complete and satisfying. It is not a fairy-tale world so much as the world of Arthurian legend, where enchantment is at once human and supernatural. It is an extraordinarily varied world; you move from a rough village inn to the stately hall of the Elves, from the dark, deadly caves of Moria to the earthy, infinitely reassuring home of Tom Bombadil the elemental. And as the scene changes, so does the style.

Action calls out some of Tolkein's best writing. The struggle between Gandalf and the Balrog, deep in Moria, is epic and demands archaic style:

> Long I fell, and he fell with me. His fire was about me. I was burned. Then we plunged into the deep water and all was dark. Cold it was as the tide of death: almost it froze my heart . . . Yet it has a bottom, beyond light and knowledge . . . Thither I came at last, to the uttermost foundations of stone. He was with me still. His fire was quenched, but now he was a thing of slime, stronger than a strangling snake.
>
> We fought far under the living earth, where time is not counted. Ever he clutched me, and ever I hewed him, till at last he fled into dark tunnels.
>
> J. R. R. Tolkein. THE TWO TOWERS (Allen & Unwin, 1954) p. 105.

And, in contrast, there is Merry's slangy account of the fantastic attack by the Ents, the tree-herds, on Isengard:

> When Treebeard had got a few arrows in him, he began to warm up, to get positively 'hasty', as he would say. He let out a great *hoom-hom*, and a dozen more Ents came striding up. An angry Ent is terrifying. Their fingers, and their toes, just freeze on to rock; and they tear it up like bread-crust. It was like watching the work of great tree-roots in a hundred years, all packed into a few moments.
>
> They pushed, pulled, tore, shook, and hammered; and *clang-bang*, *crash-crack*, in five minutes they had these huge gates just lying in ruin; and some were already beginning to eat into the walls, like rabbits in a sand-pit.
>
> Ibid., p. 172

Now plain, now bardic, now rough and clanging, the magnificent prose drives you forward through this astonishing story. It is like traditional fairy-tale in one way. It has no moral teaching. There are ideas in plenty in the three books, especially the idea behind the

Ring, that power corrupts; but this is presented as a danger, not as a moral. Time after time we realize that the Ring is changing Frodo, that it is trying to bend him to its purposes. Frodo faces this as a danger, in the same spirit as he faces Shelob or Sauron. Of course we can read morals into the books, and we are all bound to read them with thoughts of tyranny and dictatorship in our minds. But, though they reflect the climate of our time, they have the universal, dateless quality of imagination.

Tolkein's is an intensely active, bardic work. It grew out of family story-telling over many years and it is communicated very directly to the reader. With Walter de la Mare we have a country described by a poet, where appearances matter as much as events, sometimes more. Here we have come back to the land of traditional fairy-tale, but we are seeing it through a magnifying glass. Take *Dick and the Beanstalk* for example. What a beanstalk it is—not *a* beanstalk but *the* beanstalk. When Dick came upon it, that rimy afternoon in Gloucestershire, he was bound to recognize it. How sharply visualized every detail is in this brilliant tale. Here are the giant uncles in the strange land at the top of the beanstalk:

> Dick crept forward, and, leaning out a little between the bases of the balusters of the gallery, peeped down. They were intent on a game that looked like common dominoes, though the pieces or men they played with were almost as big as tombstones. In no story-book he had ever read had Dick chanced on the like of these giants. They sat like human mountains at their game, and the noise of the dominoes was like Pharaoh's chariots. And when one of them, laying down a domino on the table, mumbled, *Double!*, it was like the coughing of a lion.

Walter de la Mare. COLLECTED STORIES FOR CHILDREN (Faber, 1957) pp. 38-9.

The barn where Grackle, the young giant, lies hidden, the giants' kitchen where Dick is nearly caught, the ogre's widow, the hills Dick sees in the distance, the very hair and hide of his pony—everything is precisely and superbly described.

This is a cheerful story, because Dick is a cheerful lad who does not worry about a little danger. In most of de la Mare's work there is an undercurrent of sadness, mystery and fear. He knows what is involved in a glance into the fairy world, however brief. His apparitions have nothing to do with the gauzy and inept creatures our children see on birthday-cards. It seems hardly right to call de la Mare's beings *fairies*, even using the word in its oldest sense. Perhaps the being in *Miss Jemima* is the nearest to a fairy:

> '. . . on the other side of the flat gravestone a face appeared. I mean it didn't rise up. It simply came into the air. A very small face, more oval than round, its gold-coloured hair over its wild greenish eyes falling on either side of its head in a curous zigzag way . . .'

At least it is an extraordinarily evocative and mysterious picture. An early illustrator of this story, Irene Hawkins, did try to represent the fairy, and so put her picture some way away from the mood of the story. Robin Jacques, in a drawing for the same scene, makes you see the fairy through the raptly reflective face of the young Jemima.

Then there are the strangers in *The Three Sleeping Boys of Warwickshire* who appeared like this in the water-meadows:

> . . . of middle height, with garments like spider-web, their straight hair of the colour of straw falling gently on either side their narrow cheeks, so that it looked at first glimpse as if they were greybeards. And as they trod on their narrow feet, the frozen grasses scarcely stirring beneath them, they turned their faces from side to side, looking at the children. And then a fairness that knows no change showed in their features, and their eyes were of a faint flame like that of sea-water on nights of thunder when the tide gently lays its incoming ripples on some wide flat sandy strand of the sea.
>
> Ibid pp. 110–111.

Or the more traditional but still unique dwarf in *A Penny a Day*:

> He was of the height of a child of five; he had pointed ears, narrow shoulders, and a hump on his back. And he wore a coat made of a patchwork of moleskins. He stood there—as stock-still as the stones themselves—his bright colourless eyes under his moleskin cap fixed on her, as if Griselda was as outlandish an object to him as he was to Griselda.
>
> Ibid., pp. 55–6.

Drawing by Irene Hawkins for Walter de la Mare's *Miss Jemima* in THE MAGIC JACKET (Faber)

How could his beings fail to be unique, when he sees everything as freshly as a child would? One of his stories, *Maria-Fly*, illustrates not only the nature of a child but also of the poetic impulse. Maria, alone in a room, suddenly sees a fly. It seems to her as though she had never seen one before. She tries to communicate her vision, to the cook, to her father, to the gardener. Each one answers after his kind, each utterly fails to understand her. She goes on trying to explain:

> 'I—have—just—seen—a—fly. It had wings like as you see oil on water, and a red face with straight silver eyes, and it wasn't buzzing or nothing, but it was scraping with its front legs over its wings, then rubbing them like corkscrews. Then it took its head off and on, and then it began again—but I don't mean all that. I mean I sawn the fly—saw it, I mean.'
> Ibid., p. 354.

It is all there—the vision, the effort to communicate, the picture that comes to us. Maria, too, was a poet.

Even in this short, artless story, there is a feeling of precariousness, of one world dissolving into another. The fairy world of de la Mare is precise in detail but hazy in outline, a country unmapped and largely uninhabited. Even in a story like *The Three Sleeping Boys*, the harsh world of hunger and cold and soot, which is a version of historical fact, merges without effort into a silvery dreamland where the boys are at peace. In that incomparable piece of myth-making, THE THREE ROYAL MONKEYS, the characters are the animals of the African plain and jungle, their names fancifully modified, and the country is, on the face of it, equally recognizable. But this, too, is a magic land, the land where the traveller must seek the fabulous stone called Kiph, the land of de la Mare's poems. Here all is strange and remote. An ancient hare makes magic; Nod, youngest of the monkey princes, is at once child, pongo and fairy; there is poetic hyperbole in the descriptions of fearful mountain passes and the beautiful gardens of Tishnar. Homely, prosaic details are fused with otherworldly beauty, as in the superb passage which tells of the monkey brothers arrived at Tishnar's meadows:

> For there, in the midst between the fountains, was a long low table spread with flowers and strange fruits and nuts, and lit with clear, pear-shaped flames floating in the air like that of the Wonderstone, but of the colours of ivory and emerald and amethyst;

Drawing by Robin Jacques for Walter de la Mare's *Miss Jemima* in
COLLECTED STORIES FOR CHILDREN (Faber)

with nineteen platters of silver and nineteen goblets of gold. And presently they heard in the distance the grasshopper voices of the Hill-Mulgars, as they came stubbling along with Thimble's litter in their midst, carrying their heavy faggots and bottles and bundles, their pink eyes blinking, their knees trembling, not knowing whether to be joyful or afraid.

Walter de la Mare. THE THREE ROYAL MONKEYS (Faber, 1946) p. 226. First published in 1910 as THE THREE MULLA-MULGARS.

You believe in all these mysterious places because of the associations of the words that are used to describe them; the shorthand of poetry is easier to read (above all, easier for children to read) than the more painstaking longhand of more prosaic travellers.

Best of all de la Mare's stories is *The Lord Fish*, perhaps the most perfect example of imaginative prose, in fairy-tale idiom, of the present century. Here is the English countryside, tree, river, cottage, great house and all, but with the light of enchantment hanging over it. Here lives John, who tries to help his needy, hard-working mother, but who is led astray time and again by his passion for fishing. One day he leaps a stone wall, finds a mer-maiden in a stone tower, undergoes a transmogrification, and at last returns home with a princess for wife and a box of jewels. These are the bare bones of the story. How is it at once actual and magical, simple and full of overtones? Not with what happens, certainly, but with word after word a spell is woven round ordinary events. The house is different from any other, and yet the same:

... John suddenly found himself staring up at the walls of a high dark house with but two narrow windows in the stone surface that steeped up into the sky above. And the very sight of the house set his heart beating faster. He was afraid. Beyond this wall to the right showed the stony roofs of lesser buildings, and moss-clotted fruit trees gone to leaf. Busying to and fro above the roof were scores of rooks and jackdaws, their jangled cries sounding out even above the roaring of the water, for now close beneath him the stream narrowed to gush in beneath a low-rounded arch in the wall, and so into the silence and darkness beyond it.

Walter de la Mare. COLLECTED STORIES FOR CHILDREN (Faber, 1957) p. 239.

The changing of John when he rubs himself with the green ointment is almost clinically described, yet there is magic in it too:

... a dreadful darkness and giddiness swept over him. He felt his body narrowing and shortening and shrinking and dwindling. His bones were drawing themselves together inside his skin; his arms and legs ceased at last to wave and scuffle, his eyes seemed to be settling inside his head. The next moment, with one convulsive twist of his whole body, he had fallen plump into the water. Ibid., p. 248.

There is the Lord Fish who catches John, with grey glassy eyes and a cod-like chin and a hand that was 'little else but skin and bone'; there is the little maid with grey-green plaits and an ageless face who saves him; there is the larder where he hangs, with its glass jars of dried roots and lily-bulbs and various herbs for flavouring fish, and the great leaden casket stamped with an A for Almanara. All these things are precise and clear, but round them is an atmosphere of mystery, of other-worldliness. True, the village has a name; but the house has not, and the steward is only the Lord Fish; in short, behind the meticulous detail, the setting remains truly anonymous as it is anonymous in the tales of Grimm and Perrault.

It is noticeable that Robin Jacques's pictures for de la Mare's COLLECTED STORIES FOR CHILDREN give us no landscapes, only odd, attractive people who are not quite of this world. The landscape of this, as of other magic worlds, is to be visualized by each reader in his own way. For as he reads he will see in his mind's eye patterns and colours, scenes from real life, fragments from pictures half-remembered. Each of us makes a particular picture for each fairy-tale scene, so that illustrations do not represent the story to us. They decorate it, and help to send our imaginations off on a voyage which has no goal and no limit in time or space. De la Mare's stories reconcile the poet's skill and insight with the instinctive marvelling of a primitive mind. This is the true land of fairy-tale.

Reading List

Traditional fairy-tale and modern variants, with emphasis on the setting of fairy-tale
*Andersen, Hans. FORTY-TWO STORIES. *Faber* (1930) 1953. Translated by M. R. James. Illustrated by Robin Jacques. HANS ANDERSEN'S FAIRY TALES: A SELECTION. *O.U.P.* (World's Classics) 1959. Translated by L. W. Kingsland, with original illustrations. FAIRY TALES. World Edition, *Ward* 1951 et seq. Translated by R. P. Keigwin. Illustrated by Vihelm Pedersen.

Bonnet, Leslie. CHINESE FAIRY TALES. *Muller* 1958. Illustrated by H. Toothill.

*Browne, Frances. GRANNIE'S WONDERFUL CHAIR (1857). *Blackie* 1955. Illustrated by Barbara Freeman.

*de la Mare, Walter. *The Lord Fish*, in ANIMAL STORIES. *Faber* 1939. Wood engravings from Topsell. And in COLLECTED STORIES FOR CHILDREN, illustrated by Irene Hawkins. *Faber* 1947. Illustrated by Robin Jacques. *Faber* 1957.

*de la Mare, Walter. THE THREE ROYAL MONKEYS (1910 as THE THREE MULLA-MULGARS). *Faber* 1946. Illustrated by Mildred E. Eldridge.

*de la Mare, Walter. THE MAGIC JACKET. Illustrated by Irene Hawkins. *Faber* 1943.

Downing, Charles (retold by). RUSSIAN TALES AND LEGENDS. *O.U.P.* 1956. Illustrated by Joan Kiddell-Monroe.

Durack, Mary and Elizabeth. THE WAY OF THE WHIRLWIND. *Angus & Robertson* 1957. Australian folk-tales, brilliantly illustrated by the authors.

Duvoisin, Roger. FAIRY TALES FROM SWITZERLAND. *Muller* (1943) 1958. Illustrated by the author.

*Ewing, Juliana Horatia. THE BROWNIES AND OTHER STORIES (1870, 1885). *Dent* (Children's Illustrated Classics) 1954. Illustrated by Ernest Shepard.

*Farjeon, Eleanor. THE SILVER CURLEW 1953, THE GLASS SLIPPER 1955. *O.U.P.* Illustrated by Ernest Shepard.

Garner, Alan. THE WEIRDSTONE OF BRISINGAMEN. *Collins* 1960. Set in Alderley Edge, Cheshire, with a multiplicity of magical creatures, good and evil, and a centuries' old spell resolved by two children.

*Grimm, Jacob and W. K. FAIRY TALES. *Blackie* 1959. Edited by Amabel Williams-Ellis. Illustrated by Pauline Baynes.

Guillot, René. THE ELEPHANTS OF SARGABAL (1956 France). *O.U.P.* 1956. Translated by Gwen Marsh. Illustrated by Felix Hoffmann. Indian legend of boy leader of jungle outcasts rescuing princess: exotic and thrilling.

*Haldane, J. B. S. MY FRIEND MR LEAKEY. *Cresset Press* 1937. Illustrated by Leonard Rosoman.

Herda, H., *ed.* FAIRY TALES FROM MANY LANDS. *Thames & Hudson* 1956. Illustrated by Gerhard Grossmann, Hilde Koeppen and Ursula Wendorff-Weidt.

Jacobs, Joseph. CELTIC FAIRY TALES. *Muller* 1958. Selected by Lucia Turnbull. Illustrated by John D. Batten.

*Jeans, Angela Ainley. LISTEN TO THE WIND 1955, illustrated by Disley Jones. THE KINGDOM OF THE WINDS 1957, illustrated by V. H. Drummond. *Parrish*.

*Lewis, C. S. THE LION, THE WITCH AND THE WARDROBE 1950. *Penguin* (Puffin Story Books) 1960. PRINCE CASPIAN 1951, THE VOYAGE OF THE DAWN-TREADER 1952, THE SILVER CHAIR 1953, THE HORSE AND HIS BOY 1954. *Bles*. THE MAGICIAN'S NEPHEW 1955, THE LAST BATTLE 1956. *Bodley Head*. Illustrated by Pauline Baynes.

Lines, Kathleen, *compiler*. A RING OF TALES. *O.U.P.* 1958. Illustrated by Harold Jones.

*Lynch, Patricia. THE TURF-CUTTER'S DONKEY 1934, illustrated by Jack B. Yeats. THE GREY GOOSE OF KILNEVIN 1939, illustrated by John Keating. JINNY THE CHANGELING 1959, illustrated by Peggy Fortnum. *Dent*.

MacAlpine, Margaret. THE HAND IN THE BAG. *Faber* 1959. Illustrated by Richard Kennedy. Haunting tale of the Highlands, a delicate mixture of magic and domestic detail.

Macdonald, George. AT THE BACK OF THE NORTH WIND (1871) 1956, THE PRINCESS AND THE GOBLIN (1872) 1949, THE PRINCESS AND CURDIE (1883) 1949. *Dent* (Children's Illustrated Classics). Illustrated by Charles Folkard.

*Manning-Sanders, Ruth. PETER AND THE PISKIES. *O.U.P.* 1958. Illustrated by Raymond Briggs.

Manning-Sanders, Ruth, *ed.* RED INDIAN FOLK AND FAIRY TALES. *O.U.P.* 1960. Illustrated by Joan Kiddell-Monroe.

*Mitchison, Naomi. GRAEME AND THE DRAGON. *Faber* 1954. Illustrated by Pauline Baynes.

*Molesworth, Mrs. M. L. *The Reel Fairies*, n TELL ME A STORY. *Macmillan* 1875. And in FAIRY STORIES. *Harvill* 1957. Edited by Roger Lancelyn Green. *Ask the Robin*, in FAIRIES AFIELD. *Macmillan* 1911.

*Molesworth, Mrs. M. L. THE CARVED LIONS (1895). *Faith Press* 1960.

*Perrault, Charles. FAIRY TALES. *Penguin* 1957. New translation by Geoffrey Brereton.

Picard, Barbara Leonie. THE MERMAID AND THE SIMPLETON 1949, illustrated by Philip Gough. THE FAUN AND THE WOODCUTTER'S DAUGHTER 1951, illustrated by Charles Stewart. *O.U.P.* Exquisite fairy-tales in traditional manner.

Picard, Barbara Leonie (retold by). FRENCH LEGENDS, TALES AND FAIRY STORIES. *O.U.P.* 1955. Illustrated by Joan Kiddell-Monroe.

*Reeves, James (retold by). ENGLISH FABLES AND FAIRY STORIES. *O.U.P.* 1954.

*Reeves, James. PIGEONS AND PRINCESSES. *Heinemann* 1956. Illustrated by Edward Ardizzone.

*Reeves, James, *ed.* A GOLDEN LAND: STORIES, POEMS, SONGS NEW AND OLD. *Constable* 1958. Illustrated by various artists.

*Ross, Diana. THE WILD CHERRY 1943, THE BRIDAL GOWN 1952. *Faber.* CHILD OF AIR. *Lutterworth* 1957. Illustrated by Gri.

*Ross, Diana. THE ENORMOUS APPLE PIE 1951, THE BRAN TUB 1954. *Lutterworth.* Illustrated by Peggy Fortnum. These are all about Miss Pussy, and there are two stories about her in THE WILD CHERRY. The story that began it all can be found in THE GOLDEN HEN. *Faber* 1942. Illustrated by Gri.

*Simpson, Helen. MUMBUDGET. *Heinemann* 1928.

*Thurber, James. MANY MOONS 1944, THE WHITE DEER 1946, THE THIRTEEN CLOCKS 1951. *Hamish Hamilton.* Illustrated by the author.

*Tolkein, J. R. R. THE LORD OF THE RINGS, comprising THE FELLOWSHIP OF THE RING 1954, THE TWO TOWERS 1954, THE RETURN OF THE KING 1955. *Allen & Unwin.*

*Tolkein, J. R. R. THE HOBBIT. *Allen & Unwin* 1937. Illustrated by the author.

Vacher, Gwyneth. THE SHOEMAKER'S DAUGHTER. *Blackie* 1957. Illustrated by Peggy Fortnum. Journey of an orphan through the Forest of Nowhere.

Wells, Ann E. TALES FROM ARNHEM LAND. *Angus & Robertson* 1959. Illustrated by Margaret Paice. Folk-lore of Northern Australia linked with the adventures of a child in the present day.

Williams-Ellis, Amabel (retold by). FAIRY TALES FROM THE BRITISH ISLES. *Blackie* 1960. Illustrated by Pauline Baynes.

Zajdler, Zoë. POLISH FAIRY TALES. *Muller* 1959. Illustrated by Hazel Cook.

Chapter 6 | *The Conversation of Witches*

The Land of Faerie owes its existence to primitive fears of the natural world, but there is the human element to be considered as well. More often than not, tales of giants and elves illustrate not so much the dangers of wind and weather as of man living in a community. They offer the earliest descriptions of the human situation, couched in fanciful terms and presented impersonally.

This impersonal attitude soon became untenable. Rationalists from the sixteenth century at least had cast scorn on the race of giants and dragons, but it was left for the English critics of the nineteenth century to take the final step against the fairy world. They insisted that writers of fairy-tales should make them purposive, should give them a moral. Dismayed by the anonymous and illogical tone of Grimms' tales, which had appeared in England in 1823, they asserted that tales such as these should be brought into line with social morality.

It is easy to see why moralists thought Grimms' tales bad for children. They would naturally disapprove of stories like *The Three Dancing Princesses*, for instance, where a casual act of kindness brings what seems a disproportionate return to the hero, or like *Rumpelstiltskin*, where the miller is rewarded for his foolish boasting by becoming father-in-law to a king, or like *The Master-Thief*, which puts a premium on cunning. It never satisfied them that such tales made firm, categorical, uninhibited statements about human nature and human wishes. They felt fairy-tales should point the way to virtue. But of course no child who reads the story of Cinderella is going to think that she gets the prince because she is *better* than her sisters, only that she is nicer and more fortunate; and this is useful knowledge for anyone, child or adult. The Grimm brothers themselves certainly set great store by the victory of goodness over evil in the tales they collected. 'Notice too,' they said,

> 'that in this fairy-tale world the powers of darkness—such as robbers, witches and man-eating giants, are always foiled. Even the Devil has a grandmother, while in the case of danger from robbers or monsters, a friendly wife or daughter is likely to be at hand, who is sure to know some way of averting Fate. In short, the tales all end well and indeed usually with a suggestion of everlasting happiness. . . .'
>
> Amabel Williams-Ellis. GRIMMS' FAIRY TALES (Blackie, 1959) p. 331.

But this was not to claim a moral purpose for the tales, but only to point out that we are all, at bottom, optimists.

Of course it is not the business of fairy-tales to teach children to be good, nor, for that matter, to suggest that they should be naughty. Andrew Lang said, in the mid-Victorian period, he had 'never yet heard of a child who killed a very tall man merely because Jack killed the giants.' But the moral had come to stay. Kingsley, in THE WATER-BABIES, enforced it by a compelling narrative style and by his passionate interest in everything he wrote about. George Macdonald enforced it by the grandeur of his conceptions. No child is ever likely to forget a warning against godless living put across like this:

> One day at noon, when life was at its highest, the whole city fell with a roaring crash. The cries of men and the shrieks of women went up with its dust, and then there was a great silence.
>
> Where the mighty rock once towered, crowded with homes and crowned with a palace, now rushes and raves a stone-obstructed rapid of the river. All around spreads a wilderness of wild deer, and the very name of Gwyntystorm has ceased from the lips of men.
>
> George Macdonald. THE PRINCESS AND CURDIE (Dent, Children's Illustrated Classics, 1949) p. 238.

Mrs Molesworth and Mrs Ewing charmed children gently into the nursery virtues with their domestic sprites. Ruskin, in THE KING OF THE GOLDEN RIVER, preached his sermon in the urbane tones of a man about town. All these tones of voice may be heard in our own times. Čapek speaks with the voice of Kingsley; C. S. Lewis sounds the mythic note of George Macdonald; Diana Ross has inherited the charming moral tone of the Victorian ladies and Thurber the worldly advising of Ruskin.

Still, it will be said, modern fairy-tales have freed themselves from the need to sermonize. All the same, they have never recovered the irresponsible, inconsequent shape of the past. Certainly the demand for the pure fairy-tale still exists. The past fifteen years have seen a noticeable increase in the reprinting of volumes of traditional tales, headed by the Oxford Myths and Legends series and Muller's splendid series of national fairy-tales. British regional tales, new versions of the Arabian Nights, unfamiliar stories from Australasia, from the Eskimos and Red Indians, from Africa, as well as new versions of the Arthurian legends and the Greek myths, keep fairy-tale alive. But we are not fancy-free and presumably never can be again. If we imitate the traditional tale in the present-day, we add something of comment, of purpose. We are always trying to say something definite about people and their lives.

But our fairy-tales do not derive so much from the moral versions of the last century as from Hans Andersen, the 'father of modern fairy-tale'. Drawing from the same traditional material as older story-tellers, he turned the anonymity of folk lore to personal use. His method is certainly in tune with modern practice. He did not preach, but in his tales he expressed his own disappointments and regrets and his observations of the way of the world. In some stories, like *The Snow Queen*, it is possible to find lessons, but I doubt whether anyone who reads the story is concerned with learning them; rather, he perceives the gentle glow that comes from the character of Gerda, he recognizes the tough acceptance of life in the whole plot of Kay's enchantment and his rescue from the ice-palace, he enjoys the marvellous sequence of scenes, from the sunny beginning under the rose-trees to the terrors of the robber girl and the Lapp woman. In other stories, like *The Tinder Box*, children will see a rogue living successfully on his wits; but what child thinks the witch has been unjustly treated? Yet how much can be learned from the tales, and in how many different ways. You can observe the workings of snobbery and affectation in an Emperor or a shirt-collar, a snail or a barndoor fowl. You can see stupidity getting its deserts in a gloomy underground land of enchantment or in a provision-dealer's shop.

Hans Andersen can make a pin or a match or a lead soldier into a personality, and that is of course one of the secrets of his permanent place on children's shelves. There are plenty of writers since Andersen who have animated tin soldiers—Little Noddy, surely, has had plenty of dealings with them. But to draw tears and smiles, quite spontaneous and genuine, on account of a lead soldier with one leg and a paper doll—that takes genius. Not cleverness or wit or ingenuity but the power to compel truth out of yourself that has grown slowly out of childhood impressions. This is how writers of fairy-tale work—this is how Eleanor Farjeon worked, and Patricia Lynch, and Walter de la Mare, and Hans Andersen, the ancestor of them all. This is what he said himself, about the cottage in Odense where he lived as a child:

> That one little room which was almost filled with the cobbler's bench, bed and the turn-up bedstead on which I slept, was the whole of my childhood's home; but its walls were hung with pictures; on the chest of drawers stood pretty cups, glasses and knick-knacks, and above the workbench by the window was a shelf with books and broadsheets. In the little kitchen, above the store-cupboard, was a rack filled with plates. To me the little room appeared large and rich; the very door, whose panels were painted with landscapes, meant as much to me then as a whole picture gallery now. In the kitchen was a ladder leading on to the roof and there in the gutter between our house and our neighbour's was a box of earth in which grew chives and parsley, and that was all my mother's garden.
>
> THE MERMAID MAN: the autobiography of Hans Christian Andersen. A new abridged translation by Maurice Michael. (Arthur Barker, 1955) pp. 7-8.

It is because there is not a shadow of guile or faking here that Hans Andersen belongs to children and can give them more than anyone else—can give them, above all, a humour that rises out of household objects as often as out of people.

'Painters beget pictures,' Picasso has said, 'as princes beget children—not with princesses, but with country-girls. One never paints the Parthenon, or a Louis XV chair. One makes pictures out of a hovel, a tobacco-pack, or an old stool.' It is apt to be so, too with fairy-tales. Fire-irons, tin soldiers and porridge-bowls are hallowed by tradition and belong to the cottage world from which fairy-tales sprang. Edith Nesbit's princess 'in a simple little morning frock of white chiffon and diamonds' whose suitors are summoned by telephone is under a slight disadvantage. We are not used to this kind of drawing-room character in the magic world, nor to this kind of stage property. But there is plenty of room for humour in fairy-tale, and in our time this may well be topical. There can be magic in modern gadgets.

Richard Hughes, in a present-day story called THE SPIDER'S PALACE, describes how a little boy discovers that his torch-glass, when reversed, will turn people into toys and give toys the power to act like people. This is high fantasy, but it is presented with absolute logic and conviction:

> And he put it to his eye and looked at his father and mother, and so it was: they were immediately wooden Mr. and Mrs. Noah out of the Ark. To make sure, he took a pin, and keeping the glass firmly in his eye he tried to stick it in his mother. But it wouldn't go in, for she was now quite hard: it only scratched a little paint off. Then he took the glass away, and they were his mother and father again. But just to make sure he stuck the pin in again. This time it went right in, and his mother sat up with the most awful yell.
> Richard Hughes. THE SPIDER'S PALACE. (Chatto & Windus, 1931) p. 134.

Lorna Wood is just as ingenious in RESCUE BY BROOMSTICK. A vital history-book has been stolen and hidden in a waste-disposer. Dowsabel, the witch, gets it back by using a reversing spell, but it is then discovered that, in its pages, Henry VIII signs the Magna Carta and Boadicea invents the cinematograph. The joke has been taken to its logical conclusion, Anyone who was fortunate enough, as I was, to read the proper, unabridged stories about the Kingdom of Oz, will remember what humour and excitement and mystery Frank Baum drew out of machines and chemical experiments, and J. B. S. Haldane's MY FRIEND MR. LEAKEY follows the same prescription, with its surreptitious scientific learning.

Mr Leakey is a dragon, and this is important, for humour in a fairy-tale (one of the most obvious ways in which adults can convey their views) comes best from the more robust supernatural beings.

Fairies themselves are too ethereal for laughter. You cannot define them in human terms and so there can be nothing to laugh about. Brownies and leprechauns, giants and witches, nearer to the human race, can be imagined to act as humans do, and so can be laughed at. Barbara Sleigh's CARBONEL, a modern family story with incidental magic, is one of the best examples of this kind of humour. There is, of course, an extra twist to the humour in fairy-tales. It comes, at its best, from a delicate use of incongruity, a balance between the fairy world and our own, and is particularly well-suited to children, who are willing to believe themselves committed to both worlds.

CARBONEL is the story of Rosemary, a London schoolgirl whose mother sews for a precarious living, and who one day, when she goes to a street market to buy a broom, runs into a witch who is just retiring to keep a sweet-shop. The witch's cat, Carbonel, sold to Rosemary for her three Queen Victoria farthings, has to serve the girl unless she can unwind the spell, and for this she has to find the witch's hat and cauldron and spell-book. The story runs an exciting course as Rosemary and her new friend John, son of her mother's richest client, follow up clues, helped by the resourceful and temperamental cat, who provides most of the humour in the story. He is very much on the spot, in both magic and real world. When Rosemary suggests mending the worn broom with string, he puts her right:

> 'Good gracious, no! You can't mend magic with string! . . . You will be suggesting glue and tin-tacks next. A few weeks ago the cauldron sprang a leak, and SHE insisted on filling up the hole with one of those pot-mender things you get at an ironmonger's, at sixpence a card. And what was the result? . . . Her spells worked out lumpy . . .'

Barbara Sleigh. CARBONEL (Parrish, 1955) p. 34.

But Carbonel can also evoke a more poetic world:

> 'I took to the broomstick business like a duck to water. Oh, those were the days, when you raced together through the tumbling sky, with the Milky Way crackling below, and the wind in your fur strong enough to tear the whiskers off you! Or leaping and plunging through the midnight sky with a host of others, and the earth twirling beneath you no bigger than a bobbin!'

Ibid., p. 27.

The witch herself makes a wonderful reappearance in THE KINGDOM OF CARBONEL, as the kidnapper of the royal kittens, and her sly, dry, faintly sinister attitude to life is exactly what you would expect of a witch. And who could resist the absurd eccentricities of Lorna Wood's hag Dowsabel? Who could help laughing with her, as well as at her, when, riding on her broomstick with Jane one night, she kicks out at a weathercock and sends it spinning:

'Never could stand that bird,' she said with satisfaction. 'Too smug by half. Now he won't be sure which is east and which is west and I think I've knocked the S off South.'
Lorna Wood. RESCUE BY BROOMSTICK (Dent, 1956) p. 29.

Mary Norton's BED KNOB AND BROOMSTICK starts, in contrast. on a very ordinary note. Miss Price lives in the Bedfordshire village where Carey, Charles and Paul go to stay with an aunt:

She wore grey coats and skirts and had a long thin neck with a scarf round it (made of Liberty silk with a Paisley pattern). Her nose was sharply pointed and she had very clean, pink hands. She rode on a high bicycle with a basket in front, and she visited the sick and taught the piano.
Mary Norton. BED KNOB AND BROOMSTICK (Dent, 1957) p. 8.

When Paul first sees her lurching past his bedroom window on her broomstick, he thinks what an inefficient witch she is; in fact, being too ladylike to ride astride, she is often in difficulties, and it is because the children help her home after a fall that she confides to them her plans for study. She even does an advanced spell for them, and with the help of Paul's bed-knob they journey to distant places and distant periods, escaping from cannibals, from the police, and finally from Restoration London after the Great Fire. It is on this last journey that they meet, and bring back to their own times, the lugubrious necromancer Emelius Jones, whose neglected appearance rouses Miss Price's maternal instincts. If there is plenty of humour in these two eccentric characters, there is far more in Mary Norton's comments on the technique of witchcraft. No child could resist the description of Miss Price's workroom, or her explanation to Carey who wonders why she can't make money:

'. . . you can't get the ingredients. What people don't realize . . . is that there are very few spells that can be done without para-

phernalia. You must, if you understand, have something to turn
into something and something to turn it *with*.'
Ibid., p. 57.

or the picture of Emelius's work with his old master, who made him
do all the dirty work of collecting cats from graveyards and bats
from belfries, or Miss Price's earnest exhortation:

'I never scrape the scales from an adder . . . It takes force from any
spell except those in which hemlock is combined with fennel. The
only time I ever scrape the scales from an adder is in spells against
St. Vitus's dance, then for some reason, it gives better results . . .'
Ibid., pp. 152–3.

Mary Norton makes her comic points so well because of her close
attention to detail. In her three stories about the Borrowers, everything depends on incongruity—on creatures of another race behaving like humans—but this time humour is merged into tenderness
and poetry. The Borrowers are tiny people who live in the interstices
of human dwellings. Humans, to them, exist to supply them with
small objects, like safety-pins, matchboxes or chessmen, which they
can use for their own purposes—even to supply them with their
scraps of names. To us, as we read, the Borrowers are not miniature
humans; they are *reminders* of what humans are like.

The first of three books about these little people sounds a note of
pathos. We are told that the race is dwindling, that Pod, Homily and
Arrietty, who live under the kitchen floor of an old house in Bedfordshire, have long ago said goodbye to the Harpsichord family and the
Overmantels, and it is a long time since they saw their relations the
well-to-do Clocks. For the moment, however, the family is safe, so
long as they are not 'seen'.

One day Pod *is* seen, by a boy staying in the house, and though the
boy becomes their ally, he is the cause of their having to leave their
home in a hurry. In THE BORROWERS AFIELD we follow their fortunes as they camp in an old boot, as they search for the badger-sett
where Uncle Hendreary is said to live, and as they meet Spiller, a gipsy
Borrower who sees no need for relatives or any of the gentilities that
Homily clings to. In THE BORROWERS AFLOAT we find the little
family under a roof again, but an inhospitable one. With the help of the
gamekeeper's son they have found Uncle Hendreary behind the
skirting in a cottage; but his wife, Aunt Lupy, is unpleasant to her

Drawing by V. H. Drummond for Barbara Sleigh's CARBONEL (Parrish)

poor relations, food is short, and they are housed in a draughty garret. Urged on by young Arrietty, with her longing for the open, mother and father venture into the wilds again, and under Spiller's guidance they voyage downstream in a knife-box, hoping to find a model village they have heard of, which they believe is the perfect home. Mary Norton has said that they will find the village and settle down, in a fourth book. How passionately she makes her readers hope that they will. This is not only because her Borrowers remind us of all the dispossessed, the small and valiant and under-privileged people of this world and of all worlds. The books must be read with this in mind, but, as with Tolkein, it is an idea, not a moral. These are fairy stories, and they make their impression as much by their style as by their story.

Mary Norton is a most skilful story-teller. First, she is absolutely consistent. She is herself short-sighted, and she has a sure, sharp vision of small things. She can see *exactly* how half a pair of embroidery scissors would be used by the Borrowers, or a knob of sealing-wax or a button; and her illustrator, Diana Stanley, has exquisitely transposed this vision of littleness into drawings. Secondly, this magical world (only a few inches away from our own world of chairs and teacups) is reached by a roundabout route. These are stories within stories. At first we listen to old Mrs May telling young Kate about her brother and *his* tales about the Borrowers. Old Tom Goodenough, in the gamekeeper's cottage, Mrs Driver the cook, the gardener Crampfurl who abetted her in getting rid of the 'mice dressed up', all add their mite of detail and authenticity to the story.

But if there were still any doubt of the existence of the Borrowers, it would be dispelled by their personalities. Arrietty, bright as a button, chronicler and enthusiast; Homily keeping her integrity as a housewife through danger and misfortune (when she arrives, dishevelled and dirty, at Aunt Lupy's gracious home, she refuses to be patronized: 'Poor dear Lupy', she was saying, glancing wearily about, 'What a lot of furniture. Whoever helps you with the dusting?'); and Pod, brave as a lion, common in speech, full of sensible philosophy—('There's a lot of worse food, when you care to think of it, than a piping-hot, savoury stew made of corn-fed field-mouse.'). They are as real as many characters we or our children will meet in real life, and just as real is the setting of the stories—the dirty world

Drawing by Diana Stanley for Mary Norton's THE BORROWERS AFLOAT (Dent)

under the floorboards, the damp hedge with its safe corners, Spiller's kettle, the pile of sticks in the water where they hide from Wall-Eye the Gypsy, and the spread of Midland landscape, whole and real and touched with poetry.

If fairy-tales are universal, they are also regional. Hans Andersen or Perrault or Patricia Lynch can be placed at once in their place of origin, and many English writers can be as easily labelled. They draw their characters from British folk lore—the sproggins and drowners of Cornwall, the lob or hobgoblin of English villages—and they draw their scenes from an unchanging countryside. Mrs Ewing's tales take us back to an older England of familiar spirits, an England already threatened by the forces of industry and progress when she wrote, an England derived from Shakespeare and Drayton and even earlier writers. Kipling, too, gave us a piercing vision of a fairy past that had nothing to do with Denmark or Germany. PUCK OF POOK'S HILL and REWARDS AND FAIRIES are full of the romance of other lands and other times, but most children remember them best for the Sussex country scenes, incidental to the plot but essential to the character of the stories, for Old Hobden and Puck with his capricious ways and unruly tongue, for the bridleways older than the Romans and the magically, eternally old and new leaves of oak, ash and thorn.

Alison Uttley's stories communicate to children a picture of old England filtered through a magic haze. Stories like *The Leadminer*, with its tender lapping up of the lonely, wizened, leather-clad dwarf into the farmhouse warmth; or *Young Lambs for Sale*, with its picture of centuries-old Cotswold; or *John Barleycorn*, with its simple, unearthly evocation of the corn-spirit; or *The Merry-go-round*, where a bronze Roman whistle sets the painted horses galloping through the night; or that strange, mysterious tale of the old farm-hand who brings good luck to the place, *Orion Hardy*; each sets its own exact atmosphere. This delicate combination of history and fairy-tale can be seen at its best in *Upon Paul's Steeple*, where a chance-dropped apple-pip grows into a fine tree:

> The little boys came running as soon as school was over, from all the streets of London, up the hill of Ludgate, down the street of Fleet, carrying baskets and sticks, bags and crooks, to try to hook the lowest branches. The watchman prevented them from

Drawing by Philip Hepworth for Alison Uttley's *The Merry-go-round* in
JOHN BARLEYCORN (Faber)

throwing stones lest the precious windows of Saint Paul's should be broken.

From many a little wooden house in London came the smell of apples roast, apples baked, apples in pies, and apples in dumplings, and every spice shop was sold out of cloves. They were the sweetest, nicest apples anyone had ever tasted, and even King Charles had apple-pasties.

Alison Uttley. MAGIC IN MY POCKET (Penguin, 1957) p. 145.

This is not the only one of Alison Uttley's stories that is poised on a nursery rhyme, and this way of capturing elusive associations is used also by Eleanor Farjeon, whose numerous and varied tales are full of the vivacity and alertness of a child. One very shapely tale, *Elsie Piddock Skips in her Sleep*, grows naturally out of an old skipping-rhyme, and Sussex games provide a framework for two collections of stories, MARTIN PIPPIN IN THE APPLE ORCHARD and MARTIN PIPPIN IN THE DAISY FIELD. Martin is a resourceful countryman living in a rustic setting. At a deeper level he is a wandering enchanter, who knows the minds of men, and centuries of magic are hinted at through him. He is also a medieval jongleur, weaving an airy and delicate pattern of romantic love after the pattern of William Morris and Sydney's *Arcadia*.

THE SILVER CURLEW, a version of the English tale *Tom Tit Tot*, combines the magical and the rustic likewise. Beside sweet, stupid Doll and the petulant young king of Norfolk there is the mysterious Charlee Loon communing with birds on the beach, and the ancient, fearful Witching Wood where the Black Imp holds his court and where he binds Charlee and young Poll with spiders' webs as firm as steel.

And so to the most English writer of them all—John Masefield, whose two magic adventure stories, THE MIDNIGHT FOLK and THE BOX OF DELIGHTS should be on every child's bookshelf. These two books are built upon the past. First, upon the Herefordshire country where the poet lived as a child and which is the background of so much of his writing. They well up, especially THE MIDNIGHT FOLK, from memories of childhood, from imagination playing upon the places that were then his world. The old house, Seekings, where Kay is rapped over the knuckles by his governess; the warrens where the friendly cat Nibbins and Bitem the Fox frustrate the keeper's knavish tricks; the millpool where Kay plays with the otter;

the stable where he finds the ancient pistols of Benjamin the highwayman; the night sky where he swoops with Bat and hears the village people chatting below him; all the sounds and smells of summer days and summer nights are packed into the story, the whole feeling of a country world where time has stood still and the centuries have telescoped, where witches and cats and humans can quite easily lead parallel lives.

THE MIDNIGHT FOLK is the story of a quest for the great treasure from the cathedral of Santa Barbara, which had been entrusted to Kay's grandfather, Captain Harker, in time of revolution. Two parties are looking for the treasure, lost so many years ago—the witches, urged on by Abner Brown, whose grandfather was a mutineer on Captain Harker's ship, and the guards, Kay's old toys, who have marched off from Seekings to follow up a clue. Kay is drawn into the adventure by Nibbins, whose blood still stirs at the sound of incantations, but who wants to put things right in the old house.

The narrative is impeccable; but this may not be obvious to a child at first reading, for it is also complex. The story inches itself forward as first one party and then the other gets a little more information about what happened to the treasure and where it might be. Thus there is, inset in the adventure, a tiny sea-story of mutiny in a hot, far-off country, which is fascinating in itself. Information comes from various sources. Now Kay flies at night to a house in the north where he sees 'a wicked old woman in a very gay dressing-gown . . . reading a sprightly story'—Miss Susan Pricker, daughter of another mutineer. Now the witches get a little warmer when they call up and interrogate apparitions—a glittering child, a youth crowned with ivy-leaves, and others less helpful. Now the disreputable Rat brings a snippet of information to Kay in return for bacon-rind. Now Blackmalkin, the sneaking cat, overhears something useful to her mistress the witch.

Everywhere you feel the writer along with you, taking you into the English country or into the red muddy stretches of South American country, enjoying every picture as he draws it.

It is a real Christmas stocking of a book, packed with parcels of all shapes and colours—with adventure, by day and night, with witches and foxes, requiring wit and courage, speed and stealth; with humour in the characters of Rat the cellarman, or the riotous

Miss Susan Pricker, or the splendid witch Mrs Pouncer. And at the bottom of the stocking is the orange—the poetry shining everywhere, lighting a paragraph with an unexpected word (but just the one word that will do), making mermaids and weathercocks absolutely real, making hollow trees and lumps of sugar and brooms mysterious, as though never seen before.

THE MIDNIGHT FOLK is essentially a summer book, but THE BOX OF DELIGHTS is set in a winter landscape, in the neighbourhood of Seekings, shrouded in snow, and in the Chester Hills, sinister under a grey sky. The story started with a question in the author's mind. Exactly what would happen to the Christmas services in a cathedral town if all the clergymen disappeared? Abner Brown suggested himself as a character in this drama, and the author, with his zest for details, consulted authorities, including a Bishop, before he gave Abner his head. Like so many of Masefield's stories, THE BOX OF DELIGHTS has a vein of happy boyish humour; but there are many more threads in its rich weave. Kay is older now, and Abner Brown is more determined and more ruthless. The treasure itself is more valuable—none other than a magic box which can carry its possessor back into the past, and so to the discovery of the elixir of life. This is no ordinary adventure, though there is excitement enough to satisfy any child. There are gangsters, but there is a more primitive danger as well; magic solves problems better than kidnapping does, though Abner and his spouse (once Sylvia Daisy Pouncer, Kay's governess) try both. When Kay and Cole Hawlings, the wandering alchemist, are imprisoned underground and in danger of drowning, they escape by sympathetic magic. Kay has to draw— a man sculling a boat, with a bunch of keys, a pair of horses:

In fact, the drawings did stand out from the paper rather strangely. The light was concentrated on them; as he looked at them the horses seemed to be coming towards him out of the light, and, no, it was not seeming, they were moving; he saw the hoof casts flying and heard the rhythmical beat of hoofs. The horses were coming out of the picture, galloping fast, and becoming brighter and brighter. Then he saw that the light was partly fire from their eyes and manes, partly sparks from their hoofs.
John Masefield. THE BOX OF DELIGHTS (Heinemann, 1935) p. 378.

So even this adventure is not quite ordinary, not quite straight-forward. Masefield's sense of the past, of its colour and mystery above all, so superbly shown in his poetry and novels, works itself into this child's tale. Kay, carrying the magic box, hides behind a stockade and watches Celts fighting marauding wolves. He sees a Roman legion on the march. He comes to the walls of Troy just after the siege is over:

> After the party had gone past with the wailing captives and cursing guards, Kay went into the Skaian Gate and looked about him at the desolation. The doors of all the houses were open; the things which had not been worth carrying away lay smashed or torn in the ways. There was nobody left in the city except a stray cat or two, mewing in misery. The pigeons which had once nested in the temples were flying about in the smoke. As Kay went up towards the temples a gust of wind caught the fire; it burst out with a savage crackle and fierce flame.
> Ibid., pp. 281–2.

The past, everywhere, is as real as the present. It hangs about the mysterious stranger who comes to warn Cole, with the brooch shaped like a cross for a sign. It breathes in the study at Seekings, where Cole makes immemorial magic for the children. It is an evocation as subtle as it is strong. This return to the past is a special form of fantasy, allied to fairy-tale, owing much to it, but with different aims and feelings. In Masefield's two books it is part of a more complicated whole; but there are writers who have written fantasies simply to recall the past, in a special way distinct from historical novels, and some of these I must mention in detail in a separate chapter.

Reading List

The modern fairy-tale; humour and character
'B.B.'. THE LITTLE GREY MEN 1942, DOWN THE BRIGHT STREAM 1948. *Eyre & Spottiswoode.* Illustrated by the author. The last gnomes left in England, their adventures by stream and mill, and their departure for Ireland. Rich, evocative picture of a vanishing rural England, with light-hearted humanizing of animals and country spirits.

'B.B.'. THE FOREST OF BOLAND LIGHT RAILWAY. *Eyre & Spottiswoode* 1955. Illustrated by the author. Gnomes running a railway in defiance of enemy leprechauns: inventive and ingenious, full of wit and absurdity.

*Baum, Frank. THE WIZARD OF OZ. From 1900. Unfortunately only the first Oz story is now available in England, in an abridged version and with poor illustrations.

*Capek, Karel. FAIRY TALES (1932 Prague). *Allen & Unwin* 1933. Illustrated by Joseph Čapek.

Dixon, Marjorie and Kennedy, Richard. THE GREEN-COATED BOY. *Faber* 1957. Illustrated by Richard Kennedy. Two children wandering in search of a black goat, in Ireland, and going over the frontier of the real world.

Duggan, Maurice. FALTER TOM AND THE WATER BOY. *Faber* 1958. Illustrated by Kenneth Rownell. Fable of the world under the water.

*Farjeon, Eleanor. MARTIN PIPPIN IN THE APPLE-ORCHARD (1921) 1952, illustrated by Richard Kennedy. MARTIN PIPPIN IN THE DAISY-FIELD (1937) 1954, illustrated by Isobel and John Morton-Sale. *O.U.P.*

Guinness, Bryan and Pym, Roland. CATRIONA AND THE GRASSHOPPER. *Heinemann* 1958. Illustrated by Roland Pym. Vivacious tale of chases and parties in an entertaining land of fantasy.

Hughes, Jean. DITTA'S TREE. *Penguin* (Puffin Story Books) 1952. Illustrated by Mary Willett. An Indian tree-spirit and his unpredictable mischief and help to the villagers nearby.

*Hughes, Richard. THE SPIDER'S PALACE. *Chatto & Windus* 1931. Illustrated by George Charlton.

Kendall, Carol. THE MINNIPINS (1959 U.S.A.). *Dent* 1960. Illustrated by Erik Blegvad. Miniature race in land between mountains, fighting the Mushroom People. Allegory of individualism: clever details of local customs and characteristics.

*Kingsley, Charles. THE WATER-BABIES (1863). *O.U.P.* 1948. Illustrated by A. E. Jackson.

*Kipling, Rudyard. PUCK OF POOK'S HILL (1906), REWARDS AND FAIRIES (1910). *Macmillan*, continuously in print. Latest editions illustrated by Stuart Tresilian.

Lagerlöf, Selma. THE WONDERFUL ADVENTURES OF NILS (1906–7 Sweden). *Dent* (Children's Illustrated Classics) 1950, 1953. Translated by Velma Swanston Howard. Illustrated by Hans Baumbauer. English edition published in two parts, the second entitled THE FURTHER ADVENTURES OF NILS, and in a form slightly abridged from American edition. Superb, long, varied tale of a Swedish farmer's son who is changed into an elf as punishment for cruelty to animals, and flies with wild geese on migration. Adventures with people and animals, plenty of humour, a warm human interest.

Lofting, Hugh. THE TWILIGHT OF MAGIC. *Cape* (1931) 1958. Illustrated by the author. Droll, sober and mysterious by turns, a tale of medieval witchcraft and what the witch was really like.

*Masefield, John. THE MIDNIGHT FOLK (1927) 1957, THE BOX OF DELIGHTS (1935) 1957. *Heinemann*. Illustrated by Rowland Hilder.

Masefield, Judith. THE MARVELLOUS MERLAD. *Collins* 1952. Illustrated by Shirley Hughes. Extravaganza set in Ireland about a merboy who takes to land and has adventures with a travelling fair: tremendous gusto and humour.

*Nesbit, E. *Melisande* (1901), in MODERN FAIRY STORIES, edited by Roger Lancelyn Green. *Dent* 1955. Illustrated by Ernest Shepard.

*Norton, Mary. BED KNOB AND BROOMSTICK. *Dent* 1957. Illustrated by Eric Blegvad. A composite of THE MAGIC BEDKNOB 1945 and BONFIRES AND BROOMSTICKS 1947.

*Norton, Mary. THE BORROWERS 1952, THE BORROWERS AFIELD 1955, THE BORROWERS AFLOAT 1959. *Dent*. Illustrated by Diana Stanley. The two first stories were published in Puffin Story Books in 1958 and 1960 respectively

*Ruskin, John, *The King of the Golden River* (1830), in MODERN FAIRY STORIES, edited by Roger Lancelyn Green. *Dent* 1955. Illustrated by Ernest Shepard.

*Sleigh, Barbara. CARBONEL 1955, illustrated by V. H. Drummond. THE KINGDOM OF CARBONEL 1959, illustrated by Michael Leonard. *Parrish*.

Sleigh, Linwood. THE BOY IN THE IVY. *Faber* 1955. Illustrated by Kate Adamson. Witchcraft full of humour but with mysterious undertones.

Sleigh, Linwood. THE TAILOR'S FRIENDS. *Faber* 1956. Illustrated by Robert Spearman. Ordinary people leaving our world in a party of mysterious personages bound for a lost Celtic land.

*Uttley, Alison. CUCKOO CHERRY-TREE 1943, THE SPICE-WOMAN'S BASKET 1944, illustrated by Irene Hawkins. THE WEATHER-COCK 1945, illustrated by Nancy Innes. JOHN BARLEYCORN 1948, illustrated by Philip Hepworth. THE COBBLER'S SHOP 1950, illustrated by Irene Hawkins. *Faber*.

Uttley, Alison. MAGIC IN MY POCKET. *Penguin* (Puffin Story Books) 1957, illustrated by Judith Brook. A collection from the above and the volumes of animal stories. (See Chap. 4).

*Wood, Lorna. THE PEOPLE IN THE GARDEN 1954, RESCUE BY BROOMSTICK 1956, THE HAG CALLS FOR HELP 1957, HOLIDAY ON HOT BRICKS 1958, SEVEN-LEAGUE BALLET SHOES 1959, HAGS ON HOLIDAY 1960. *Dent*. Illustrated by Joan Kiddell-Monroe.

Chapter 7 | *Travellers in Time*

Every piece of fiction is written twice over—first by the author and then by the reader. The author is making a journey into a new world and he leaves signposts which will help the reader to find the way there in his turn. In a time fantasy the journey is a double one. The child who reads goes first on a straight road, introduced to a character or characters like himself and belonging to his own time. These characters take over the function of guide and the reader follows them back into the past, forgetting his own world and taking the world of the traveller with him. He becomes the traveller—or, if he does not, the journey has been in vain. For this impressive and exciting kind of fantasy exercises the imagination in a way that no other does.

You have, then, a story within a story, and one depends absolutely on the other. This kind of book is very different from the straight historical tale. HOUSE OF ARDEN by E. Nesbit, Alison Uttley's A TRAVELLER IN TIME, Edward Eager's THE TIME GARDEN— these give you far more than just a story of Elizabeth's reign. They give you, in various moods, the *feelings* of boys and girls moving in history but still remembering their own times. The reactions of the children to what they see and hear, the way they are changed by their experience—it is for these things that we make the journey. What we learn on the way is incidental. We may come back knowing some of the facts of the Babington plot, or with a picture in our mind of an Elizabethan feast, or with a more lively impression of Queen Elizabeth herself. But the child who reads these books will have learned something beyond fact. He, too, will be a little changed by his imaginative experience.

In every one of these time fantasies there is one question we can justifiably ask. Has the author made us believe in his manipulation of time? Has his illusion been successful? There are various ways in which writers have helped the reader through the double journey, and one is by a magic talisman. Masefield's THE BOX OF DELIGHTS has such a talisman. Isolated and illuminated by a poet's hand, it is so real to a child that he can believe in everything that the box causes to happen. Magic clings round it as it clings round Frances Browne's story-telling chair or round Desdemona's handkerchief. These objects are focal points. They collect and concentrate the magic of a story. So, in THE GAUNTLET, Ronald Welch uses a mailed glove as the way back to twelfth-century Wales. In THE FIFTH OF NOVEMBER, L. A. G. Strong's boy hero snatches up a piece of crumbling stone and plaster from the torture-chamber of the Tower of London, and sleeps with it under his pillow; only then, in his dreams, does he live through the story of Guy Fawkes. Hilda Lewis, in THE SHIP THAT FLEW, pricks the imagination with a little model ship, which young Peter found in an antique-shop, a Viking ship which grows to fit its intended crew and which can take them anywhere in space and time. The ship is not only a conveyance; its history and fate are important to the story. The children discover it had been the property of the Norse god Frey, and at Asgard they bargain with him for it, before they re-trace its adventures in ancient Egypt and play some part in the rescue of Pharaoh's son from his enemies.

E. Nesbit, whose magic has always a sensible, even prosaic beginning, understood this device very well. In THE STORY OF THE AMULET the magic object has two functions. It is the means by which the children reach the past, but it is also the object of their journeyings. At the beginning of the story they only possess half of it, rummaged from out of a tray in a junk-shop. To get their heart's desire, they must find the whole amulet at some stage before it was broken. If they can do this, they will somehow be able to bear the whole object back to their own time, even though they know that one half was completely crushed in the past. This is straining credulity to the utmost, but so persuasively does E. Nesbit establish the magical nature of the amulet, so skilfully does she mix fantastic events with historical background, that we believe everything, even that the amulet does end up, years after the children are dead and gone, in a case at the British Museum.

We believe it, in the end, because E. Nesbit believes it, and because in the realm of fact she is so sure and safe. With relatively few details at her disposal about Egypt or Babylon or Atlantis, she strikes a drum-note of awe, distance and magnificence. She gives the reader a feeling of the past.

THE STORY OF THE AMULET, for all its scholarly background and vivid detail, is no text-book. There is plenty of incidental humour, especially coming from the Psammead (the central figure of FIVE CHILDREN AND IT, now making a brief appearance). His grudging assistance, his grumblings and exactions, his fear of damp and love of praise, provide an acceptable contrast to the more thoughtful parts of the book. E. Nesbit shares with her readers the doubts and terrors of a journey to the distant past. She never talks down to them; she believes they are capable of appreciating mature distinctions of right and wrong, good and evil. On the other hand, unlike some writers of fantasy, she never plunges her young characters into adventures beyond their scope. Although the scenes in THE STORY OF THE AMULET are impressively accurate, there is nothing in any of them which could not have come from the imaginations of intelligent and well-read children thoroughly acquainted with the galleries of the British Museum. And from time to time, as they face angry rulers or clever priests, a word or a phrase will remind us that they are children, distinct and individual, meeting each situation as a child would meet it.

Obviously it is the amulet, the magical object, which holds together the various episodes of this exciting story. In some time fantasies it is a place, a building or a hill or a piece of country, which has accumulated magic through the centuries. Here the author is on safe ground. Most of us have at some time or another had a flash of understanding of the past when our knowledge of history has been awoken by a particular place, a local repository of great events.

Two striking stories, THE CHILDREN OF GREEN KNOWE and THE CHIMNEYS OF GREEN KNOWE, by Lucy M. Boston, are built round an old home, partly Norman, where a small boy stays with his great-grandmother Oldknow. Green Knowe (based on a real house, and lovingly described) sits four-square in the story, with its large, partly wild garden, and its topiary work, including the terrifying Green Noah which involved Tolly in the most exciting of his adventures. The story is warmed by the feeling of past generations—old walls, old toys, old tales of bygone Oldknows. At first Tolly wonders about these ancestors, then he studies their portraits, then, slowly, begins to see them—children of the seventeenth century, with their old names (Linnet, Toby, Alexander), their odd way of talking, of coming and going, of snatching Tolly up in their long-past exploits. It is not historical fact, but atmosphere, that the author is after, the feeling of a past century linked to the present by the spontaneous laughter of children and the superstitious terror of the great moving bush whose fall portends the end of the magic.

For it is magic, a curious, oblique, almost conversational magic, built round little things—a pet squirrel, a patteran in the garden, a chaffinch that flies in at Tolly's bedroom window. In the first book, THE CHILDREN OF GREEN KNOWE, it is a very simple magic, a matter of companionship across time. THE CHIMNEYS OF GREEN KNOWE has a more strictly planned story. This time Tolly makes a friend from the end of the eighteenth century, blind Susan, daughter of a seafaring Captain Oldknow, who brought back from the West Indies a little black boy to be her servant and companion. Tolly learns their story, chiefly from his great-grandmother, snatch by fascinating snatch, as she sits mending the old patchwork quilt in which pieces of the Captain's corduroy and his wife's muslin, of black Jacob's monkey-suit and the striped apron of the sneaking servant Caxton, are all stitched.

So they sit at night, not old woman and child, but two friends playing a game of pretending, and by day Tolly ranges the house, tapping the walls to find the jewels which were lost when the new wing was burnt down, and 'listening' to the house which is 'full of secrets'. He adds to his grandmother's tales. Once or twice he becomes an actor in old dramas, but his treasure-hunt, once he has collected enough clues from the past, is brought to a successful conclusion in the present when, exploring among the roof-timbers, he finds the chimney of the blocked-up room that had belonged to the evil servant, and drags out the jewels that mean new life for the old house.

In these beautifully written stories, imagination spans time. They are not fairy-tales. There is nothing supernatural in them; this is the magic of personality and of atmosphere. The author's intention in this has been understood entirely by her son, who is her illustrator. To illustrate *directly* what happens would be to break the spell of the fantasy. Peter Boston's pictures are backgrounds, establishing the place where strange things happen. For THE CHILDREN OF GREEN KNOWE he has devised illustrations in a unique combination of green on black which seem almost to emanate from the story, and the black and white drawings for THE CHIMNEYS OF GREEN KNOWE have a strange, appealing delicacy. So, in text and pictures, Green Knowe comes to life with its odd corners, its stone walls imposing yet 'gentle and curving to touch, almost warm, to be patted like living creatures'; full of past generations, enshrining layers of experience.

Drawing by Peter Boston for L. M. Boston's THE CHIMNEYS OF GREEN KNOWE (Faber)

Alison Uttley's exquisite story, A TRAVELLER IN TIME, re-creates the past by the same method. Thackers, the house where young Penelope stumbles upon the past, is based on a farm-house where the author spent her early years, and where she heard her father talk of the Babingtons and their championing of Mary Queen of Scots as though they were neighbours in the present. The tunnels which Anthony Babington had planned and started were tradition only when Alison Uttley heard of them, but very strong tradition, passed on to her by people who believed it. Her imagination, as she tells us in her foreword, seized on these tales:

Many of the incidents in this story are based on my dreams, for in sleep I went through secret hidden doorways in the house wall and found myself in another century. Four times I stepped through the door and wandered in rooms which had no existence . . . and I talked with people who lived alongside but out of time, moving through a life parallel to my own existence.
Alison Uttley. A TRAVELLER IN TIME (Faber, 1939) p. 12.

Just so Penelope, a visitor from London to her aunt and uncle at the farm, strays through a door and finds herself talking to an aunt kneading dough in a wooden trough in an Elizabethan kitchen; finds that this is the favourite country house of the Babingtons and that Anthony is hopelessly committed to the cause of the tragic queen. Through her aunt, housekeeper to the family, she meets and talks to the Babingtons. At first her visits to the past are brief and she is not anxious about her return; but as she is swept up into the plot, she grows more aware of danger—to herself as well as to the Babingtons. Her whole heart is engaged, and she tries to communicate to them her knowledge of what must be Mary's fate. Her distress when nobody will listen to her gives poignancy to the simple incidents of the story. When she sees Mary sewing with her ladies in Wingfield Manor, she recognizes her loneliness and remembers her danger. 'Oh, take care! They read your letters.' she calls outside the window, and turns away from the past, miserable because she cannot warn the queen, afraid lest she should be too deeply involved in her fate. All the same, she cannot wish for the end of her visions, and as she grows older and realizes that the power cannot last, she regrets the clear sight of younger days:

There was a clatter of hooves from the court-yard and Master Anthony rode out with two horses. Francis sprang to his mare's back and away they went, down the drive and along the winding valley. I waited there, shivering with cold, but the hoofbeats were only the clamour of the brook's waters, and nobody returned.
The peacefulness of Thackers which had held the seasons for five hundred years flowed through me, giving me strength and courage as it had done to those others, uniting me and them. I knew I had seen them for the last time on this earth, but some day I shall return to be with that brave company of shadows.
Ibid., pp. 330–1.

More than the story of the romantic Babingtons, or the atmosphere of the old house, or the mysterious movements in time, the character of Penelope dominates the book, and it is her wondering and her fear that are the real reason for it.

Personal experience, transmuted by imagination and fine writing—these are found also in Philippa Pearce's TOM'S MIDNIGHT GARDEN. In this story, time loses its limits for two people. First, for Tom, a schoolboy sent to stay with a rather unenterprising aunt and uncle while his brother has measles. The Kitsons live in a flat in a large converted house, and Tom, disturbed by rich food and lack of exercise, lies awake at night listening to the unregulated and eccentric chimes of the grandfather clock in the hall. He is soon to prove the truth of the clock's motto—Time No Longer; for though he intends to keep his promise not to stir out of bed between bedtime and breakfast time, he is given an hour outside time.

One night the clock strikes thirteen. Tom goes down to investigate, opens the back-door and finds himself not in the concrete yard with dustbins and clothes-lines but in an apparently limitless garden. In this garden it would seem that Tom is a ghost; or so he appears to Hatty, the small girl he meets there and who accepts him as a playmate in her Victorian world. He believes that he can share everything that happens to Hatty before he has to return to the present. This is not to be. Although time stands still in Tom's world while he is in the past, it does not stand still for Hatty. She is growing up even as Tom plays with her, and the magic, the wonder of the garden, the transcending of time must come to an end with the ending of her childhood. This familiar ending to time fantasies is beautifully handled, with great sympathy for the boy who suddenly sees his companion as a young woman. And there is a bold twist to the ending which sends the whole book back on itself, sends the reader rethinking the whole. For Tom, on the very day he is due to go home, meets the owner of the house, old Mrs Bartholomew, who lives in seclusion upstairs. He climbs to her flat, opens the door—and finds that she is Hatty. So, did he go back in the past, or did she create the past with her dreams as she lay in bed, an old woman?

The subtlety of this circumstance is something children may pay more attention to if they reread the book in their late teens. As a child's story it is magnificent. It is at once philosophical, swift and gay. The conversations of Hatty and Tom are natural, the incidents

Drawing by Susan Einzig for Philippa Pearce's TOM'S MIDNIGHT GARDEN (O.U.P.)

probable and presented with beautiful clarity. The style is impeccable —loose-jointed and flexible, colloquial when the occasion demands, at other times rhythmical and poetic. The fantasy will be real to children because it is real to the author; she has carried out C. S. Lewis's advice that 'the matter of our story should be part of the habitual furniture of our minds.' This means that although in some ways the book is too old for an eight-year-old, in other ways it is exactly right. The immediate mysterious sympathy between Tom and old Mrs Bartholomew can be paralleled in another magnificent story, BARBOCHE by Henri Bosco, which tells how young Pascalet (who appeared earlier in THE BOY AND THE RIVER and THE FOX IN THE ISLAND) goes on a journey with his old aunt Martine to revisit the village where she lived as a child. Her vision of the past merges into the present, as two pieces of film scenery can melt together. Where she sees fine formal gardens and prosperous cottages, Pascalet sees ruin, weeds and decay; but such is the bond between the two, and the atmosphere of magic into which they journey, that he can almost see the village of the past as well as of the present.

The mysterious half-magic of this story rises partly from the Provençal landscape, partly from the superstitious, dreamy characters of young Pascalet and his aunt. TOM'S MIDNIGHT GARDEN, likewise, is a book about people and their feelings. It is also, very much, a book about Time. The author is preoccupied with Time and its problems. Is it circular? Is it continuous? If Hatty carves Tom's private mark on a tree (which in present Time stands in the middle of a new housing estate), will the mark be visible to Tom in the present? And, if so, was it made *now* or *then*? Tom, always conscious of being in two worlds, never finds the answer to this, but he does make one firm attempt to conquer the limits of Time. He visits the garden on one occasion in winter, and finds Hatty skating. As he has no skates, he makes a plan; he begs her to wrap up her skates and hide them in her secret hiding-place (which, in the present, is in Tom's bedroom). Tom then returns to the present, finds the skates, takes them back into the past, and is soon skating blissfully on the Fens, the skates mysteriously duplicated. This bold stroke succeeds by its simplicity. The author, wisely, attempts no explanation. As Edward Eager makes one of his characters say, in THE TIME GARDEN, when a red handkerchief exists simultaneously in two periods, 'it's all part of the Mystery of Time.' Authors who try an elaborate analysis, or who lay down rules for a journey into Time, hold up the action of the story and only succeed in bewildering the reader.

Past may be linked with present in ordinary, non-magical terms. One of the neatest links I know of this kind is in a short story by Margaret J. Baker in TIP AND RUN. Two children, helped by a Tudor stone-mason who descends from a stained-glass window, go back to the Victorian period, where they find that two small cousins are ill. They need blankets; the children get to the village and choose some, but the shopkeeper refuses to accept their modern money. There is only one thing to do; they run off with the blankets, and pay when they return to the present, by post. The nineteenth-century bill, with the twentieth-century notes, is taken to the manager:

'I recollect it well,' he said to himself. 'I was just a lad and fresh to the job with shoes that pinched. It's proper money, the little lass said, and they've got to have them. We'll pay, it's a promise. She's honest enough for credit, I thought, but the manager, he were a tartar. "No credit," he said, and she and the boy took the blankets and ran. We traced them in the carrier's cart to Sunflower Hampton. A terrible snowy night it were, and I could have sworn I saw their footprints in the snow leading straight for the church door. But when we looked inside, they weren't to be seen. I've puzzled about it from that day to this.'

Slowly he dipped his pen in the ink-well, and beside the item in the ledger he wrote the words *Account Settled in Full*.

Margaret J. Baker. TIP AND RUN. (Brockhampton, 1958) pp. 34-5.

It is a masterly ending, fantasy comfortably equated with reality. This little story is meant to entertain, but it has a crisp certainty in the handling of Time.

There is one problem in time fantasies which cannot be written off by the word *mystery*. If you embroil your characters in the past, are they to be passive spectators or are they, in effect, to alter the course of history? Of course any author who tried to alter accepted fact drastically would court disaster. Professor Branestawm says the last word on this, when he and his friend Colonel Dedshott go back in time and participate in the Squiglatanian revolution:

'This is all wrong, you know ... it was the king's troops who won really. We've done something nasty to history, I'm afraid. I had no idea we should alter the battle like that.'

Norman Hunter. THE INCREDIBLE ADVENTURES OF PROFESSOR BRANESTAWM (Penguin 1950) p. 17.

Alison Uttley, as we have seen, lets Penelope remember what the fate of Mary Queen of Scots was, but the girl has no power to communicate this to her friends in the past. In E. Nesbit's fine story, HOUSE OF ARDEN, Elfrida finds herself dancing round a maypole in Tudor times, watched by Henry VIII and his new Queen Anne Boleyn. She can only say, 'Mind your darling head', and nobody heeds her. The touch of sadness here fits better in the story than the more exciting way of letting children from the present make mischief in the past. Richard Arden, for example, chats about the Gunpowder Plot before it is discovered and is promptly put in the Tower; so is Eliza, in THE TIME GARDEN, when she informs her royal namesake that she will soon be having Essex beheaded.

It is safer, and perhaps wiser, to confine yourself to domestic pictures in the past or to obscure or imagined events. The fourteenth-century siege which Ronald Welch so vividly reconstructs in THE GAUNTLET takes place in an unknown castle on the Welsh marches. Patricia Lynch, in ORLA OF BURREN, uses legendary material, about Granuaile, piratical and romantic queen of Galway in Elizabethan times, and in FIONA LEAPS THE BONFIRE she tells of Queen Maeve and Cuchullain. Other writers offer, as it were, lessons in social history, avoiding great events but giving their characters the power to enter the lives of ordinary people. E. Nesbit's HOUSE OF ARDEN and HARDING'S LUCK are really adventure stories, stories about a quest for treasure through the past. Edred and Elfrida and their cousin Richard, through the magic made by the snappish white Mouldiwarp, badge of their house, and by Dickie's magic seeds and coral, visit many periods, but they are nearly always involved in the private affairs of private families. In any case, history is not the main purpose in these excellent stories. They are studies of character, of brother and sister relationship, of the reaction of children to danger and perplexity and responsibility beyond their years, to their duty as landowners.

THE GOLDEN SHORE by Elinor Lyon, on the other hand, has a serious historical purpose. The two young people concerned have ancient Greece much in mind. Penelope's father is a schoolmaster who is coaching her cousin John for a scholarship. An essay subject, 'Describe in your own words the life of an ancient Greek peasant', starts the ball rolling. Grumbling about this, John urges Penelope out of doors. They jump a stream, fall in on the far side, and find themselves in an unknown world, where a group of Hellenes, threatened by barbarian invasion, have entrenched themselves behind the stream (in the children's world the Lifferli, to the Greeks Lethe). The waters of Lethe have had their effect on John and Penelope. They are only dimly aware of being out of their own time, but they throw themselves eagerly into the new skills and occupations they are offered. The adventures in the story are familiar enough—battles and chases which can be found hundreds of times over in stories—but they are lifted from ordinariness by the author's historical sense, her splendid picture of the Greeks clinging to their old customs and traditions. Because of her imaginative sympathy, her story is likely to teach children, indirectly, far more about Ancient Greece than a more factual story might, and I would put this book, well-written and compelling as it is, on a level with E. Nesbit's excursions into the pre-Christian world.

The use of the river Lethe makes this story something more than a piece of factual history. Though far from the poetry of Alison Uttley or Philippa Pearce, it has a strong element of fantasy in it. Other books which have an even stronger element of the didactic have sacrificed something of poetry, I think. Noel Streatfeild's tour de force, THE FEARLESS TREASURE, pursues ideas of inheritance and social obligation through various periods of British history. It is informative and brilliantly pictorial; but although the six children concerned are guided into the past through imagination, the boy or girl who reads the book—and it is best for the over-twelves, I think—will find their interest caught rather than their emotions. The same is true of Meriol Trevor's SUN SLOWER, SUN FASTER, in which the author sets out to survey the Catholic faith—first to illuminate its tenacity through persecution, neglect and corruption, and then to trace faith itself back to a primitive sun-worship which clinches the title of her book. Four people go back to various scenes in history—Bristol when Brunel's ship, the *Great Western*, sails in; Bath, visited by James II; the Norman Abbey in Bristol; a Saxon village, and so on. We watch these people affected in different ways by the religious aspect of what they see, and the doctrinal aim of the story really puts any feeling of poetry or magic out of the question.

There is no reason, of course, why this device of a journey in time should not be used in various ways. There is a good deal of humour to be got out of a character from the past visiting the present—like Norman Matilda in THE SHIP THAT FLEW, whose piece of Bayeux tapestry enlivens a present-day village fête, or Victorian Louisa (in Elizabeth Denys's light-hearted adventure, SEVEN DAYS' WONDER) who so much enjoys car-rides and television. This is all good fun and is not meant either to create a magical atmosphere or preach a moral. A visit to the future is a different matter.

Inevitably the writer, when he projects himself forward in imagination, takes with him his own idea of the present. Usually he will be suggesting the consequences, good or bad, of a logical change from our own pattern, that pattern being always discernible. When the children in THE STORY OF THE AMULET have a glimpse of the not-very-distant future, they see a London fresh and clean and full of flowers, where people are gentle and generous-hearted. All Edith Nesbit's Fabian principles and desires are behind the picture, which is made more telling when the woman they are talking to looks out of the window for a moment into the past and recoils with dismay from its ugliness.

Light, air, flowers, honesty and grace—ideals natural enough to writers of our time—these are the points, too, round which Meriol Trevor builds an ambitious story, THE OTHER SIDE OF THE MOON. This is not exclusively a children's book, though, on the face of it, it is one more venture to the Moon, with a boy in his teens as chief character. But there is no restriction of either terror or teaching, and in its imaginative sweep it occasionally approaches the three extra-terrestrial novels of C. S. Lewis (OUT OF THE SILENT PLANET, PERELANDRA, THAT HIDEOUS STRENGTH). Meriol Trevor describes two races on the Moon. The inhabitants of Cordeluc, with their twin kings, romantic as well as democratic, their language going back to Creation, their conviction that they are in touch with the First Giver of Life, represent the ideal man, a man who has taken from the past simplicity, myth-making and knight-errantry, and has turned his back on the worst elements of mechanization. These men of Cordeluc live on 'the other side of the Moon', in a small area of warmth and fertility, whereas the Half People live on the edge of the dead side, in underground cities ruled by dictators and always at war. The description of the people shows how they derive from our own times:

> . . . they all seemed to wear uniform, or if not, their ordinary clothes looked like uniforms, for they were mass-produced in standard sizes in a factory which Brett showed them. Men and women alike wore loose trousers and a sort of blouse jacket, with a belt. Everyone wore a tag on his shoulder with his name and number, and the same on his or her cap . . . Everybody looked grim or gloomy or cross or worried; they all stared at the visitors but none of them said anything, though they chattered to each

other in an ugly language full of hisses and guttural croaks.
Meriol Trevor. THE OTHER SIDE OF THE MOON (Collins, 1956)
p. 120.

A few Half People win the right to return to Cordeluc, and a few
of the noble folk are either stolen or tempted over to Coldeaston,
where they are brainwashed and kept as citizen-slaves. This is the
fate that threatens the men of the *Moondart*, when they are lured
into the city after a sojourn with the twin kings. The odd combination
of social satire and magic in the book (the quest of the Moonstone
is fairy-tale with a religious note) is only made possible, as so often
in fantasy, by the careful drawing of the characters, each influenced
one way or the other by the people on the Moon. Gil has the clear,
unprejudiced courage of a schoolboy; Tracy Kingville, the American
playboy, has his own jocular bravery; the bigoted scientist, Oliver,
recoils from too much knowledge; the pilot belongs by nature to the
Half People; while Anselm, the navigator, who alone can touch the
Moonstone, is the good man, the scapegoat. Together, these men
stand for humanity. The moral is not pressed too much, the thrilling
story is not hampered by it, but it is there all the same.

No journey in time is completely lacking in magic, even if it
teaches a lesson; but time fantasy is freer and goes nearer to the
heart of the matter. It makes the reader feel in tune with the past
or the future; it gives him the feeling of moving naturally in strange
worlds, the heir to many places and many times.

Reading List

*Baker, Margaret J. TIP AND RUN. *Brockhampton* 1958. Illustrated by Terence
  Freeman.
*Bosco, Henri. THE BOY AND THE RIVER (1955 France) 1956, THE FOX IN
  THE ISLAND (1956 France) 1958, BARBOCHE (1957 France) 1959. *O.U.P.*
  Translated by Gerard Hopkins. Illustrated by Lynton Lamb.
*Boston, L. M. THE CHILDREN OF GREEN KNOWE 1954, THE CHIMNEYS
  OF GREEN KNOWE 1958. *Faber.* Illustrated by Peter Boston.
Capon, Paul. FLIGHT OF TIME. *Heinemann* 1960. Illustrated by Marina Hoffer.
  Four teenagers discover a time-machine and journey to 2600 A.D. and
  1960 B.C.

Chauncy, Nan. TANGARA. *O.U.P.* 1960. Illustrated by Brian Wildsmith. Beautifully written, touching story of a girl in Tasmania going back in time and making friends with the last blackfellows.

Dawson, Carley. MR WICKER'S WINDOW. *Faber* 1955. Illustrated by Lynd Ward. Quest for jewelled tree belonging to Chinese princess, starting in present-day Washington and moving back to the eighteenth-century port of Georgetown.

*Denys, Elizabeth. SEVEN DAYS' WONDER. *Collins* 1959. Illustrated by Margery Gill.

Dickinson, William Croft. BORROBIL 1944, illustrated by John Morton-Sale. THE EILDON TREE 1947, illustrated by James S. Richardson. *Cape.* Two children are admitted to a fairy past.

Dickinson, William Croft. THE FLAG FROM THE ISLES. *Cape* 1951. Illustrated by Eric Tansley. The same children meet James IV of Scotland and play their part at Flodden Field.

*Eager, Edward. THE TIME GARDEN. *Macmillan* 1958. Illustrated by N. M. Bodecker.

Fitzroy, Olivia. THE HUNTED HEAD. *Cape* 1956. Illustrated by Raymond Sheppard. Boy returns to eighteenth century and re-enacts adventure of his ancestors with Bonny Prince Charlie.

*Hunter, Norman. THE INCREDIBLE ADVENTURES OF PROFESSOR BRANE-STAWM (1933). *Penguin* (Puffin Story Books) (1946) 1950. Illustrated by Heath Robinson. (see also Chap. 9).

*Lewis, C. S. OUT OF THE SILENT PLANET 1938, PERELANDRA 1943, THAT HIDEOUS STRENGTH 1945. *Bodley Head.*

*Lewis, Hilda. THE SHIP THAT FLEW. *O.U.P.* 1939. Illustrated by Nora Lavrin.

*Lynch, Patricia. ORLA OF BURREN 1954, illustrated by Joan Kiddell-Monroe. FIONA LEAPS THE BONFIRE 1957, illustrated by Peggy Fortnum. *Dent.*

Lynch, Patricia. THE BOOKSHOP ON THE QUAY. *Dent* 1956. Illustrated by Peggy Fortnum. Boy who loves reading wanders at night in Dublin, meets and talks with Swift.

*Lyon, Elinor. THE GOLDEN SHORE. *Hodder & Stoughton* 1957. Illustrated by the author.

Lyon, Elinor. DAUGHTERS OF ARADALE. *Hodder & Stoughton* 1957. Illustrated by the author. Three children reconstruct a Stuart incident in their family history.

Maddock, Reginald. THE TIME MAZE. *Nelson* 1960. Illustrated by Robert Hodgson. Two boys diverted in a magic cave to prehistoric times and then to the future.

*Nesbit, E. THE STORY OF THE AMULET (1906) 1957, FIVE CHILDREN AND IT
(1902) 1957, illustrated by H. R. Millar. THE HOUSE OF ARDEN (1908)
1949, HARDING'S LUCK (1903) 1949, illustrated by Desmond Walduck.
Benn.

Pardoe, M. ARGLE'S MIST 1956, ARGLE'S CAUSEWAY 1958, ARGLE'S ORACLE
1959. *Routledge.* Illustrated by Audrey Fawley. Three children and a schoolmaster mysteriously visit Britain in the time of Cymbeline, Hampshire in the
twelfth century, and Greece at the time of Alcibiades and Socrates.

*Pearce, A. Philippa. TOM'S MIDNIGHT GARDEN. *O.U.P.* 1958. Illustrated by
Susan Einzig.

Sauer, Julia. FOG MAGIC. *Viking*, New York 1943. Illustrated by Lynd Ward.
Girl in Novia Scotia joins life of village of long ago, now lost; a beautiful
and impressive story.

Severn, David. THE FUTURE TOOK US. *Bodley Head* 1958. Illustrated by Jillian
Richards. Two schoolboys go forward to Kent and London in 3,000 A.D.

Severn, David. DREAM GOLD. *Bodley Head* 1949. Illustrated by A. K. Lee. Two
schoolboys in Cornwall follow in dream an ancient adventure of pirates and
treasure.

Severn, David. DRUM-BEATS! *Bodley Head* 1953. Illustrated by Richard
Kennedy. Children in co-educational boarding school see into Africa and the
fate of an expedition lost years before.

*Streatfeild, Noel. THE FEARLESS TREASURE. *Michael Joseph* 1953. Illustrated
by Dorothy Braby.

*Strong, L. A. G. THE FIFTH OF NOVEMBER. *Dent* (King's Treasuries of Literature Series) (1937) 1940. Illustrated by Jack Matthew.

*Trevor, Meriol. SUN SLOWER, SUN FASTER 1955, illustrated by Edward
Ardizzone. THE OTHER SIDE OF THE MOON 1956, illustrated by Martin
Thomas. *Collins.*

*Uttley, Alison. A TRAVELLER IN TIME. *Faber* 1939. Illustrated by Phyllis
Bray.

Wallace, Kathleen. THE PRIZE ESSAY. *Heinemann* 1953. Illustrated by Richard
Kennedy. Mature story for girls of fourteen and over. Two schoolgirls
begin to see and talk to the Brontës, while studying their lives and work.
Very moving and done with masterly tact.

*Welch, Ronald. THE GAUNTLET. *O.U.P.* 1951. Illustrated by Terence Freeman.

Chapter 8 | *Magic Carpets*

The setting of fairy-tale is customarily (though not invariably) an enchanted country which we must seek in what Jung called the collective unconscious. We may more properly call those stories *fantasy*, which bring the magic and the irrational into our own world. Fantasy takes known objects and scenes and reshapes them in its own terms. This, at least, is one way of classifying the numerous tales which are not fairy-tales, although they may have traditional elements. Some will be only arbitrarily sorted. Where, for example, can we put THE PHOENIX AND THE CARPET, or THE LITTLE MATCH GIRL, or, for that matter, ALICE IN WONDERLAND?

The very simple dramatizing of a child's experience, through an animal or a toy that comes to life, though it is technically fantastic, can be very near to fact, just because the child takes it literally. A four-year-old has only to tie a bonnet on a kitten and force it into a doll's pram to make it, instantly, a baby. To this child there is nothing out of the way in Mrs Tiggy-Winkle wearing an apron and wielding a flat-iron. Nor is the everyday world really changed. Plates and spoons, cats and foxes, may change their rôle and their clothes in stories, but to a child they are not essentially different. Merely, the story has gratified his wish for a world where nothing is impossible; it is still the world he knows. Fantasy for young children is best if it is a matter of one simple incident which, for a time, enlarges and irradiates the everyday world.

In two volumes of enchanting stories from Norway, LITTLE OLD MRS PEPPERPOT and MRS PEPPERPOT AGAIN, by Alf Prøysen, we meet an ordinary housewife with one unusual habit. From time to time, unexpectedly, she shrinks to the size of a pepperpot, and while she is small she can understand the speech of animals. The accidents that rise from this are all founded on the facts of everyday.

The magic shines over a grocer's shop with a drawer of macaroni, a small girl's doll, a brass bedstead, a magic fulfilling the unspoken wish of many a child to be able to enter the world in a different guise. There is shrewd psychology in these tales. Mrs Pepperpot (a very real character, in words and in pictures), is quick to exploit her power, even if she cannot have it to order. For a long time she has suspected mice of raiding her larder, but one day she learns otherwise, when she goes small and they describe to her a 'monster' who can only be her husband; with quick opportunism, she appoints a mouse as her 'penny watchman' and stops her husband's marauding. Then there is her neighbour, who has earned the nickname Mrs Calamity because of her love of omens. Mrs Calamity has a habit of stealing plants and one day she sets to work on Mrs Pepperpot's best geranium; but Mrs Pepperpot, going small, makes the most of her chance. Following the thief, she enlists the help of a wagtail, a black cat and a magpie, and with one stroke puts an end to her neighbour's superstition and her thieving ways. Everything that happens is just one remove from the familiar world of a bustling woman. These simple tales have some of the same attractive ingredients as Mary Norton's more complex stories about the Borrowers.

Drawing-magic is another device of this simple kind. Look at, for instance, that delightful little tale, THE MAGIC BUTTON by Kathleen Guthrie. One day, as Kitty draws a mouse and a caterpillar, she rubs the top button of her blouse, thinking at the same time how wonderful it would be if they could talk to her. At once, of course, they do, and the three of them go for a glorious spin round the town on thistledown parachutes. Kitty is taken out of her world and yet she never leaves it. The direct style and the comical drawings fit perfectly together; this is a beautiful exercise in creative imagination.

The magic in a pencil is not always so simple and light-hearted. Most stories that use this device take it at its face value, but drawing is, after all, one of the forms of sympathetic magic, and fear lurks behind it. This is one of the compelling fears, like the thought of infinity, which comes to strong imaginations. It would be possible for a timid child to read, say, the drawing incident in THE BOX OF DELIGHTS (see pp. 373–9) and remain unmoved, but an imaginative child would very likely feel a pang of terror as Kay's pictures come to life. This is not a harmful thing, I am sure, but a necessary stretching of that child's poetic feeling. A fascinating story by

Catherine Storr, MARIANNE DREAMS, illustrates this point.

This is the story of a girl, kept in bed by illness, who finds a pencil with magical properties. There begins a dream-relationship with Mark, who is also ill. The two children have not met, though the same tutor visits them both, but through Marianne's drawings they share a weird adventure, besieged in a bleak house on a moor by huge, one-eyed stones which, each day, move nearer and nearer. Marianne's ordinary world is confused and shifted as the adventure gets more and more alarming, until the children escape in the healing beams of a lighthouse which she had sketched on the horizon.

The story is sometimes frightening, but the terror is held in check because the children are learning to control it through the pencil. Using their wits, they think out, step by logical step, what they can draw that will be most useful, and they deduce by observation, gradually, that safety lies in light. In one way this story can be read as a fantastic adventure, but it is also a study of children coming to terms with some of the harsher aspects of life. It is a little allegory, wonderfully turned.

This is certainly a book for the child older than the little girl who can light-heartedly imagine herself flying on a piece of thistledown and talking with a mouse and a caterpillar. All the same, everything develops from Marianne's simple, child-shaped drawings. Reality is always there—that is the secret—from the simplest stories about agreeably odd happenings to those dream-stories which, as it were, create a country through imagination, almost map the country of the imagination itself. Palmer Brown has written two exquisite stories, BEYOND THE PAWPAW TREES and THE SILVER NUTMEG, which are fantasies within fantasy, for the country where Anna Lavinia lives and her house shielded by a high wall are both real and unreal. Here are the domestic events of an ordinary world, with mother making preserves (pawpaw preserves) and little girl enjoying her pets. But the air is different; this is a country unknown to travel-agencies. Anna Lavinia's mother likes to believe what she sees, but the child's father, who has been absent for a long time, is, in his wife's words, 'always chasing rainbows', and his daughter inclines to his point of view:

Though she had not seen him for more than two years, Anna Lavinia remembered clearly his bright red beard and the pocket microscope which he always carried to examine the motes in sunbeams. He often promised to let Anna Lavinia look at them too, but somehow he never got around to it.

Palmer Brown. BEYOND THE PAWPAW TREES (Methuen, 1956) pp. 8–9.

So, in this book, she sets out on a visit to her aunt Sophia Maria prepared for all that may happen, dealing equally well with the matter-of-fact fat lady in the train and with the mirage on which a town is perched, and where she finds her aunt and her father. She has found something else, too, on her journey, a silver key which her father has been searching for; together they take it back to the desert oasis and find 'fourteen small iron pots all full of gold'. It is real gold, as Anna Lavinia's father assures her, and at last she knew 'why her father was always chasing rainbows, and she felt sure that her mother would feel better about it when she knew too.' This is having the best of both worlds!

Drawing by Palmer Brown for his THE SILVER NUTMEG (Methuen)

In THE SILVER NUTMEG, Anna Lavinia, still exploring, goes through a dew-pond into an upside-down world where gravity does not exist, and where a permanent band of recoverers pull down things that float out of their proper sphere. Anna Lavinia and the boy who is her companion in this world enjoy playing together, and they enjoy too the discovery that the sad lady, his aunt, was once betrothed to Anna Lavinia's wandering uncle (an engaging character who peddles spices and who is united to his love in the end). The odd, entrancing illustrations, feathery and delicate, encrusted with detail, underline this fascinating amalgam of fantastical and familiar. The tale is made of the very spirit of childhood, curious, aware and reaching out to the unknown.

Under water, too, or reflected, is the world Theresa Whistler has imagined in THE RIVER BOY. This is the story of Nathaniel, who lives in an old house remote in deep country, a boy whose imagination keeps him company, who wants something and at last finds it in his dreams—his reflection, the river boy. For Nathaniel's valley has no river, but in his dreams and reveries he and the river boy play in a wonderful stream, and journey down it towards the sea. The journey itself is symbolic of growing up. When Nat reaches the sea and sees the last of the river boy, he realizes as well as we do that the adventure is over. The fantasy swings at will between the simple, concrete wishes of a boy and the half-formed wishes of his mind thrusting towards his older self. Beside the delights of finding birds' nests, seeing a mill at work or scything corn, there are intimations of deeper desires. At the mill, Nat feels the presence of an unseen people. He is drawn strongly towards the farm seen across the valley:

> It was then that he realised with a strange, sharp surprise, that the tower cast no shadow at all. All round it beneath him the twelve roofs lay in the bright sunlight of evening, which was drawing from his own feet already so long and dark a shadow, stretching out far beyond the shadow of the stack. Yet the whole farm, and the ancient tower, and the flowering trees, lay in a circle of untroubled radiance. Gazing at them long and silently, Nathaniel felt as though something he had always minded had been put right, as though he had found something he did not know he had lost.
> Theresa Whistler. THE RIVER BOY (Hart-Davis, 1955) p. 115.

It is because he struggles to reach the farm by his own efforts that the dream momentarily swings into a nightmare, to a long vision of the river boy lying motionless in the snow, tended by an old woman —Nature herself. Then Nat finds the sea and enters upon the next, rational stage of everyday life, refreshed, taught, enlivened by the imaginary journey.

The meaning of the story will rise in the mind of an intelligent child long after he has enjoyed the concrete images, the beautiful pictures that children naturally create in a dream. A white horse in moonlight, a village with its church, 'like a string of goslings behind a grey goose', a snail 'waving delighted horns in the air', an old mill at work—the floor trembling, the three cats whisking about 'in the mealy gloom', the miller himself with every crease of his clothes giving off flour 'as a puffball spurts brown dust when you stamp on it'. I can't praise too highly this unusual, shining book, with its exquisite drawings, its rich, graceful style and its overtones of meaning. This is indeed the transformation of one world into another, for while there is nothing here outside a boy's experience, there is nothing quite ordinary in this river world. The ordinary and familiar have become magical, new and vibrating with colour and light.

The balance between real and unreal, between fact and imagination, is the key to good fantasy. You can accept the improbable (that is, you can believe in it with your imagination) just so far as you can believe in the realistic beginnings from which the fantasy springs. Belief is taxed to its utmost when the fantasy is closest to the real. The works of Rosemary Anne Sisson, to take an example, are at first glance realistic: they are best called romantic. In THE IMPRACTICAL CHIMNEY-SWEEP we have a rustic scene idealized but still only one remove from the world we know. The story tells how John William, who climbs chimneys for his father, loses his job because he prefers to watch the sunrise from the top of Lord Summerset's chimney-stack. John William's sense of values provides the point of the story. Setting out with a horse and cart, he sweeps his way from house to house in country unknown to him, picking up as wages various objects which seem useless but which come in handy in the end:

Then Miss Ellen kissed John William and gave him the sea-shell, and he said goodbye to her and to Commander Peters and to Jane, and he went away inland, with his brush over one shoulder and his bundle of flints over the other, and his leather halter pulled up tight with the silver buckle. And long after the little white house was out of sight, and the sea was only a blue and silver gleam behind him, he put Miss Ellen's shell to his ear, and there he could hear the waves breaking on the shore and the wide sea singing, singing in the wind.

Rosemary Anne Sisson. THE IMPRACTICAL CHIMNEY-SWEEP (Macmillan, 1956) p. 136.

Drawing by Theresa Whistler for her THE RIVER BOY (Hart-Davis)

And John, whom his father scorns for his unworldliness, ends up with a beautiful gypsy bride and a blessing from the Romany queen:

'You shall climb chimneys all your life . . . and you shall never grow too stout for it. At the end of every chimney you shall see the silver stars, and the soot shall never blind you to them.'
Ibid., pp. 158–9.

The events of this odd story are offered as fact, as something that happened. At the other extreme are two remarkable books by William Mayne which push real-life adventure just to the edge of fantasy, but never beyond, through the imaginations of the central characters. THE BLUE BOAT, which shows this method at its simplest, is the story of two small boys spending a spring holiday in a prim seaside villa with a prim landlady. Escaping from her fussing, they play by a mere where they borrow a boat—a magic boat, it seems to them, for they come upon it just after they have wished for it. By the mere, too, they meet a giant, a goblin and an alchemist, and the fact that they later discover these to be friends lying up between circus seasons makes no difference to their enjoyment. It is all, to use Hugh's splendid word, 'disordinary', and they separate fact and fantasy, partially and happily, as children naturally would:

Christopher sat in the back of the car and heard no more of anyone's conversation. He was sorting out all the muddling facts that had appeared to him, starting with the goblin and ending with the friendliness of the giant. It was easy, he thought, for Hugh to think they were slightly magic; but whatever Hugh thought or imagined there was no magic, no sudden land of goblins and giants and princes beyond the Mere. Yet they had been there, without any sort of fancying at all, and seen the goblin and the giant, and been called princes . . .
The explanation came to him gradually: it had to, because it troubled his mind all the time to find himself in a place he did not believe in. If the goblin pretended to be a goblin, and the giant pretended to be a giant, and really they were friends . . . But they are goblin-sized and giant-sized . . . Yet they are only pretending, and playing a game, and we are playing it too . . . If I play it instead of trying to make it into sense, will that be better?
It was better, he found at once. He looked at Mrs Wrigley in the front of the car, and found she was a witch, quite certainly . . .

Pretending certainly, that is . . . And Dad was a king . . . That could very likely be so, because he was a kingish man used to ordering people and sending them to do things.

William Mayne. THE BLUE BOAT (Oxford University Press, 1957) pp. 122–3.

In A GRASS ROPE there is a deeper feeling of mystery. Set in the Yorkshire dales, this is a treasure hunt, like so many of William Mayne's books, but with the difference that one of the characters, young Mary, believes so firmly in magic that her interpretation of events dominates the story rather than her parents' common-sense or Adam Forrest's grammar-school reasoning. The treasure, they know, belonged to Sir Owland (an ancestor of Nan and Mary) who lost a pack of hounds and a hunting unicorn and, with them, all his wealth, which was said to be 'fastened' to them. The older children follow up clues, in story-book fashion: but Mary plaits the traditional grass-rope to catch the unicorn, and goes off in the night down an old mine-shaft, which she firmly believes is the gate to fairyland. Down in the darkness she finds a creature she takes for the unicorn (it is a fox-cub fallen into the shaft); groping in the grass she finds some wire, twists it into a collar and lead, and fastens one end to the fox, the other to a 'white peeled stick'. When she is found and pulled out by her anxious family, the wire is found to be the silver collars joined together of the long-dead hounds, the 'white stick' a piece of an animal's skull with a central horn. So strong is William Mayne's power of fantasy that most children will refuse, as Mary does, to listen to the father's rational explanation of this. As Mary says, when she sees the collars being polished, 'One for each of us, and one for each animal . . . And all because I believe in fairies.'

It is certainly not inappropriate to use the word 'magic' of a story where the author makes you aware of the irrational all the time, the poetic below the events of ordinary life, and does this while keeping his characters absolutely real, not eccentric or peculiar, but people with character and drive and personal idiom.

Mayne's particular contribution to the fantastic adventure is the way he makes the vision of certain of his characters override actual events. In these two books, which have simple, almost hackneyed plots, the tone is set by Mary's belief in fairyland and by the interpretation Hugh and Christopher put on the people they meet. All else—narrative, clear-cut dialogue, implied description—follow along behind, brilliant but subsidiary. The same compulsive imagination runs through an odd, intriguing story, THE DOUBLING ROD, by Ada Harrison. This is the story of the Hinnabels, who by chance find a forked stick which has the power to duplicate any object or event. The Hinnabels gradually come to understand, and sometimes to fear, the power of the rod. They use it to get back an Etruscan bronze figure which is stolen while Mr Hinnabel is keeping it for a museum, but the rod only works because the Hinnabels believe in it. The magic is not really from outside; it depends on character, and is believable because of this. There are plenty of adventure stories like this one which have been given a new life and vigour by a small, easy touch of magic—for instance Meta Mayne Reid's stories, in which a group of Irish children are instructed by Tiffany, the cat, in magical lore. The magic does not advance the plot noticeably in any of these stories, but it adds tension and glamour to stories that are otherwise familiar enough.

Meta Mayne Reid blends magic and reality without any self-consciousness, and so does Janet McNeill in her amusing stories of Specs McCann, school stories which, without the touch of fantasy, would still be notable for their wit, their complete lack of cliché in word or event, their precisely delineated characters. But Specs, an Irish boy at boarding-school, has 'queer things' happen to him. He is taught the crawl by a mermaid, he hatches a dragon from an egg found in a cave, he changes a master into a white rabbit; the droll joke runs through two volumes and is always fresh and entertaining. Sometimes the fantasy is extreme (as with the dragon); sometimes it is subtle, as in *Specs and the Cuckoo Clock*, a small masterpiece. Tusky, a rival schoolboy, has planted a moth-ball in Specs's clock, and has made Specs look a fool, for he was sure the bird had laid it; but Specs has the last word:

Tusky came in at the end of the period to borrow a dictionary. He looked rather excited and pleased, but we didn't make any remark and just handed the book over. It was half a minute to five and he hung about looking up his word. Then the doors on the clock opened and the cuckoo came out. 'Cuck–' she said, and stopped. For a moment she hung there with her little wings stretched wide, and her bright little eyes looked at Tusky. She knew who'd made a fool of her. Then she went into her house and shut the doors with a tiny vicious bang.

Tusky didn't say a word. He just stood there, looking at the clock and his face got redder and redder. Then he turned and went out. Specs went over to the clock. It was still ticking busily. He bent down close to the little doors. 'Thank you, ma'am,' he said. Janet McNeill. MY FRIEND SPECS MCCANN (Faber, 1955) pp.95–6.

How easily the author bounces from one mood to another, how lightly she carries off the joke, not a matter for laughter so much as for smiles, for beyond it there is a mystery, something more than the mere fact of a small boy exercising, sometimes outrageously and inappropriately, an unusual gift. And the more seriously you take the magic, the more you are kept in bounds by the shrewd psychology, the accurate picture of small boys at school.

With the intrusion of fantastic creatures into an everyday world, the factual foundation is most important. The swing between fact and fancy produces an agreeable humour. We believe in the odd things that happen to Specs McCann because he is such a real boy. How does Barbara Euphan Todd make us believe in *her* fantastic characters? For she makes a band of scarecrows settle down with such success in everyday life that you constantly forget they are fantastic. Some credit, certainly, is due to her illustrators, who have presented her scarecrow characters in different but always in interesting ways. To John Harwood, who illustrated WORZEL GUMMIDGE AND SAUCY NANCY, it is the woodenness of the creatures that is most striking; he makes you see the humour of sticks and clothes suddenly animated. Jill Crockford is very much aware of the magic of the transformation, and in her drawings there is an off-beat poetry that suits the stories perfectly.

Then, the scarecrows come to life by association with the human characters, so very real themselves—the children, Tom and Susan and towny Robin, the farmer's wife, who looks after them at Scatterbrook, the egregious Mrs Bloomsbury-Barton. But there is more to it than this. That adventures happen at all depends on the premise that Worzel Gummidge is alive, that he can walk and talk, and that the same power is extended to his wife, Earthy Mangold, lugubrious Hannah Harrow, and the rest of the crew. But *what* happens de-

Drawing by John Harwood for Barbara Euphan Todd's WORZEL GUMMIDGE AND SAUCY NANCY (Hollis & Carter). Below: Drawing by Jill Crockford for WORZEL GUMMIDGE AND THE RAILWAY SCARECROWS (Evans)

pends on character, and most of all on the intentions of Gummidge himself, with his Will Rogers brand of philosophy that matches so well his bottle-straw feet and his hedgehog hairbrush. Whatever humans do, whatever he does to them, to Gummidge 'humans is daft'. When Earthy Mangold, as a new scarecrow, says she would rather try to learn being a human first, Gummidge storms at her:

> 'Go and be human then . . . Go and live complicate. Spend your mornin's bringin' mud into the house, and your arternoons takin' it out again, and puttin' rags into water, and hangin' 'em out to dry.'
> 'Is that what humans does?' asked Earthy.
> 'Ooh, Aye! I've caught 'em at it. It's enough to make anyone sulk.'
> Barbara Euphan Todd. EARTHY MANGOLD AND WORZEL GUMMIDGE (Hollis & Carter, 1954) p. 41.

and he is just as rude when John asks him the time:

> 'Humans is daft, the way they goes on about time. I allus defies it. The human as started choppin' days and nights into hours, and hours into minutes did a great deal o' harm. Time goes wriggling on just like a worm, and it don't make no differ if you chops it up or not. All humans is daft.' Ibid., p. 52.

Most of the adventures in these books arise simply from Gummidge's mistaken self-confidence. He is prepared at a moment's notice to take on the semblance of an elephant-trainer, an amateur naturalist (what he calls a badger-badgerer) or almost any variant of village worthy, and the authentic, crabby, racy tone echoes through all his impersonations; perhaps at its most typical when he opens the Scatterbrook bazaar, after borrowing the clothes belonging to Lady Piddingfold, the guest of honour:

> Mr Perkins interrupted quickly by saying, 'I will now ask our kind friend, Lady Piddingfold, to say that the bazaar is open.' He bowed towards Worzel Gummidge, who seemed to have got his fingers knotted together in the strings of the sponge-bag.
> 'All right,' he said in his loudest, crossest voice. 'If you say the thing's open, it *is* open. I didn't come here to start arguments. It's never been shut that I know of.' Then he coughed violently, and walked away.
> Barbara Euphan Todd. MORE ABOUT WORZEL GUMMIDGE (Hollis & Carter, 1938) p. 65.

This is rollicking humour, but now and then we are pulled up short by moments of poetry, when the children see the country purely, as it should be seen. Robin's night ride on Dapple Grey, the merry-go-round horse (in WORZEL GUMMIDGE AT THE CIRCUS), with the animals and scarecrows crowding round him, is one such moment, and so is the description of John and Susan waking at dawn in the railway cutting where they have spent the night with Gummidge and his friends (in WORZEL GUMMIDGE AGAIN). These stories are popular partly because they give children an outlet for their wish to be rude, dirty and untrammelled; Gummidge carries on, for them, a perpetual mutiny against the world of grown-ups. At the same time he satisfies their latent desire for mystery and magic.

Talking animals are more difficult to draw successfully than fantastic semi-humans, at least when they are to be involved in human affairs, and I would give high praise to Margaret J. Baker for her handling of Homer the tortoise. This pedantic personage first appeared in a story called, suitably, NONSENSE! SAID THE TORTOISE, in which he was bought by three sisters from a local pet-shop. His name is important. In this first book Homer is very useful to Lettice's younger sister Mouse in a spelling-test at school, acting as a crib in her desk. In HOMER SEES THE QUEEN he gets into the British Museum Reading Room and establishes friendly relations with a professor. In HOMER GOES TO STRATFORD he is quite equal to conversations about The Bard, as he calls him, and eventually insinuates himself into an open-air performance of *A Midsummer Night's Dream*. Homer is a splendid character and the adventures which result from his unusual accomplishments are almost all well chosen and reasonable; but there is one point where Margaret J. Baker has gone too far. Fantasy must be consistent. It must have its own limits, and the extra-human events must not clash too seriously with the events of the real world. In NONSENSE! SAID THE TORTOISE Homer has one adventure which illustrates the perfection of fantasy, and one which is, I think, in the wrong key.

First, the good example. Homer is confiscated at school by Miss Weston, a mistress whom most of the girls find prim and alarming. The girls, anxious about their pet, creep out at night and peer in at Miss Weston's window:

They stood on tip-toe peering through a slit in the curtains. Miss

Weston was sitting in a rocking-chair before the gas stove with a mug of cocoa in her hand and a chessboard arranged on the table by her side . . . Sitting on the opposite side of the table, studying the chessmen and shifting one very cautiously with his clubbed foot, was Homer, looking very pleased with himself.

'Checkmate, I think,' he said, 'and thank you for a most enjoyable evening.'

'Not at all,' said Miss Weston, 'your skill was really too much for me. You play a really remarkable game. Now if you have everything for the night, I think I will retire. It's past one o'clock and those children will require all my energies tomorrow.'
Margaret J. Baker. NONSENSE! SAID THE TORTOISE (Brockhampton, 1949) pp. 61-2.

Miss Weston's sang-froid is beautifully conveyed, and there is not a word wasted in this delightful scene. Later in the book, however, Homer's gift is used in a way I find indefensible. In the garden of Sir George Clewisham's mansion the tortoise overhears two men plotting to steal his jewels. He tells the children and they warn Sir George, but too late; Homer has to settle the crooks himself, by shouting at them as they get over the wall, so that they drop the jewels. Now this is too serious an affair to be settled by fantasy; the whole balance of the incident is upset.

A similar point comes up in THE MAGIC WALKING-STICK, a pleasant adventure story by John Buchan, in which an Eton schoolboy finds a stick which will carry him anywhere he wants to go. Bill gets involved in the affairs of young prince Anatole of Gracia and his wicked uncle Kuno, and uses the stick to rescue Anatole and to maroon Kuno, first on St Kilda, then in the Highlands, and finally (a nice Buchan touch) in a suburb of Moscow. Nobody is going to question the logic of all this, for the adventure is an unreal Ruritanian affair. But earlier on the magic has been used in a more questionable way. Bill's aviator uncle is lost in the Sahara on a record-breaking flight. Bill finds him, gives him food and sends a rescue-party from the nearest French frontier-post. Now this puts the fantasy into direct contact with real life, where the danger is too serious, too stringent to be solved by fantastic means. Again, the balance of a story has been spoiled.

This is a mistake that E. Nesbit never made. She tells us exactly how far the magic is supposed to go and coaxes us to believe in it by her cunning detail and by the moderate amount of oddity that we are asked to believe. In that classic wish-story, FIVE CHILDREN AND IT, there are two limits to the magic power which the Psammead exercises, often grudgingly, on behalf of the children. First, it is over by sundown. Secondly, only the children can perceive its effects. These conditions keep the story within bounds and lead to some amusing situations. When Robert wishes to be in a besieged castle, the servants are quite unaware of the change in circumstances, and serve a normal lunch to the children, who hungrily go through a pantomime of eating. There is another twist to the siege incident, for Cyril, pouring water through a hole over the portcullis, in lieu of the customary boiling oil, unfortunately chooses the first moment of sunset, with the result that Martha, back from her day out, receives an undeserved wetting.

Situations like this have a purpose. Reconsideration is the keynote of the book. In the gayest way, E. Nesbit explodes the very idea of the magic wish. Delightful as each day seems at its outset, before the magic has ended some disaster or disconcerting mistake is bound to make the children think again, so that they gradually learn to be careful and to avoid casual wishes. To be rich beyond the dreams of avarice is, after all, not much use when the local shopkeepers do not recognize your currency.

Nobody can fail to believe in E. Nesbit's fantasies, for they are so firmly rooted in character and in circumstance. Everything that happens joins on somewhere to the ordinary world. In THE PHOENIX AND THE CARPET, when Anthea and the rest have used their magic carpet, under the Phœnix's instructions, for several quite exacting journeys, it begins to wear rather thin. E. Nesbit means this literally. A clergyman, transported to a desert island to marry the cook and the burglar, appears only as half a man and half a shadow, because he is standing on a worn part of the carpet, and there comes a moment when two of the children actually fall through a large hole—fortunately on to a handy roof-top. Similarly, THE MAGIC CITY is a series of dream-fantasies based firmly on the conditions of Philip's life. He has built the city out of anything that comes to hand. The citizens whom he finds terrorized by the Giant Sloth turn out to be his Halma men; the city is saved by Cæsar, who marches his forces out of *De Bello Gallico* to attack the barbarians who have already escaped from its pages; the animals are ark-animals, under Mr Noah's rule. As for the city itself, Mr Perrin, the carpenter, says:

'All the cities and things you ever built is in this country. I don't know how it's managed, no more'n what you do. But so it is. And as you made 'em, you've the right to come to them—if you can get there. And you have got there. It isn't every one has the luck, I'm told. Well, then, you made the cities, but you made 'em out of what other folks had made, things like bricks and chessmen and books and candlesticks and dominoes and brass basins and every sort of kind of thing. An' all the people who helped to make all them things you used to build with, they're all here too. D'you see? *Making's* the thing. If it was no more than the lad that turned the handle of the grindstone to sharp the knife that carved a bit of a cabinet or what not, or a child that picked a teazle to finish a bit of the cloth that's glued on to the bottom of a chessman—they're all here. They're what's called the population of your cities.'

E. Nesbit. THE MAGIC CITY (Benn, 1910) pp. 105–6.

Beyond the magic happenings, too, there is the feeling of human relations—Philip's growing friendship with Lucy, his advances towards the step-brother he so strongly resented; there is a feeling of growing up, of stretching, of youthful experience. Gay and rollicking though the book is, there is enough wisdom in it to fill out hundreds of wishy-washy family stories of today.

The same sturdy realism anchors to the earth the tugging, sky-bound stories about Mary Poppins by P. L. Travers. Mary Poppins occupies in the Banks family the place filled in Miss Nesbit's books by the Mouldiwarp, the Psammead and the Phœnix. Like them, she is crusty, unpredictable and fond of speaking her mind. Magic is something she is obliged to perform and which she feels will do her charges no good. But she cannot help being magic, for she is an elemental. Sun and stars defer to her at a sky-fête; she is an old friend of the Greek gods; she appears out of the sky on a kite-string; she orders the elements and promotes the unlikely everywhere. That is one side of her. The other side is the Nannie, with her expressive sniff, her despotic commands, her love of the last word.

These lively stories take you into a madder, more completely fantastic world than the world of E. Nesbit, though with the same homely domestic foundation. There is *Bad Wednesday*, a terrifying piece, when Jane is whisked into the world of a Royal Doulton bowl; there is *Mrs Lark's Andrew*, a splendid piece of nonsense about a respectable dog and a mongrel; there is *The Marble Boy*, an incident in the park which combines sharp social comedy with a deep apprehension of the antique; there is the vivid *Hallowe'en*, where comic characters and natural objects all obey Mary Poppins as, with her Dutch doll hair and her immovable, bourgeois hat, she foots it through the night. She is always respectable. When, in *Peppermint Horses*, she whirls the children up into the sky, she is still very much the Nannie:

'I'll race you to the oak tree, Jane!' cried Michael, as she trotted up.

'Quietly, please! No horseplay, Michael! Put your hats straight and follow me!'

Mary Poppins, on her parrot umbrella, rode past them at a canter. Neatly and primly, as though she were in a rocking chair, she sat on the black silk folds. In her hand she held two leading strings attached to the Twins' pink sticks.

P. L. Travers. MARY POPPINS OPENS THE DOOR (Peter Davies, 1944) pp. 124-5.

These stories depend mainly on the character of this strange personage, and because her character is so important, Mary Shepard's illustrations are of the first importance too, for they present Mary Poppins to us visually in a way that establishes her for ever. It is because of Mary Poppins, because she is as she is, that these books are at once gay and serious, superbly entertaining, but always probing into depths of mystery and poetry.

This deeper meaning is essential in fantasy. For the characters involved, there is no need for very deep thought. They can enjoy the pleasure of realizing their dearest wishes, only occasionally speculating about their origin. Sometimes (as in E. Nesbit's stories) they can be changed a little, can learn a little from their adventures, as they miraculously travel the world, change their shape, or exploit the power of a button, a lamp-post or a pencil. But the reader who vicariously enjoys these delights should expect something more. The fantasy should exercise his imagination. For the characters in the story there is little time for Why and How. Questions are blown away as they rush from one adventure to another. But the reader can and should ask How and Why. He should be left with a sense of expansion, as if he himself had been flying on a magic carpet and breathing an air more rarefied than his accustomed oxygen, a world which he wants to know more about. Then, and only then, has the fantasy fulfilled its purpose.

Drawing by Mary Shepard for
P. L. Travers's MARY POPPINS OPENS
THE DOOR (Collins)

Reading List

Fantasy starting in everyday life

*Baker, Margaret J. NONSENSE! SAID THE TORTOISE 1949, HOMER SEES THE QUEEN 1956, HOMER GOES TO STRATFORD 1958. *Brockhampton.* Illustrated by Terence Freeman.

Bourne, Holly. PERIWINKLE. *Heinemann* 1959. Illustrated by the author. Two children take home a mermaid from a fish-shop, with amusing consequences.

*Brown, Palmer. BEYOND THE PAW-PAW TREES (1954 U.S.A.) 1956, THE SILVER NUTMEG (1956 U.S.A.) 1957. *Methuen.* Illustrated by the author.

*Buchan, John. THE MAGIC WALKING-STICK. *Bodley Head* 1932.

Forester, C. S. POO-POO AND THE DRAGONS. *Michael Joseph* 1942. Illustrated by Robert Lawson. Ordinary family copes with two large, affectionate dragons.

*Guthrie, Kathleen. THE MAGIC BUTTON. *Brockhampton* 1959. Illustrated by the author.

*Harrison, Ada. THE DOUBLING ROD. *Bodley Head* 1957. Illustrated by Robert Austin.

Hopp, Zinken. THE MAGIC CHALK (1948 Norway). *Ward* 1960. Illustrated by Gian Berto Vannio. Inspired nonsense, for all ages from about six. Travels of Jon and his companion Sofus (whom he has drawn) in an astonishing world.

Howard, Jean. THE THIRTEENTH IS MAGIC (1950 U.S.A.). *World's Work* 1958. Illustrated by Adrienne Adams. Boy and girl in New York flat have adventures with an enchanted pencil.

Lang, E. H. THE CURIOUS ADVENTURES OF TABBY. *Faber* 1956. Illustrated by Shirley Hughes. Small girl has all her most extraordinary wishes granted.

*McNeill, Janet. MY FRIEND SPECS MCCANN 1955, SPECS FORTISSIMO 1958. *Faber*. Illustrated by Rowland Friers.

*Mayne, William. THE BLUE BOAT 1957, illustrated by Geraldine Spence. A GRASS ROPE 1957, illustrated by Lynton Lamb. *O.U.P.*

*Nesbit, E. FIVE CHILDREN AND IT (see Chap. 7).

Nesbit, E. THE PHOENIX AND THE CARPET (1904) 1956, THE MAGIC CITY 1910 *Benn*. Illustrated by H. R. Millar.

*Norton, Mary. THE BORROWERS, etc. (see Chap. 6).

*Prøysen, Alf. LITTLE OLD MRS PEPPERPOT (1957 Sweden) 1959, MRS PEPPERPOT AGAIN (1958 Sweden) 1960. *Hutchinson*. Translated by Marianne Helweg. Illustrated by Björn Berg.

*Reid, Meta Mayne. CARRIGMORE CASTLE 1954, TIFFANY AND THE SWALLOW RHYME 1956, THE CUCKOO AT COOLNEAN 1956, STRANGERS AT CARRIGMORE 1958. *Faber*. Illustrated by Richard Kennedy.

Ropner, Pamela. THE GOLDEN IMPALA. *Hart-Davis* 1957. Illustrated by Ralph Thompson. African adventure, with a legendary animal helping a girl.

Severn, David. FOXY-BOY. *Bodley Head* 1959. Illustrated by Lynton Lamb. Child on lonely visit to country aunts makes friends with a boy of the wilds.

*Sisson, Rosemary Anne. THE IMPRACTICAL CHIMNEY-SWEEP. *Macmillan* 1956. Illustrated by Fritz Wagner.

*Storr, Catherine. MARIANNE DREAMS. *Faber* 1958. Illustrated by Marjorie-Anne Watts.

*Todd, Barbara Euphan. WORZEL GUMMIDGE (1936). *Hollis & Carter* (1943) 1946. *Penguin* (Puffin Story Books) (1941) 1946. Illustrated by Elizabeth Alldridge.

Todd, Barbara Euphan. WORZEL GUMMIDGE AGAIN (1937). *Penguin* (Puffin Story Books) 1949. Illustrated by Will Nickless.

Todd, Barbara Euphan. MORE ABOUT WORZEL GUMMIDGE (1938) 1951, WORZEL GUMMIDGE AND SAUCY NANCY 1947, illustrated by John Harwood. WORZEL GUMMIDGE TAKES A HOLIDAY 1949, illustrated by Will Nickless. EARTHY MANGOLD AND WORZEL GUMMIDGE 1949, illustrated by Jill Crockford. *Hollis & Carter.*

Todd, Barbara Euphan. WORZEL GUMMIDGE AND THE RAILWAY SCARE-CROWS 1955, WORZEL GUMMIDGE AT THE CIRCUS 1956, WORZEL GUMMIDGE AND THE TREASURE SHIP 1958, *Evans.* Illustrated by Jill Crockford.

*Travers, P. L. MARY POPPINS 1934, MARY POPPINS COMES BACK 1935, MARY POPPINS OPENS THE DOOR 1944, MARY POPPINS IN THE PARK 1952. *Collins* (formerly *Peter Davies*). Illustrated by Mary Shepard.

Ward, Patricia. THE SILVER PENCIL. *Collins* 1959. Illustrated by Nicole Hornby. Pencil writes messages which lead Anne to adventure.

*Whistler, Theresa. THE RIVER BOY. *Hart-Davis* 1955. Illustrated by the author.

White, T. H. MISTRESS MASHAM'S REPOSE. *Cape* 1947. Adult novel, for any imaginative child of twelve or over. Girl living at Stowe discovers descendants of Lilliputians on island in lake. Brilliant fantasy anchored by precise detail.

Drawing by Björn Berg for Alf Prøysen's MRS PEPPERPOT AGAIN (Hutchinson)

Chapter 9 | *Climates of Humour*

The preamble to the Penguin edition of THE MAGIC PUDDING, a humorous tale by Norman Lindsay, ends with the recommendation: 'For ages from eight to eighty, allowing for brief blind periods now and again in between.' It is these blind periods (brief, perhaps, but numerous) which make it difficult to write specifically humorous books for children. I doubt whether many small children really recognize humour as such at all. To do so, they need the experience to sort out the incongruous from the congruous, the likely from the unlikely; and, for them, the distinction hardly exists. They will almost always accept ALICE IN WONDERLAND, for instance, as serious fantasy. Alice's rapid changes in size, the behaviour of the sheep in the wool shop or the flutterings of the White Queen, seem to them exciting and odd rather than laughable.

Perhaps an appreciation of humour begins, most usually, at seven or eight, with practical jokes and the more innocent types of coarseness. This is the period when THE MAGIC PUDDING, or Coppard's PINK FURNITURE, or William Pène du Bois's gay fancies, or Professor Branestawm's nightmarish adventures come into their own; the period when children will read and enjoy comic verse of all shades of wit from Eliot's PRACTICAL CATS to Ian Serraillier's ballads or the ingenious rhymes of Eleanor Farjeon—not necessarily finding their full measure, but enjoying the smiles they provoke.

Children of later school age do not so often look for funny books. Humour *in* stories suits them better. Humour in school stories (though by this time Billy Bunter is a bit of a bore); humour in a sophisticated family idiom, as in Elizabeth Enright's stories about the Melendys, or in William Mayne's choir-school tales; humour in fairy-tale, when the ordinary world is turned upside-down. All kinds of humour by the way, but not humour for its own sake.

This is hardly a 'blind period'. It is a period of change, when the young spontaneous laugh is less frequent than it was before. The capacity for enjoying humour and nonsense will return, and later, too, will come the real blind spots, which are the result of character rather than of age. For adults can, and very often do, laugh at the humour in children's stories (and not only in a retrospective way), but it may be doubted whether children are ever well served by truly adult humour—that is, by humour deliberately keyed to adults.

I do not mean that children will not laugh at humorous books written for adults. They will, of course. They delight in the geometrical absurdities of Leacock about the landlady's bed and her catering, or in the difficulties Bertie Wooster has with the social niceties. They enjoy the Edwardian slapstick of THREE MEN IN A BOAT. But these are forms of humour which belong to a Peter Pan world, where the regular and the orthodox are turned upside-down and destructiveness has a special licence. Adults and children happily meet here and find something they both need, and this may be the reason why so many fathers (perhaps fewer mothers) can still pick up Richmal Crompton's *William* books and find pleasure in them.

For children, though, humour *must* be simple and spontaneous. A manufactured, elaborate joke will not do. I do not mean by this that jokes for children have to be short. On the contrary, a child can wear a joke a long time without getting bored (as parents know only too well), so long as it is a lively and natural one. THE MAGIC PUDDING, which I have already mentioned, is a case in point. This is a splendid, racy, jovial Australian story which is, in fact, one simple expanded joke. Bunyip Bluegum, travelling for pleasure, joins up with Bill Barnacle the sailor and Sam Sawnoff, the penguin, who have already as their companion Albert, a magic, self-perpetuating pudding. Albert is coveted by a Possum and a Wombat, whose plots and stratagems lead them finally into court in the backblocks town of Tooraloo—after which the three friends build a house in a tree, with a paddock for Albert, and settle down to a life of peace and gastronomic bliss. The one point—the to-ing and fro-ing of the Puddin' —is magnificently varied, in a story that moves quick and sharp as the crack of a stockwhip, never overdoing a detail, never missing a chance for one more absurd variation on the theme. It is the simplicity that does the trick.

Take, for instance, our first glimpse of the Puddin':

Bunyip Bluegum was too much of a gentleman to invite himself to lunch, but he said carelessly, 'Am I right in supposing that there are onions in this pudding?'

Before Bill could reply, a thick, angry voice came out of the pudding, saying—

'Onions, bunions, cows and crabs,
Whiskers, wheels and hansom cabs,
Beef and bottles, beer and bones,
Give him a feed and end his groans.'

'Albert, Albert,' said Bill to the Puddin', 'where's your manners?'

'Where's yours?' said the Puddin' rudely, 'guzzling away there, and never so much as offering this stranger a slice.'

'There you are,' said Bill. 'There's nothing this Puddin' enjoys more than offering slices of himself to strangers.'

Norman Lindsay. THE MAGIC PUDDING (Penguin, 1957) p. 15.

One word too many, and the joke might become tedious; but it never does.

Drawing by Norman Lindsay for his THE MAGIC PUDDING (Angus & Robertson)

This wonderful little story has in it both the types of humour that particularly appeal to children—the humour of situation (horse-play and accident) and verbal wit. The various stratagems of pudding-thieves and pudding-owners, illustrated in rollicking style, are introduced by absurd touches. When the friends come upon the thieves disguised by curious headgear, the Possum stumps them by remarking 'No removing people's hats. Removing hats is larceny, and you'll get six months for it.' Bunyip Bluegum's solution is to stand to attention and strike up God Save the King, whereupon the crooks are revealed. In the other vein, there are conversations in the height of lunatic vigour, like the one between Bill Barnacle and Henderson Hedgehog the deaf Horticulturist:

> 'Have you seen a SINGED POSSUM?' roared Bill.
> 'To be sure,' said Henderson, 'but the turnips are backward.'
> 'Turnips be stewed,' yelled Bill in such a tremendous voice that he blew his own hat off. 'HAVE YOU SEEN A SINGED POSSUM?'
> 'Good season for wattle blossom,' said Henderson. 'Well, yes, but a very poor season for carrots.'
> 'A man might as well talk to a carrot as try an' get some sense out of this runt of a feller,' said Bill, disgusted. 'Come and see if we can't find someone that it won't bust a man's vocal chords gettin' information out of.'
> Ibid., pp. 49–50.

Or, in a different idiom, the Kookaburra's rude come-back to the staring sailor, 'all I can say is that if yer don't take yer dial outer the road I'll bloomin' well take an' bounce a gibber off yer crust'.

There are echoes of ALICE IN WONDERLAND all through this book, but its raw, violent, bustlingly energetic humour is unique. In the same vein, and coming from an equally rollicking and energetic writer, are Eric Linklater's two adventure stories for children, THE PIRATES IN THE DEEP GREEN SEA and THE WIND ON THE MOON. Linklater is a superb writer and his greatest virtue is that he never writes down to children. Certainly his subjects are chosen to suit them. THE PIRATES IN THE DEEP GREEN SEA is a phantasmagoria of cutlasses, treasure-chests and talking octopuses which has clearly grown out of bedtime stories, and in THE WIND ON THE MOON the hilarious incidents arise from the one comic circumstance of two sisters unexpectedly turning into kangaroos. But if the subjects of his adult novels, like POET'S PUB or THE MERRY MUSE, are more sophisticated, the technique is the same in all Linklater's books— the bubbling up of nonsense, the rollicking slapstick, and the verbal wit to tempt the discriminating child—like the description of Davy Jones's Locker, where:

Above the throne two mermaids had arranged some branches of coral in the handsomest style, and now, below the coral, they were hanging a long broad ribbon of pale blue on which, in darker letters, was written:

FLOREAT ETONA

And in smaller letters below the motto—for the benefit of sailors who had forgotten their Latin—was the English translation: *Let Eton flourish.*
Eric Linklater. THE PIRATES IN THE DEEP GREEN SEA (Macmillan, 1949) p. 235.

Adult writers who write one or two children's books for special occasions are rarely as generous with their skill as Linklater has been. The answer is, I imagine, that he has kept the natural love of a good joke in which adults and children can meet as equals (though they rarely do).

The success of these comedies for children comes partly from their closeness to real life. A child can readily imagine himself under the sea with Hugh and Tim without, as it were, taking a step out of his own backyard, and yet there is a fantastic twist that provokes laughter. William Pène du Bois, similarly, strikes humour out of the familiar, but turns it with a swift movement into the unlikely and the surprising, in THE GREAT GEPPY, the story of a horse-detective, and his magnificent travelogue THE 21 BALLOONS, which tells of the adventures of Professor William Waterman Sherman on the island of Krakatoa. Much of the humour in this book derives from absurd scientific inventions, like the labour-saving house of the M's (which, after nearly twenty years has come a good deal nearer to reality) or the super-ingenious aerial merry-go-round which the Professor so much enjoys.

The mechanical erudition of small boys is flattered by this book, and no less by Norman Hunter's THE INCREDIBLE ADVENTURES OF PROFESSOR BRANESTAWM, which is illustrated, appropriately, by Heath Robinson. The humour here is based entirely on physical things, on absurd machines or phenomenal absence of mind (always a popular subject). There is the nightmarish story, *The Wild*

Waste Paper, with its echo of M. R. James; there is the wry logic of *The Too-Many Professors*, when the Professor comments on his invention to bring pictured things to life:

> 'It is rather a pity,' said the Professor, spraying a picture of a box of chocolates to life, 'that it costs more to make the liquid for doing this than it would cost to buy the things.'
> Norman Hunter. THE INCREDIBLE ADVENTURES OF PROFESSOR BRANESTAWM (Penguin, 1946) p. 123.

and there is the almost brutal slapstick of *Pancake Day at Great Pagwell:*

> The Professor struggled out of his pancake just in time for another one to drop over him. Two pancakes were on the clock, four were draped over the light. The Mayor was eating his way through a complete set of pancakes of varying sizes that had fallen in front of him. The four firemen put their helmets on and brandished their axes, but only succeeded in smashing two cups, one saucer and the sugar basin. Mrs. Flittersnoop put her head gingerly out from under the table and was immediately gummed to the carpet by a three-foot pancake two inches thick that had just shot out.
> Ibid., pp. 189-90.

Each story enshrines one piece of absurdity, expanded but never overdone, provoking laughter, and, as well, reaching down to the creative energy of schoolboys. Jay Williams and Raymond Abrashkin take the idea of absurd scientific invention as far as possible in two light-hearted stories, DANNY DUNN AND THE ANTI-GRAVITY PAINT and THE HOMEWORK MACHINE. Simple and entertaining though they are, these stories are not merely farce. The children who so much enjoy feeding their school problems to a computer, in the second story, are very well drawn, and this makes their difficulties credible and amusing. Besides, there is an implied comment on the dangerous side of automation that gives the book ballast. Their chief purpose, all the same, is to promote fun and laughter over ordinary things going wrong.

This is the kind of humour which is often found mixed with other elements in the pages of the Jennings stories. I am doubtful whether, in fact, books are ever written with the *sole* intention of making children laugh; but in so far as they are, they do this, almost always, through the element of fantasy. There is, in other words, another world lurking behind the laughter, a world where what seems funny here may in fact be perfectly serious and logical there. Leila Berg's stories about Chunky, besides showing brilliantly the bustling activity of comical small boys, has a touch of this other-worldliness. So has A. E. Coppard's PINK FURNITURE, to an even more marked degree. The story of Toby Tottel's quest is in the finest tradition of meaningful nonsense:

> Then he went on, and on and on he went until he came to the house of the Baldheaded Woman who was renowned for her surpassing wisdom. But she was absent now; only her son was left at home, and his name was Stinker. It was a good name for him. He was a lanky man, with long black gloves and a very high beaver hat, and he always walked backwards and never saw anybody coming. Whenever it rained his boots became dusty, and in times of drought he carried an open umbrella and got wet as a herring.
> A. E. Coppard. PINK FURNITURE (Cape, 1930) p. 28.

The books I have discussed so far have been perfectly understandable in terms of our own world, and have made relatively little demand on the imagination. But nonsense of this kind, of the Edward Lear kind, is mysterious. It is poetry first, humour afterwards. It can carry a child out of himself or it can let him down with a bump, if he resists it with a matter-of-fact attitude.

Nonsense can, of course, be simple and easy. For children of five or so there are Donald Bisset's enchanting bits of idiocy, ANYTIME STORIES and SOMETIME STORIES, with stories where pencils talk and even a silence can have an existence. Sheer absurdity is only valid when the writer is completely committed to it, as Rowland Emett so obviously is in his railway fantasies, ANTHONY AND ANTIMACASSAR and NELLIE COME HOME. This is absurdity verbal and visible. A child can take in his stride a sentence like this: 'The last thing Anthony saw as they left the Branch Line was the Woodchopper chopping the steam into infinitesimal pieces in a fit of amazement and despair.' It is to be enjoyed slowly, like the accompanying drawing, with its shapely but fantastic detail.

There is no age limit for nonsense, and it is possible for anyone to enjoy the Norwegian tale, THE SINGING TOWN by Thorbjørn

Egner, about the town of Kardemomma, and a band of comic-opera thieves who learn to be good citizens.

I am always a little surprised when foreign humour translates and transplants well, but this vividly coloured tale, with its interspersed songs, its world of eccentric tram-cars and odd people, has been warmly welcomed by English children. Tove Jansson and her Finnish books about the Moomins have, perhaps, a smaller and more select band of admirers. Here we have something very subtle, nonsense stories full of melancholy wisdom and terror, neither wholly fantasy nor wholly humour. It is impossible not to compare these stories with the work of Edward Lear and Lewis Carroll. Who would not see cousinly resemblances between the Hattifatteners and the Dong with a Luminous Nose, or between the Moomin parents and Mr and Mrs Discobolos, or between Snufkin and some of Lewis Carroll's touching small animals? The resemblance in each case is not one of feature or idiom; it lies in the mature atmosphere of the stories, the sunny sky of comedy in which there is always drifting a distant cloud of sadness and unease.

The Moomins are presented by their creator in drawings which also have this strange, melancholy feeling. They look, these endearing little animals, like hippopotamuses at the head end (but lively, twinkling hippopotamuses) and they are neatly porcine in body. The Moomins who concern us live in a lonely valley with various peculiar friends—the Snork Maiden, flapping her long eyelashes, who comes of Moomin stock; lively, restless Snufkin, son of an old family friend; the Hemulen, moody and stamp-collecting, who comes to stay and never leaves. Whether these creatures are pure inventions or whether they are based on folk lore figures I do not know. In any case, they are extremely real to me, for their personalities have been cleverly established by what they say and what they do. And in the world they live in there is plenty doing. In COMET IN MOOMINLAND there is danger not only from outer space but also from flood and drought. In MOOMINSUMMER MADNESS the peaceful valley is disturbed by a volcanic eruption which brings an earthquake and a tidal wave. In FINN FAMILY MOOMINTROLL the finding of a Hobgoblin's magic hat precipitates events in which natural and supernatural are both represented. Indeed, the supernatural, or the feeling of it, is never far from this wide, tundra landscape. MOOMINLAND MIDWINTER, perhaps the oddest and most enchanting of all the books, is, simply, a poem to winter, and the poetry is never swamped by the absurd things that happen to Moomintroll when he wakes half-way through hibernation.

Certainly there is humour in these stories, but I doubt whether reviewers or publishers are right in classifying them as 'humorous'. There is, to be sure, the continuous, muted, delightful humour of odd creatures doing ordinary everyday things. Sniff and Moomintroll looking through the Observatory telescope in the Lonely Mountains, respectfully listening to the scientists as they explain the comet; Moominmamma making a cake to welcome her son back from a dangerous adventure; the Snork Maiden adjusting her hair before thanking Moomintroll for rescuing her from the poisonous bush Angostura; Moominpappa, like any mildly arrogant family man, reading extracts from his memoirs to a politely inattentive family.

There is the humour of idiosyncrasy, in the character of the Hemulen aunt, who, in EXPLOITS OF MOOMINPAPPA, is such a nuisance to the roving young men, and who suggests as suitable entertainment for them 'a little sock-darning contest' or 'a nice history quiz', or, in the same book, there is the Carrollian note of parody in Moominpappa's conversation with a chance-met ghost:

The room had suddenly grown cold with an icy draught, and the ghost sneezed.

I don't know how you'd have felt, but for my part I immediately lost much of my respect. So I crawled out from under the bed and said: 'Cold night, sir!'

'Yes,' replied the ghost in an annoyed tone. 'A bleak night of fate resounding with the horrible wails of the phantoms of the gorge!'

'What can I do for you?' I asked politely.

'On a night of fate like this,' the ghost continued stubbornly, 'the forgotten bones are rattling on the silent beach!'

'Whose bones?' I asked (still very politely).

'The *forgotten* bones,' said the ghost. 'Pale horror grins over the damned island! Mortal, beware!' The ghost uncurled, gave me a terrible look and floated back towards the half-open door. The back of his head met the door-jamb with a resounding bang.

'Oop!' said the ghost.

I didn't hide my delight.

With a last hiss the ghost glided downstairs and out into the moonlight. Down on the ground he turned and bade me farewell with three horrible laughs.

Tove Jansson. THE EXPLOITS OF MOOMINPAPPA (Benn, 1952) pp. 112–14.

But all this is humour that belongs to no particular age, and to some ages it will not really seem to be humour. Tove Jansson has done as Lewis Carroll and Lear did. She has corkscrewed her way down into a world of childhood where the unlikely is readily accepted, where incongruity seems entirely natural and at the same time can be comic. But she has kept her adult wits about her, so that we are always aware of shape and logic and order in an unusual world. As with ALICE IN WONDERLAND, these Moomin books are folk lore and fantasy to young children, humour to older boys and girls, and poetry to all. For what binds the elements of nonsense, absurdity, satire and wit together is an underlying note of seriousness, of speculation, an implication of the uncertainty of human wishes and human knowledge. Most compelling of all Tove Jansson's creatures, to me, are the Hattifatteners, those wraith-like people who, like the lemmings, are governed by migratory compulsions. Moominpappa describes them thus:

In that moment I caught sight of a whole flotilla of small ships putting out to sea. Light as butterflies they went gliding away over their own reflections. All were manned by a silent crew: little grey-white beings huddling close together and staring out towards the horizon.

'Hattifatteners,' Hodgkins said.

'Hattifatteners!' I whispered excitedly. 'Putting out on their endless voyages . . .'

'Mind you don't touch them if there's a thunderstorm about,' said Hodgkins. 'Makes them electric. Sting like nettles.'

Ibid., pp. 62–3.

Put beside this extract any of the poems of Edward Lear, with their haunting refrain of vanishing, loss, plaintive longing (*The Courtship of the Yonghy-Bonghy-Bò*, or *Calico Pie*, or most of all, *The Dong with a Luminous Nose*) and you can see the same deep humour of the heart, the humour of poetry which knows no geographical limits nor age limits either.

Lewis Carroll, explaining his portmanteau word 'frumious' in *Jabberwocky*, ended like this:

If your thoughts incline ever so little towards 'fuming', you will say 'fuming-furious'; if they turn, by even a hair's-breadth, towards 'furious', you will say 'furious-fuming'; but if you have that rarest of gifts, a perfectly balanced mind, you will say 'frumious'. Lewis Carroll. THE HUNTING OF THE SNARK (Zodiac Books, 1948) Preface, vii.

A perfectly balanced mind. Yes, it is this above all that is needed in a true nonsense book, a book that is going to remain the treasure and activating possession of child and adult alike. A mind balanced between the spontaneous, irrational, exploratory laughter of a child, and the poetically irrational, energetic, appraising laughter of a well-stored older mind. Let us see how far Lewis Carroll has satisfied both these sections of the thinking, laughing public.

Tragedy may be the obverse side of humour, and it may therefore be natural to find in the realm of nonsense a melancholy belonging properly to it. But melancholy, sometimes tilting into apprehension, is also to be expected in Lewis Carroll's works, as in Lear's, because of their temperaments. To both of them, nonsense provided an escape, a world of fantasy in which they could forget that they were not entirely at ease in their own world. In ALICE IN WONDERLAND and THROUGH THE LOOKING-GLASS Carroll celebrates the wonder of childhood as he saw it, from his own needs. Alice he described* as 'loving and gentle, loving as a dog and gentle as a fawn; courteous—courteous to *all*, high or low, grand or grotesque, king or caterpillar; trustful, curious—wildly curious with the eager enjoyment of life that comes only in the happy hours of childhood.' But if he was trying in these two books to satisfy a child's curiosity and spontaneous love of life, he put into them, too, his own doubts, his fears and nightmares, and something of the barbarity of childhood as it survived in himself. Alice as he saw her gives us one facet of childhood, but there are others. There is the near-cruelty of the Pig and Pepper chapter in ALICE; there is the devastating truth of remarks like those of the Gnat in the sequel:

*From an article in *The Theatre*, April 1887, quoted in Puffin edition of THROUGH THE LOOKING-GLASS, 1948, p. 13.

'Crawling at your feet,' said the Gnat (Alice drew her feet back in some alarm), 'you may observe a Bread-and-Butterfly. Its wings are thin slices of Bread-and-butter, its body is a crust, and its head is a lump of sugar.'

'And what does *it* live on?'

'Weak tea with cream in it.'

A new difficulty came into Alice's head. 'Supposing it couldn't find any?' she suggested.

'Then it would die, of course.'

'But that must happen very often,' Alice remarked thoughtfully.

'It always happens,' said the Gnat.

Lewis Carroll. THROUGH THE LOOKING-GLASS (Penguin, 1948) pp. 69–70.

Obviously, these are books which have a special meaning for different ages. Alice's character, which young people take for granted, can seem, when they are older, rather tiresome and priggish; and perhaps she is never (except for Carroll himself) more to anyone than a centre round which the delightful and peculiar creatures can revolve. My own memory of the two books from my childhood is one of very mixed pleasure. I enjoyed the puns and nonsense verses, but I can remember more vividly the pathetic scenes, and particularly the upsetting effect Bill the lizard had on me, when he was hurled from the rabbit's roof by a giant Alice and when he sat helpless and mortified in the jury box, trying to write with his finger on his slate because Alice had confiscated his squeaking pencil. It was the helplessness of childhood I noticed then, not the sombre, crazy philosophy of the White Queen and the Mad Hatter, or the energetic proliferation of jokes and puns.

Anyone can make jokes, but nobody can write another ALICE IN WONDERLAND. I feel this all the more after reading the gallant attempt of Yates Wilson to do just that, in MORE ALICE. It is clearer to me than ever that Lewis Carroll was not trying to be funny and that he could only be funny because he was not trying. Yates Wilson is held up by his publishers as a writer who can echo 'the master of pure nonsense—Lewis Carroll.' But Lewis Carroll was no master of pure nonsense. His books are not *pure* nonsense, nor were they intended to be so. Yates Wilson, on the other hand, has produced a crazy procession of creatures with no substance behind them,

Drawing by Yates Wilson for his MORE ALICE (Boardman)

though his drawings are deliberately reminiscent of Tenniel. The concord of thought and laughter in ALICE is regrettably absent. For instance, when Ethelred is arming for battle, his courtiers answer his call for his accoutrements of battle with loud cries about his 'ACCOUTRITHINGUMMIES.'

This rather hoary joke is the kind which adults think children enjoy, though I doubt if they often do. In any case, Lewis Carroll could never have made it, for long words always have their rights in his books; they are written on the assumption that the reader will either recognize long words or at least respect them if they are unknown. Many of the jokes in this latter-day ALICE are good, but they are none of them natives of Carroll's world. You can see this clearly if you compare the description of Ethelred arming for battle with Carroll's similar scene. Here is Wilson:

> Alice crept into a corner to watch proceedings.
>
> 'I can't wear *that* shirt in battle,' Ethelred was roaring. 'I wouldn't be seen dead in it—hand me that flour-bag instead—that's it—now my spats.'
>
> 'HIS SPATS!' everyone chorused. 'Not *those*,' as a well-meaning young lobster was rushing towards the King with a string of fish. 'SPATS! not SPRATS!'
>
> 'Help me on with my hot water bottle!' yelled Ethelred.
>
> 'I wonder why he wants *that*?' Alice thought.
>
> 'In case the field needs airing,' said Ethelred as though he had heard her. 'Now my fire-irons!' he roared, '*and* my bellows, idiot—now my morning paper in case we find some fish and chips —that's it! Now my armour. Not *that* way—here, give it to me— *ouch*! this armour hasn't been warmed—now my visor—not *that* way, fool, I haven't got eyes in the *back* of my head—oh *you*! That's more like it . . .'
>
> Suddenly there was a silence and a stillness, broken only by Ethelred's surprised cry, 'I'm *ready*!'
>
> 'He's ready!' yelled everyone.
>
> There was a mad dash for the door and in a moment the room was empty and the noise of the stampede faded on the afternoon air.
>
> Yates Wilson. MORE ALICE (Boardman, 1959) pp. 60-2.

This is pantomime humour. All the directions are here for the clowning and the by-play; nothing is left to the imagination. If the modern idiom, and the occasional vulgar adverbs and verbs, did not put this very far from Carroll, the technique of the humour would do so, for Carroll's account is infinitely reserved, depending on hints and suggestions:

> 'Of course you agree to have a battle?' Tweedledum said in a calmer tone.
>
> 'I suppose so,' the other sulkily replied, as he crawled out of the umbrella: 'only *she* must help us to dress up, you know.'
>
> So the two brothers went off hand-in-hand into the wood, and returned in a minute with their arms full of things—such as bol-

sters, blankets, hearth-rugs, table-cloths, dish-covers and coal-scuttles. 'I hope you're a good hand at pinning and tying strings?' Tweedledum remarked. 'Every one of these things has got to go on, somehow or other.'

Alice said afterwards she had never seen such a fuss made about anything in all her life—the way those two bustled about—and the quantity of things they put on—and the trouble they gave her in tying strings and fastening buttons—'Really, they'll be more like bundles of old clothes than anything else, by the time they're ready!' she said to herself, as she arranged a bolster round the neck of Tweedledee, 'to keep his head from being cut off ', as he said.

'You know,' he added very gravely, 'it's one of the most serious things that can possibly happen to one in a battle—to get one's head cut off.'

Op. cit., pp. 89-90.

Wilson's numerous exclamation marks are of no more consequence than his loud verbs—'he roared', 'he yelled', and all the rest; they are signs of weakness, and their absence in the lunatic paragraphs of Carroll is a matter for thankfulness; for, above all, Carroll was a dignified writer. He never pestered his readers.

I would put THE MAGIC PUDDING on a level with ALICE in its lively inventiveness; and for the poetry of oddity, A. E. Coppard makes as strong an impact on me. But ultimately anyone who tries to imitate Carroll has to reckon with his style, and this is inimitable. His is the tongue of the university man, scholarly, urbane, a little diffident, absolutely uncondescending but conscious of superiority, repressed but generous. It belongs to the Establishment, to a particular way of life which is now part of history.

In some ways it is a bad thing that these two books have the air of the Establishment round them. Not that we would want to do without the gravity and stylishness of ALICE simply because people nowadays do not live as the author had lived; but because the fact of their special flavour has given rise to an absurd amount of snobbery about the books. They are spoken of with reverence; two words quoted from them, by a dignitary of the church or state, bring roars of sycophantic laughter; they may not be criticized. All this is absurd. No book is as good as this. And the result of this persistent adulation is that children nowadays either read ALICE in the potted form in which she appears in comic papers, or they read her with the adjurations of their parents ringing in their ears and feel let down when they have finished (if, indeed, they ever do finish). In many middle-class circles it is as important to know ALICE as it is to use the word napkin and not the word serviette; but this intellectual snobbery cuts the ground from under Carroll's feet, for it makes the books tiresome and gives them an artificial importance. Let us take ALICE down and dust her off and consider her critically and then give her to our children without any sermons. Let us not tell them they will be amused, or that this is a book they must like or be for ever beyond the pale. Let them discover it for themselves. They will discover it, in their own time, and re-discover it many times in the rest of their lives.

Drawing by Rowland Emett for his ANTHONY AND ANTIMACASSAR (Faber)

Reading List

*Berg, Leila. THE ADVENTURES OF CHUNKY. *O.U.P.* (1950) 1958. Illustrated by George Downs.

Berg, Leila. TRUST CHUNKY. *Brockhampton* 1954. Illustrated by Peggy Fortnum.

*Bisset, Donald. ANYTIME STORIES 1954, SOMETIME STORIES 1957. *Faber.* Illustrated by the author.

*Bois, W. Pène du. THE GREAT GEPPY (1940 U.S.A.) 1942, THE 21 BALLOONS (1947 U.S.A.) 1949. *Robert Hale.* Illustrated by the author.

*Carroll, Lewis. ALICE IN WONDERLAND (1865), THROUGH THE LOOKING-GLASS (1872). Continuously in print in various editions, e.g. *Dent* (Children's Illustrated Classics) 1954, with original illustrations by John Tenniel.

*Coppard, A. E. PINK FURNITURE. *Cape* 1930. Illustrated by Nancy Bankart Gurney.

*Crompton, Richmal. JUST WILLIAM. *Newnes* 1922. Numerous other titles, latest WILLIAM'S TELEVISION SHOW, 1958. Illustrated by Thomas Henry.

*Egner, Thorbjørn. THE SINGING TOWN (1951 Sweden). *Methuen* 1959. Translated by Evelyn Ramsden, verses translated by Leila Berg. Illustrated by the author.

*Emett, Rowland and Mary. ANTHONY AND ANTIMACASSAR 1943, NELLIE COME HOME 1952. *Faber.* Illustrated by Rowland Emett.

*Hunter, Norman. THE INCREDIBLE ADVENTURES OF PROFESSOR BRANESTAWM (see Chap.7).

*Jansson, Tove. FINN FAMILY MOOMINTROLL (1949 Finland) 1950, COMET IN MOOMINLAND (1946 Finland) 1951, THE EXPLOITS OF MOOMINPAPPA (1950 Finland) 1952, MOOMINSUMMER MADNESS (1954 Finland) 1955, MOOMIN, MYMBLE AND LITTLE MY (1952 Finland) 1953, MOOMINLAND MIDWINTER (1957 Finland) 1958. *Benn.* First two translated by Elizabeth Portch, the rest by Thomas Warburton. Illustrated by the author. The language of the original works is Swedish.

*Jerome, Jerome K. THREE MEN IN A BOAT (1889). *Herbert Jenkins* 1953.

*Leacock, Stephen. NONSENSE NOVELS. *Bodley Head* (1911) 1921.

*Lear, Edward. THE BOOK OF NONSENSE (1846). THE COMPLETE NONSENSE OF EDWARD LEAR, edited by Holbrook Jackson. *Faber* 1947.

*Lindsay, Norman. THE MAGIC PUDDING (1931). *Angus & Robertson* 1952. *Penguin* (Puffin Story Books) 1957. Illustrated by the author.

*Linklater, Eric. THE WIND ON THE MOON 1944, illustrated by Nicolas Bentley. THE PIRATES IN THE DEEP GREEN SEA 1949, illustrated by William Reeves. *Macmillan.*

*Williams, Jay and Abrashkin, Raymond. DANNY DUNN AND THE ANTI-GRAVITY PAINT (1956 U.S.A.) 1959, THE HOMEWORK MACHINE (1958 U.S.A.) 1960. *Brockhampton.* Illustrated by E. J. Keats.

*Wilson, Yates. MORE ALICE. *Boardman* 1959. Illustrated by the author.

Chapter 10 | *Fossils and Formulas*

In one sense, all children's stories are based on fantasy; they take place in a world that is not fact, not even fictionalized fact, but a special place created out of imagination for that particular story and for no other. All the same, as we move from the younger age-groups to stories for ten-year-olds and upward, we find more demand for tales set in a normal everyday environment. Imagination must still be at work, however prosaic a story may be, but it now works in a different way. A kettle, in a story for a six-year-old, may grow legs and walk; a kettle, in a family story for a ten-year-old, will be an adjunct to boiling water. Yet it may still be the means by which a child enters a world of fantasy, a world of dreams and wishes, if it is used in a story where a girl changes her status — a school buffoon who becomes a heroine at a Guide picnic, or an unwanted orphan who becomes the central figure in a happy household. The innumerable sub-divisions of family stories and adventure stories have one thing in common. They all gratify the wishes of young people—to be richer, to be more clever, to be famous, to be in another country, to be older, to be *different*.

So fantasy and imagination are still there. But because family stories require a realistic background, they are more susceptible to the danger of second-rate writers. The writer of true fantasy makes his own world and, consequently, makes his own pace, his own atmosphere, his own conditions. Family stories are less easy to vary. Certain types of story become popular and are eagerly imitated; children, seizing upon a favourite plot, demand more of the same thing. A formula is born, and a formula, in the end, can kill life and originality for all but the genuinely talented writer.

Take school stories, for instance. How can children distinguish between the Toms, Dicks and Harrys who jostle and compete in boys' classrooms; or between innumerable madcaps of the Fourth recognizable only by the colour of their tunics or the length of their hair? How can they distinguish between one set of ink-stained desks and another? How many writers have managed to bring life to the apparently monotonous and restricted subject of school days?

It is the fashion to trace the inadequacy of boys' school stories back to writers like Talbot Baines Reed. Frank Eyre thinks that Reed brought the school story 'to a perfection of unreality from which there was no escape possible.'* George Orwell, in his celebrated essay on school stories, drew up a formidable list of their failings. They displayed, he said, an unreal world, jingoistic, Conservative, rooted in privilege, xenophobic, rabidly class-conscious and apparently denying the very existence of sex. His strictures, part and parcel of the time when they were pronounced, seem out of place nowadays, when school stories are infinitely more varied in scope and setting. Where Orwell would lump all writers of school stories together, we can look back and see them as individuals, and we can see that— as in any sphere of literature—some were genuinely creative, others were merely copying. In effect, some set a model, others worked to a formula. Certainly, if a boy of fifteen wants to know what a traditional public school is really like, he will be well advised to read an adult novel rather than a boys' school story. Vachell's THE HILL, E. F. Benson's DAVID BLAIZE, D. Wynne Wilson's EARLY CLOSING and Alec Waugh's THE LOOM OF YOUTH—any of these will give him a picture of school as a living and complete world; while, in a story written for boys, schoolmasters, adults generally, will be treated as background characters, as the natural enemies of boys. Only in STALKY AND CO. shall we find any attempt to present a school as a community in which masters and boys have the same right to personality.

There are other basic restrictions. *Competition* is the theme of most school stories, and the games-field is the customary source of drama. When we are in the classroom, lessons will never be interesting in themselves, but only because of the prizes attached to them. The Nightingale scholarship, in THE FIFTH FORM AT ST DOMINIC'S, the university scholarship in Richard Bird's THE WHARTON MEDAL, are the centre of scene after scene, but, quite rightly in the context,

*TWENTIETH CENTURY CHILDREN'S BOOKS. Longmans, Green & Co., for the British Council, 1952, p. 51.

we have no idea what books the heroes of these contests had to read. That interesting type, the scholar, has no place in school stories. The clever boy must be odd, or mischievous, or a buffoon, to earn his place. So you get the odd impression that school life consists of a series of cricket and football matches and school speech days, enlivened by petty larceny, cribbing and gang warfare.

Still, I can see no reason why a good school story should not be written within these limits, and it has often been done. The exclusion of any emotional complications between boy and boy (or boy and girl) in the pages of Talbot Baines Reed was chiefly due to the literary conventions of his day, but even today I very much doubt whether most of the boys for whom school stories are designed (that is, boys up to the age of thirteen or fourteen) will not be more interested in the drama of a cricket-match than in the drama of the head prefect or the girl next door. They do not as a rule enjoy political or social comment in their stories. The books which take a mature view of such problems—books like DAVID BLAIZE, with its tentative but honest study of homosexual love or Florence Crannell Means's SHUTTERED WINDOWS, with its striking study of the colour problem in Carolina— are outside the school story formula; and first-class books can be produced within the formula, using the day-to-day events of school life. They can be exciting events, familiar as they are: but they will only be exciting if there are strong characters.

It is characterization that makes certain writers live on, long after the boarding-school formula seems to be worked out; and I would name Talbot Baines Reed as one of them.

The most exciting event in THE FIFTH FORM AT ST DOMINIC'S is the stealing of an exam paper, but there is scope here for the clash of character, made more exciting because it takes place in a small, close community. Two boys are rivals in the Nightingale prize—the cad, Loman, and the clever, odd, unpredictable Oliver Greenfield. Loman has been consorting with a publican, who is now black- mailing him; he desperately needs the money the prize brings. Oliver is ambitious; he wants the honour of winning. When the vital paper disappears from the headmaster's study, and Oliver subsequ- ently wins the prize, the school and staff reach the obvious conclusion. He receives his award to the sound of hissing, and an investigation begins. The scene, in essentials, is familiar enough. But few writers have matched Reed's sure direction of every detail to the one purpose of revealing character. The repercussions of the theft—Oliver's bravado and cynicism, the passionate, miserable loyalty of his young brother (a new boy), the casual support of his friend Wraysford, and the barbed, wayward encouragement of lame Tony Pembury—these are enough to make of an ordinary school story a really telling drama; and even if boys take the book up initially as a story, they will probably, as I have done from my childhood days, remember not the plot but the people.

Lesser writers have grafted on to school routine the most sensational events in order to produce excitement. But it did not help L. C. Douthwaite, a practised writer of school stories, when in THE LUCK OF ST BONIFACE he brought in a gang of crooks to steal the boxing cup, and threw in, at the end, a monastic treasure as a makeweight. His story, written twenty years after the masterpieces of Talbot Baines Reed, seems far more old-fashioned now than the lively rags and initiation ceremonies in THE COCK HOUSE AT FELLSGARTH, or the central problem of THE WILLOUGHBY CAPTAINS, which turns on the simple fact of a senior boy being taken from a good house to be head of a bad one.

Fifty years after their first appearance, Reed's stories are still real and alive, in narrative and in dialogue. They are not likely to become fossilized even by their slang—and in fact Reed uses slang far less than most writers of school stories and always dramatically. With the seniors, it is occasional and idiosyncratic; with the juniors, it is a special language, born of the younger boys' natural desire for uniformity. In the same way, slang is the badge of such lively characters in modern school stories as Specs McCann or Anthony Buckeridge's Jennings. Here are Jennings and his friend Darbishire getting ready for a cross-country run:

Darbishire had found his gym shoes by this time, but as he bent down to put them on he uttered a wail of dismay.

'Oh, fish-hooks! Some gruesome specimen has pinched my laces! I bet it was Atkinson. He broke one of his yesterday and he was snooping round my locker while . . .'

'There's no time to worry about that now. You'll just have to wear them as they are!' Jennings danced with impatience as the sound of Mr. Carter's referee whistle was wafted through the window. 'Quick, Darbi, they're starting!'

'But what about my laces? I can't go with my shoes flapping about my ankles. They're about a hundred sizes too big for me, anyway, and they'll fall off as soon as I try to get up speed.'

Jennings rounded on his friend with some heat. 'Now look here, Darbishire; I'm doing you a supersonic favour by letting you be my partner for this run, seeing that you only go as fast as a sea-lion on its flippers.'

'Yes, I know, but . . .'

'And you heard what Old Wilkie said about getting a move on. If we don't get going right away, he won't need a watch to time us with—he'll need a calendar!'

Anthony Buckeridge. OUR FRIEND JENNINGS (Collins, 1955) pp. 42–3.

The greatest achievement of Buckeridge, among other school story writers, is to make his small boys individuals, in dialogue and in habit, as well as giving them the typical group-character which is so striking in any preparatory school. The same is true of William Mayne. In his three choir-school stories the dialogue is curiously formalized and yet so apposite that it gets nearer to the *real* talk of boys than anything I have read later than TOM SAWYER. Here are one or two of them nursing a dramatic secret, talking to their headmaster:

'Can we explain in a few days' time?' said Trevithic. 'We're busy, you see, sir.'

'So long as you have a member of the staff in your confidence, to give you leave for late meals; and you don't break rules in front of the juniors, Trevithic, you may do what you like,' said Mr. Ardent. 'And you must never be late for Mr. Sutton.'

'I've set one or two rules at naught,' said Trevithic. 'Will you punish me on Monday, sir?'

'With pleasure,' said Mr. Ardent. 'And now it would be tactful if you wiped up the crumbs and washed your plates.' Then he asked Owen: 'When did you last have your hair cut?'

'Last term, sir,' said Owen. 'There's no one to do it at home.'

'I'd rather do it here,' said Mr. Ardent. 'As soon as you've washed up, what about a lawn-mowing session in the senior bathroom? You have a very wild, woolly, Welsh look.'

'Sheep-shearing, sir,' said Trevithic. 'Couldn't we make

cushions for the choir-stalls, and fill them with our own hair-clippings?'

'You'd better suggest it to the Dean and Chapter,' said Mr. Ardent.

William Mayne. A SWARM IN MAY (Oxford University Press, 1955) pp. 145–6.

From the dialogue and the narrative in Mayne's books you are always aware, too, of the extreme *concreteness* of the junior world (not an easy thing to get into a book). Mary's delight in the 'white stick' in A GRASS ROPE, the absorption of Owen in the ball and key he has found, in A SWARM IN MAY, the map on the damp wall in THE WORLD UPSIDE DOWN—all these objects are crucial to the stories, but they are also important to the children who handle or observe or find them, for their shape or texture or colour. This is one of the most important qualities of Mayne's work and links him with writers like Walter de la Mare and Elizabeth Coatsworth and Laura Ingalls Wilder, writers who have a particular faculty for reliving the life of the senses which a child cannot communicate directly to an adult. In A SWARM IN MAY the whole atmosphere of school is summarized, for me at any rate, in this little snatch of description:

They were in their places. The organ stopped. Mr. Ardent lifted his head. 'Enter not into judgement with thy servant, O Lord; for in thy sight shall no man living be justified.'

Owen found with his right hand the five small marks under the edge of the stall, where his fingernails fitted: he had been making the marks for two terms now. When they knelt he found with his left toe the crack in the flagstones that helped to hold his foot where it would not go to sleep. Silverman pushed against him and left a sticky hand-mark on the woodwork.

Ibid., pp. 21–2.

When a boy reads a passage like this, he is likely to make his own mental picture, and for this reason such descriptions can only be given to us through the flexible medium of words which each of us can make our own. Illustrations are too restricting here, as they are, too, in the case of the dramatis personæ of a story. C. Walter Hodges, who has illustrated these three choir-school stories, has tried to draw some of the individuals in them (perhaps at the request of the publisher), but I cannot believe that anyone who enjoys these stories could want to be given someone else's impression of the features of the lordly Trevithic or the egregious Sandwell. On the other hand,

Trevithic.

when the illustrator *comments* on a scene, not reproducing it but getting at the quickening spirit of it, he is making a valuable contribution to the truth of the stories; and these are among the most spontaneous and the most living of all school stories.

But now we must come to the arch-fossil, the original fly in the ointment—Billy Bunter. Pictorially speaking, it is not correct to speak of Bunter as a fossil, for he has undergone evolutionary change. The first illustration in which the fat boy appeared, on the title-page of *The Magnet* of March 1908, is relatively normal. To be sure, Bunter is eating jam-tarts, but his figure is only that of an ordinary plump boy, his spectacles are of orthodox size. Two months later he has put on a little weight, in a picture of a picnic to which the caption is, 'It was certainly a mistake to leave Billy in charge.' And so the thing goes on. It is interesting to watch over the course of years as the artistic bicycle pump is applied and Bunter gradually

Drawing by C. Walter Hodges for William Mayne's CATHEDRAL WEDNESDAY (O.U.P.)

becomes the gross, grotesque figure which our children know from the pages of the last *Magnets* of 1940, from the frontispieces of the Bunter books still continuing, and from the television screen.

It is very different, however, on the printed page. Frank Richards conceived Bunter in 1908 as a character in a magazine story, a serial. He has been kept alive, virtually unchanged in age and temperament, from 1908 to the present day (with a break between 1940 and 1947). The chief virtue of Greyfriars School, as of other schools in comics of yesterday and today, is their *familiarity*. The stories rely on a few simple formulas of plot and character, instantly recognized, endlessly repeated. Hurree Singh's Babu English, based on the word 'terrific' and on certain self-coined abstract nouns, has never been changed; nor have the hearty ejaculations of Cherry or the mouthings of Bunter.

Each of Bunter's familiar characteristics was taken from real life, as Richard tells us in his autobiography. His girth came from a Fleet Street editor; his spectacles from a relation who had goggled at Richards when he was a boy; his postal order gag came from an acquaintance who was always borrowing on the expectation of a cheque; his fatuousness under cross-examination from 'an eminent public figure' of late Victorian times. Thus Bunter was born whole and immutable. At his very first appearance he was preoccupied with food, he used the onomatopœic expressions like 'Yarroo' and 'Gerumph' which shatter television valves in hundreds of homes today. To be sure, in the early days he was an incidental bit of comic relief for the trials and heartburnings of Harry Wharton, designed to be the chief character of the stories. But that 'little chatterbox', 'little Bunter', 'the smallest boy in the form' (not sarcastic, then) had soon pushed himself forward; and now that the fat boy has been given a new lease of life in full-length books, it is his name which stands for the series. They are the Bunter books, and it is his scrapes, infinitely blown up from trivial incidents, which make the stories. For Bunter's appeal must come from familiarity in childhood. Nobody could approach in middle-age paragraphs like this:

'Prime!' gurgled Billy Bunter.

Bunter did not find it easy to utter even that monosyllable. His capacious mouth was packed to capacity, with luscious, purple grapes. He gurgled happily through delicious grapes that seemed to melt in the mouth.

It was a happy fat Owl! Smithy, for once kind and sympathetic, had done the thing well. That bunch was the biggest and best that money could buy. Probably it would have pleased an invalid, —had there been an invalid, and had it reached that invalid. Certainly it pleased William George Bunter. His little round eyes were still red, and still exuded water, from the application of the onion, but otherwise, his fat face beamed . . .

Frank Richards. BILLY BUNTER'S BOLT (Cassell, 1957) p. 40.

Nostalgia, alone, can carry you through this sort of thing. Pleasure remembered is worth having; but the books to look out for are those which can be picked up and reread, with new understanding, in middle-age, or which can revive a parent's interest in school stories by a new slant. These books will never become fossilized, although they may be written well within the boarding-school formula. THE WILLOUGHBY CAPTAINS, William Mayne's CHORISTER'S CAKE and A SWARM IN MAY, Antonia Forest's AUTUMN TERM and END OF TERM—these stories, by Orwell's prescription, are all limited; but there is as much in them as in the most vigorous tale whose plot Orwell would have approved.

Antonia Forest is probably unique in the field of school stories for girls. Writing in the present day, she has boldly chosen the now old-fashioned setting of an exclusive boarding-school; she has completely cut across the silliness and triviality which resulted from half a century of Angela Brazil and her imitators; she has drawn girls who are totally feminine and yet do not tiresomely rebel against a very orthodox and restricted life. She uses the situations that would naturally develop between vigorous personalities living at close quarters. The rivalry between seventeen-year-old Rowan Marlow and Lois Sanger, in AUTUMN TERM, is displayed on the games field, in the classroom, on a Guide trek, and it is always seen as a surface tension reflecting far deeper dissatisfactions and ambitions.

Because Antonia Forest concentrates on character, I can absolutely accept her limited sphere of action. I mind very much whether Nicola Marlow or the spoilt Pomona gets the spare front desk in Form 3 Remove; but when E. Brent Dyer, a prolific writer, writes ten or twelve pages of drama concerning the dire consequences of tilting your chair while working, I cannot see the incident as she (presumably) does, for the characters involved are so shadowy and uninteresting.

In E. Brent Dyer's stories about the Chalet School, and Elsie J. Oxenham's series about the Abbey School, we have another clear case of fossilization. The appeal of these books, like the appeal of Bunter, is one of familiarity. I remember THE ABBEY GIRLS well from my own girlhood. It was in 1920 that the quaint school morris-dancing club first found its way to the Abbey and caught up in its sociable and rather absurd activities the lonely girls, Joy and Joan. I remembered nothing about the book except the vaguely medieval atmosphere and the elaborate descriptions of the Queen's dresses. Rereading this book, and pursuing the sequels up to the present day, I was astonished to find that the atmosphere in the books published in the 'fifties is almost unchanged. The same other-worldly, decorative background; the same gracious Abbey girls, grown up now but still with the sentimental vision of adolescence; the new generation of schoolgirls untouched, apparently, by the passage of time. The same may be said of the Chalet girls, who have been working for bazaars and getting into mischief continuously since 1925. Indeed, many of the later volumes are filled out with the reminiscences of Old Girls.

These are survivals, and they must eventually suffer the fate of other books, creatures and tribes that prolong existence in a world that has passed them by. The school story is keeping alive by renewing itself, as all literature must do. The boarding-school story can live now only in the hands of exceptional writers like William Mayne and Antonia Forest. It is the day-school story which has been most interesting in the past ten years or so, partly because the greater proportion of readers go to day-schools, partly because home and school can be neatly and profitably welded together.

It is a relief to escape from the wooden unrealities of Angela Brazil and her descendants to the fresh and vigorous life of a girls' day-school as some recent writers portray it. Alice Lunt's SECRET STEPMOTHER has for heroine a girl who resents her inoffensive young stepmother and refuses to admit her existence. Janet's attitude leads her into troubles large and small, as her young sister escapes from her control and gets into mischief, as the headmistress, misled by Janet's excuses, investigates what seems to be a case of parental neglect. This is a fresh, topical drama in which all the characters come to life, and JEANNETTE'S FIRST TERM, even mo.e remarkably, fills with interest the simple theme of two friends moving up to a Secondary Modern school. Mary Harris has made a striking contribution, too, to the girls' school story. It is a sad fact that the emotions of girlhood, so often roused by unworthy causes, can be tedious to read about. There is nothing very new in the story of EMILY AND THE HEADMISTRESS, but the friendship growing between Emily and Miss Robinson in the holidays has unexpected point. A later story, SERAPHINA, goes deeper. I know few books which relate school and home life so intelligently. Seraphina is an orphan. When her beloved grandmother dies she goes to live with an aunt, a smart woman who runs a hairdressing salon and has no sympathy with moods and fancies. She packs her niece off to a boarding-hostel attached to the local grammar school. An awe-inspiring headmistress, a high standard of work, a very mixed collection of girls, these tax Seraphina and sometimes worry her; and then there is Stephanie, so fascinating, so secretive about her home. The growing friendship between these girls and their sharing of hopes and sorrows is described with real insight and the book has a quiet but impressive authenticity.

Drawing by Roger Payne for E. W. Hildick's JIM STARLING AND THE AGENCY (Chatto)

In the same way, E. W. Hildick has given a good shake to the drooping form of the boys' school story. Jim Starling is certainly a pleasant change from the usual straw-hatted hero, just as Cement Street Secondary Modern for boys, in the town of Smogbury, is a pleasant change from the ancient walls of St Boniface's. The novelty of Hildick's setting and of his working-class characters may at first distract readers from the vigour and skill of his writing. His plots are cleverly worked out, his characters fully realized, his style racy and workmanlike. I know few school stories of any kind which give me so completely the impression of a school from the boy's point of view. Here is an art-lesson in progress:

> For the next ten minutes or so the boys of 3B worked away busily with their sticks of charcoal, sketching their ideas on large sheets of paper. Then, as they decided they had enough to work upon, they began to mix their paint. Hamer walked round, quietly giving advice, exploding only occasionally whenever he caught someone drawing too carefully. Then he would shout: 'Don't spend all morning drawing, lad!' or 'Fill the paper, don't niggle away in one corner!' or 'Use bold, free, happy strokes! Happy strokes! Happy strokes!' And every time he said 'Happy strokes' he'd fetch the unfortunate boy a clump at the back of the head.
> E. W. Hildick. JIM STARLING (Chatto & Windus, 1958) p. 34.

and here is one of those curious moments when you see the school, as it were, from an oblique angle:

> The changing-room was up a few steps from the corridor. At the other side you went down another few steps and through a door into the gym itself. Jim had never really thought about this before, but now it seemed very strange that the changing-room should be raised up like that. In fact, everything seemed strange: the silence of the changing-room itself, with all the pants and shirts hung up, limp and bedraggled, like dish-cloths, and the shoes lying about as if the owners had had to leave them in a hurry and run for their lives (which they had, in a way, with Hilton snapping at them to look sharp and banging a slipper against the doorpost). Then the muffled clump-clumping from the gym—that sounded strange, too—and the commands of Hilton suddenly making the clumping stop or go faster. And the smell of the dust and sweat and rubber was strange . . .
> Ibid., pp. 50–1.

The books about Jim Starling are excellent, but I have not the least doubt that Mr Hildick would have made just as much of a success if he had chosen to write a story about a public school. Public school or primary, Smogbury or Fellsgarth, boys and girls at home or away from home, what does it matter so long as the book has its own atmosphere and its own compulsion? 'School stories' are fettered by formulas; good stories about schools make use of them at their own choice.

Children will always want school stories; their appeal is universal, the appeal of sorrows and triumphs felt by any child, even if they are in an unfamiliar setting. Can the same be said of the pony book? Is its popularity over the last twenty years or so a passing fashion or is it permanent? Certainly the universal emotions of childhood can be found here, but you often have to dig deep to find them. The basic formula promises to be good—the idea of children learning a technique and winning success in it. True, it is a special technique and relatively few children come anywhere near even starting to learn it; but this does not seem to matter. Hundreds of children who have no pony, and may probably never ride, want pony books. Some, (especially town children) because of the idealized charm of country life; some just for the pleasure of learning about a technique; some because the dream formula (I WANTED A PONY, WISH FOR A PONY, GAZE AT THE MOON are typical titles) is so consoling; all, I believe, because horses make a direct appeal to the feminine need to be dominated and at the same time to be maternal (for pony books are written chiefly for girls). Above all, there is the appeal that any story has which deals with achievement. In almost every pony book success comes first and matters most; the ponies take second place. They are not animal stories. Only in a very few (Kitty Barne's moving tale of ROSINA COPPER among them) do you get to know what a horse or a pony is like.

There is one thing I do not like about pony books—their exclusiveness. It does not matter that hundreds and thousands of the girls who read them have no ponies; it *does* matter that they should be made to feel (as they are, far too often) that they could not qualify for this magic world, either, on grounds of class. In many pony books there is a distasteful feeling of clubmanship. I find myself impatiently waiting to read one in which the lower middle-class girl who comes by a pony, especially if her father is *nouveau riche*, turns out to have a perfect seat. The procession of delicately nurtured, or well-bred, children, or ordinary children adopting the current manners of the horsy fraternity, is apt to be as wearisome as a pageant produced by amateurs. Out of a hundred or so pony books (leaving out the few memorable exceptions) I can remember only a series of crash-caps and crashes, and books that must be remembered for their plots are going to have only a short life—although it must be admitted that horse-mad girls cherish this monotony, in text and in illustrations.

I think there is light on the horizon. Pony books, which must move with the times if they are to get new readers, are bound to be affected by the rise of pony clubs since the war, with their varied membership; and perhaps these same pony clubs will gradually work another necessary change. It is obvious that the young hero or heroine must succeed, must win her pony or her rosette. But the reader demands (or should demand) that success is *won*; it must not come easily. Few readers, whether they know about ponies or not, are likely to accept the situation in I WANTED A PONY, by Diana Pullein-Thompson, where Augusta discovers in a few minutes what everyone else (including the vet) has failed to deduce in months about the grey pony—that its unpleasant habit of tossing its head is *not* due to a brain-tumour but to the fact that an unusually broad forehead makes all bridles uncomfortable. This contrivance to bring the pony within Augusta's limited means is unusually bad, but there are many books far more skilfully written, among them Joanna Cannan's GAZE AT THE MOON and M. E. Atkinson's pleasant HUNTER'S MOON, where good fortune and coincidence still dominate the story, to the loss of the really important element—character.

If the gymkhana story has its improbabilities, how much more so has the pony adventure story. It is a relief to get away from the collecting ring, but the author who makes her young riders outwit crooks, sometimes quite dangerous crooks, has to be very good to win permanent belief from her readers. Here again the secret lies not in convincing detail but in character. You very seldom get anything as good as Ann Stafford's FIVE PROUD RIDERS, which triumphantly carries off a most unlikely tale about international spies in the New Forest because the children who bring them to justice—Jill, responsible and full of sense, superior Nigel, and the bumptious, resourceful little John—are so real.

Head and shoulders above other writers of the pony adventure story is Mary Treadgold. Her books will satisfy the most ardent pony-fancier, but her talent is entirely unhampered by formula. WE COULDN'T LEAVE DINAH is set in a Channel island coveted by the Nazis as an invasion base. The story is an exciting one. The Nazis come to Clerinel and are helped by the Beaumarchais family. Peter Beaumarchais is leader of a pony club, and the Templeton children are horrified to discover that his home is a centre of collaboration. Besides, Mick and Caroline should not be in Clerinel at all. In the confusion of sudden evacuation they are left behind and from their hiding-place they discover the dangerous activities of the Nazis, and the unpleasant fact that fat Nannerl, the Commandant's daughter, is riding Caroline's beloved Dinah. The spy plot is beautifully adapted to the capacities and characters of the children, and the same is true of the later story, NO PONIES, set in the South of France, where stolen ponies are used for transport in an underground railway carrying Nazi-trained agitators into other countries. In each case, a sensational plot is kept within bounds by exceptionally good character drawing (and also by exceptionally good writing).

It is character, again, which makes the stories of Monica Edwards popular with children who may or may not already love ponies. But hers are not, in the strict sense, pony books. It is true that she started well within the formula, making her first appearance with WISH FOR A PONY, where two girls on Romney Marsh lived, talked and dreamed ponies, did the worst chores at the local riding stables in the hope of rides, and ultimately, by a piece of story-book fortune, had a pony almost drop into their laps. No, it is not out of the ordinary for its plot, this book, but there is something unusually lifelike about the girls and their home background. It is not surprising to learn that the book was written to please Monica Edwards's daughter and that she and a school friend were models for the characters of Tamzin and Rissa; while the Marsh setting which appears in entrancing glimpses throughout the story had been familiar to the author from her childhood. In this simple, unostentatious story was the beginning of an attractive series in which adventures with ponies and boats rise naturally from the characters and their environment, and are pursued in a very probable manner. Smuggling at Westling, in THE SUMMER OF THE GREAT SECRET; the traffic in horse-flesh in CARGO OF HORSES; a man caught in quicksands, in HIDDEN IN A DREAM; floods on the estuary, in STORM AHEAD; foot-and-mouth disease in NO ENTRY; poaching by French fishermen in THE NIGHT-BIRD; bird protection in STRANGER TO THE MARSH when a pair of hoopoes nest in the ruined castle; oiled seabirds in OPERATION

SEABIRD; it is a wonderful list of subjects, topically and intrinsically interesting, and not one of these books has anything stilted about it. The children develop as time goes on. We know their ages and we see their capacities widening as their experience grows. In the latest story, NO GOING BACK, Meryon and Tamzin discover an adolescent love for each other which alters the happy relationship of the group; the author's sense of proportion and her sensitiveness in this matter are notable. And though ponies play their part in the stories, they are not the object of adulation or of excessive care. Sometimes they are used as casually by the girls as their boy companions in adventure use their bicycles. Monica Edwards is not setting out to please horse-obsessives. She writes stories full of common sense and with a sound knowledge of young people, and in a rare and effective way she puts these young people firmly in their environment. Their homes, the village where Tamzin's father is Vicar, the neighbours they respect and the visitors they examine with caution—everything is part of a balanced whole.

The same warm realistic atmosphere is conspicuous in her second cycle of stories, about Punchbowl Farm, which are based even more closely on her own family, and which are some of the best stories one can offer to girls of ten or so. The risk of using real life, sometimes in great detail, was worth taking. The Thorntons, learning to farm from scratch, have adventures which are perfectly credible. This is because Monica Edwards, since she is using real life, gives her young readers all of it—the disaster to the beautiful mare Moonstone as well as the romantic finding of the old diary, loss of crops or stock as well as successes, quarrels and disappointments as well as halcyon days in the country.

In these splendid, humorous, human stories, with their direct, accomplished style, we are a long way from the pony story that is written to a formula, and another kind of story shows the same wide range of accomplishment. Ballet, acting, circus-life—these, for their colour and drama, have been favourite subjects for children's stories for many years. Here is the success formula again, perhaps now better called the Footlight Formula. Hundreds of girls dream of winning public acclaim on the stage, and tales of spectacular successes are available in their hundreds to console children who feel their life is entirely drab and ordinary compared with the life of a child acrobat or a television star.

Now the disadvantage of this formula, as we have already found in the case of pony books, is that success is prescriptive. However skilfully the author mixes the rough with the smooth, it is soon obvious that the understudy is going to get the star part or that the young equestrienne is going to save the horses in the burning circus tent. A good writer, while she may accept the necessity of success, will concentrate on the clash of characters, which can be particularly interesting in the egotistical world of show business. I do not want to be too solemn about this. There are plenty of excellent stage stories where the stage atmosphere matters more than the characters. They live in the memory for less time than those where character is paramount, but they can be most agreeable to read. Pamela Brown, for instance, communicates brilliantly the feeling of crowded excitement, ups and downs, flurry and hurry of back stage, whether it is audition, rehearsal or performance. If you want to accept her books, you must accept the Footlight Formula as a whole. The six children in the Blue Door series have far more successes than failures as they pass through acting school and gain experience in repertory, cabaret, television and touring. In these books the children, lively and talented, are interchangeable, but the smell of grease-paint is authentic. Theatrical dress-shop in HARLEQUIN CORNER, Thames launch in SHOWBOAT SUMMER, greenroom in UNDERSTUDY—the atmosphere is always wonderfully real.

Real, of course, only up to a point. Children's stories about the theatre are more often than not about child actors. Too much of the danger and difficulty of real life must be left out if the subject is a girl or boy in the late teens (unless, as Pamela Brown does, you keep your character at the permanent emotional age of fourteen or so), and children of ten or twelve who want to read about the stage will naturally enjoy theatrical technique more than theatrical perils. A girl of thirteen or so will do better to read some of the best adult novels of the theatre, like Clemence Dane's BROOME STAGES, or George Moore's superb study of an opera-singer, EVELYN INNES. Margot Benary's CASTLE ON THE BORDER, written specifically for children, gives an unusually realistic view of an amateur acting company in Germany, but even this exceptionally mature writer has cast something of a rosy glow over her book to suit the young reader.

By far the most successful theatre stories for children are those which, with children as their subjects, can show rivalries and ambitions unaffected, as yet, by the awkward, sordid, bewildering adult world. Here Noel Streatfeild is outstanding. Her young actors, skaters and ballet pupils are infatuated by the theatre. They are ambitious, self-centred, as deeply obsessed by technique as any young aspirant for a jumping rosette. She even succeeds, sometimes, in conveying that intangible but unmistakable thing, star quality— in Posy, for instance, youngest of the three girls in BALLET SHOES, who, when the brilliant teacher falls ill, inquires at once what is to happen to her own career; or in Rachel in WINTLE'S WONDERS, whose talents are discovered almost by accident, but whom you recognize at once as a dedicated dancer.

Though Noel Streatfeild knows her theatre as well as Pamela Brown does, she does not put it first. She has an insatiable curiosity about people, and especially about theatrical children, with their peculiar, hard-working, rigidly organized life; and she is curious, too, about the effects of publicity and performance on young people. Her books, for all the detail and skill of their backgrounds, are primarily studies in character. Mrs Wintle's dancing-school is the battlefield for her daughter Dulcie, a conceited little girl who wants the best parts in all the shows, and the two children, Rachel and Hilary, who are taken into the family and threaten to steal some of Dulcie's thunder. The same theme, of the poor and modest child coming to the fore, is brilliantly used in WHITE BOOTS, in the rivalry of Harriet Johnson, daughter of a poor (but well-connected) green-grocer, and Lalla Moore, a well-to-do orphan whose aunt is pushing her into the limelight in the world of ice-skating. In all Noel Streatfeild's books we have portraits of the professional child, set off by the occasional brave souls who resist the dazzle of the footlights, like Petrova in BALLET SHOES, whose heart is in motor-engineering, or Hilary, in WINTLE'S WONDERS, whose attitude is entirely refreshing, when she is offered a star part:

'What do you want me for? I won't be any good.'
The producer was thoroughly amused.
'I'm sorry if I've inconvenienced you. But there's a comic robin in this new children's play which I thought would suit you.'
'Has he anything to say?'
'No, it's all mime with a little dancing.'
Hilary gave in grudgingly.

'Well, I suppose I'll have to be him.'

The producer laughed.

'Don't you want to? Most children would jump at the chance, I thought I was doing you a good turn.'

'Well, you aren't. All I want to be is just an ordinary Wonder, and look what happens to me. My first engagement is to understudy Dulcie, which nobody could like, and now I've got to be a robin. Wouldn't you rather have somebody else? There are heaps of Wonders who'd be better than me.'

The producer gave Hilary's hair an affectionate rub.

'You're a card. But no, thank you, I'm sticking to you.'

Noel Streatfeild. WINTLE'S WONDERS. (Collins, 1957) pp. 232–3.

The intrusion of such a robust point of view into the somewhat rarefied air of the theatre saves these stories, full of technical detail as they are, from becoming too specialized for the general reader. Noel Streatfeild has her feet firmly on the ground, and children who reread her books when they are older will bless her for this.

Theatrical children, of course, are not ordinary, and neither are circus children. In THE CIRCUS IS COMING, still perhaps Noel Streatfeild's most popular book, she emphasizes the oddity of circus characters by bringing into Cob's Circus a prim little hero and heroine, Peter and Santa, who have to shake down, after a suburban upbringing, in the heady atmosphere of sawdust and performance. In the same way Howard Spring, in the incomparable SAMPSON'S CIRCUS, brings real life abruptly into relation with the exotic. To Howard Spring, character is the mainspring of children's writing, and character that is recognizable—sharply, pictorially drawn. Most of his characters are outsize—like lively Charley Chaffinch, the villainous Aristide Elverdingen, and the imposing Mr Sampson himself. This is how young Jo describes him:

An extraordinary figure came down the steps with slow dignity. Through the telescope I could pick out every detail: the enormous body, so fat that it was difficult to see where the legs ended and the stomach began; the tiny feet shod in boots with brilliant toes, dove-coloured cloth uppers and buttons; the grey trousers with a broad stripe of black braid down the sides; the black frock-coat pulled so tight that it looked as though it might burst asunder, scattering a hail of buttons, at any moment. There was a white camellia in Mr. Sampson's buttonhole. On his head was a tall grey topper, and between the topper and the bright scarlet of his tie was a face like an immense Dutch cheese, ornamented with moustaches waxed to long fine points.

Howard Spring. SAMPSON'S CIRCUS. (Faber, 1936) pp. 72–3.

Like TUMBLEDOWN DICK, this is a book where good writing and genial humour go hand in hand, without in the least falsifying the hard knocks of the world.

Howard Spring is, of course, on good ground for the creating of characters, for circus people are outsize. Far more difficult is the task of those who want to present musicians as they are, present them as ordinary people and yet indicate their particular quality. Kitty Barne has done for the technique of concert playing much what Noel Streatfeild has done for acting. Her stories are serious and professional, as well as entertaining. She does not let her characters win success easily, nor does she make them larger than life. In SHE SHALL HAVE MUSIC, for instance, we follow eight-year-old Karin Forest through a discouraging period, when she has no piano to exercise her talent on; we follow her as she clings to Rosalba, romantic and tasteless in execution, because she can teach her at least something; and because we have seen her difficulties, we can readily believe in Karin's success on the concert platform. I think only one writer for children has really succeeded in making you *feel* a musician's character. Elfrida Vipont's LARK IN THE MORN, with its rather sentimental sequel, THE LARK ON THE WING, really make you believe in the special talent, as well as the dedication to music, of Kit Haverard. It is no small achievement to describe the awakening of creative imagination in a schoolgirl without any shadow of exaggeration or falseness. Elfrida Vipont has done just this. Kit Haverard is playing a game of King Arthur with her friends:

At length Elaine, cruelly forsaken, proceeded to pine away. The action was becoming far too slow, thought Pony. 'Buck up and get on to the dying part,' she urged. Elaine did not seem to hear her. Nowadays, Kit had a way of losing herself in the play, which irritated Pony very much. She seemed to be taking their games more seriously than ever, whereas Pony was beginning to feel a little self-conscious about them. None of the other girls in her form played pretending-games. 'Can't we skip a bit of this?' she suggested.

Kit lay back on the sofa, humming to herself. The words of Elaine's song from *The Idylls of the King* were running through her mind. Somehow or other, they were fitting themselves into a kind of tune as they went along. She began to sing tentatively; her voice was uneven and uncontrolled. The others scarcely listened. They were used to Kit's oddities by now, but they did wish she would hurry up, and Pony itched to sing it for her . . . suddenly something seemed to break down in Kit. As if she had indeed been transformed into the lovelorn child of the story, she lost herself . . .

Pony and Helen stared at her. They had never heard her sing like that before. Pony pulled herself together to break the spell.

'What's up with thee, Elaine?' she began, in the fatherly tones of the Lord of Astolat. 'Art thinking of yonder knight?'

Kit said nothing. There were tears in her eyes.

'Look out!' whispered Helen. 'She's going to cry. For goodness' sake let's play something else.'

Pony nodded assent and plumped down on to the sofa. 'Cheer up!' said she. 'It was awfully nice, but don't let's do any more of it. The part where she goes down the river is a bit dull, isn't it? Let's try something else.'

Kit shook herself slightly and sat up. 'All right,' she said gruffly. 'Don't mind. Anything you like.'

'Right-o!' said Pony, taking the situation in hand. 'We'll do the last battle and you can be Arthur. You'd like that, wouldn't you? Helen can do Modred and Bedivere, and I'll be Lancelot.'

'But he wasn't there,' protested Helen.

'Can't help it,' rejoined Pony. 'And how do you know, anyway?' Elfrida Vipont. THE LARK IN THE MORN. (Oxford University Press, 1948) pp. 61-3.

There is in this book an extraordinarily easy swing of emotion, a sure sense of timing, and beyond these technical skills, an understanding of a dedicated personality. It is not often that books written for girls, even for older girls, go as deep as this story does. It is not often that you find the familiar and hackneyed success formula bursting out into fresh and pulsating life, into a book which offers as much for an adult reader as it does to girls aspiring to be adults.

Reading List

1.*School Stories*

Allan, Mabel Esther. A SCHOOL IN DANGER 1952, OVER THE SEA TO SCHOOL 1954, AT SCHOOL IN SKYE 1957. *Blackie.* Illustrated by Constance Marshall. Lively tales of an unorthodox school in Skye, with good characters.

*Benson, E. F. DAVID BLAIZE 1916, DAVID OF KING'S 1924. *Hodder & Stoughton.*

*Bird, Richard. THE WHARTON MEDAL, in THE RICHARD BIRD OMNIBUS. *O.U.P.* 1937.

*Buckeridge, Anthony. JENNINGS GOES TO SCHOOL 1950, ACCORDING TO JENNINGS 1954, OUR FRIEND JENNINGS 1955. *Collins.*

*Douthwaite, L. C. THE LUCK OF ST BONIFACE. *Jarrold* 1925.

*Dyer, E. Brent. TOM TACKLES THE CHALET SCHOOL. *Chambers* 1955. Numerous other titles, earliest THE SCHOOL AT THE CHALET 1925, latest JOEY AND CO. IN TIROL 1960.

*Forest, Antonia. AUTUMN TERM 1948, END OF TERM 1959. *Faber.*

Garrard, Phyllis. NEW ZEALAND SCHOOLGIRL 1958; contains HILDA AT SCHOOL, THE DOINGS OF HILDA, and HILDA'S ADVENTURES. Also HILDA, FIFTEEN. *Blackie* 1944. A schoolgirl in the back-country; cheerful, unconventional tales with a pleasing family background.

*Harris, Mary K. EMILY AND THE HEADMISTRESS 1958, SERAPHINA 1960. *Faber.* Illustrated by Sheila Rose.

*Hildick, E. W. JIM STARLING 1958, JIM STARLING AND THE AGENCY 1958. *Chatto & Windus.* Illustrated by Roger Payne.

*Hildick, E. W. JIM STARLING'S HOLIDAY 1960, JIM STARLING AND THE COLONEL 1960. *Heinemann.* Illustrated by Roger Payne.

Kästner, Erich. THE FLYING CLASSROOM (1933 Germany). *Cape* 1934. Translated by Cyrus Brooks. Illustrated by Walter Trier. Bavarian boarding-school, schoolboy feuds, play-acting, etc.

*Kipling, Rudyard. STALKY AND CO. *Macmillan* (1899) 1951.

Lloyd, Marjorie. ONE SUMMER TERM. *Methuen* 1959. Illustrated by Astrid Walford. Boarding house in day school on Welsh Marches. Excellent characterization and clash of personalities.

*Lunt, Alice. SECRET STEPMOTHER 1959, illustrated by D. G. Valentine. JEANETTE'S FIRST TERM 1960, illustrated by Dorothy Parsons. *Dent.*

*McNeill, Janet. Books about Specs McCann (see Chap.8).

*Mayne, William. THE WORLD UPSIDE DOWN 1954, illustrated by Shirley Hughes. A SWARM IN MAY 1955, CHORISTER'S CAKE 1956, CATHEDRAL WEDNESDAY 1960, illustrated by C. Walter Hodges. *O.U.P.*

Mayne, William. THE MEMBER FOR THE MARSH. *O.U.P.* 1956. Illustrated by Lynton Lamb. Somerset grammar school boys and their weekend pursuits in marshy country. Superb characterization, dialogue and setting.

*Means, Florence Crannell. SHUTTERED WINDOWS. *Houghton Mifflin*, New York 1943.

*Oxenham, Elsie J. THE ABBEY GIRLS (1920) *Collins* (Schoolgirls' Library) 1951. Many other titles, of which the latest is TOMBOYS AT THE ABBEY. *Collins* 1957.

*Reed, Talbot Baines. THE FIFTH FORM AT ST DOMINIC'S (1907). *Blackie* 1951.

*Reed, Talbot Baines. THE WILLOUGHBY CAPTAINS (1887), THE COCK HOUSE AT FELLSGARTH (1893), THE MASTER OF THE SHELL (1894), TOM, DICK AND HARRY (1894), A DOG WITH A BAD NAME (1894). *Religious Tract Society* 1931.

*Richards, Frank. BILLY BUNTER STORIES. *Magnet* 1907–1940. BILLY BUNTER books. *Cassell*. Latest, BUNTER THE BAD LAD 1960. Illustrated by C. H. Chapman.

Sterling, Dorothy. MARY JANE. (1959 U.S.A.) *Constable* 1960. Colour problem in Southern school; sympathetic, well-turned story.

Strong, L. A. G. WRONG FOOT FOREMOST. *Pitman* 1940. Amalgamation of two schools and the difficulties of an individualist.

Tring, A. Stephen. THE OLD GANG. *O.U.P.* 1947. Illustrated by John Camp. Small-town grammar school and its feud with Modern school; realistic without effort.

Tring, A. Stephen. PENNY DREADFUL 1949, PENNY TRIUMPHANT 1953, PENNY PENITENT 1953, PENNY PUZZLED 1955, PENNY DRAMATIC 1956. *O.U.P.* Illustrated by Terence Freeman. Day-school girl of dash and zeal, her adventures at school, at home and on holiday.

*Vachell, H. A. THE HILL. *Newnes* (1905) 1925.

*Waugh, Alec. THE LOOM OF YOUTH. *Cassell* (1917) 1929.

*Wilson, D. Wynne. EARLY CLOSING. *Constable* 1931.

Wodehouse, P. G. MIKE. *Black* 1909. Reissued as MIKE AT WRYKYN. *Herbert Jenkins* 1953. Conventional public-school story of some merit, with flashes of true Wodehouse wit.

2.*Pony Stories*

Anderson, C. W. THE HORSE OF HURRICANE HILL (1956 U.S.A.) 1958, AFRAID TO RIDE (1957 U.S.A.) 1959. *Brockhampton*. Illustrated by the author. A horseman writes with understanding of people and their pleasure in horses: excellent drawings.

*Atkinson, M. E. HUNTER'S MOON. *Bodley Head* 1952. Illustrated by Charlotte Hough.

*Barne, Kitty. ROSINA COPPER 1954, illustrated by Alfons Purtscher. ROSINA AND SON 1956, illustrated by Marcia Lane-Foster. *Evans*.

Baxter, Gillian. TAN AND TARMAC. *Evans* 1958. Illustrated by Anne Gordon. South Kensington riding-school: glimpses of horses in show business, with refreshingly professional attitude to riding.

*Cannan, Joanna. GAZE AT THE MOON. *Collins* 1957. Illustrated by Sheila Rose.

Cumming, Primrose. THE WEDNESDAY PONY. *Blackie* 1939. Illustrated by Stanley Lloyd. Butcher's children try to improve on their pony but find him best in the end; a lively and unusually realistic tale.

Cumming, Primrose. NO PLACE FOR PONIES. *Dent* 1954. Illustrated by M. Tulloch. Children sent to Sussex guest-house find lack of freedom a handicap, but mystery horse adds excitement to their lives.

Cumming, Primrose. FLYING HORSEMAN. *Dent* 1959. Illustrated by Sheila Rose. Boy kept from flying career by illness comes to terms with himself and with the horsy family he works for. Unusually good character-drawing.

Davis, Lavinia. PONY JUNGLE. *Collins* 1944. English children in America fraternizing over pony-express service, camps, gymkhanas and the like.

*Edwards, Monica. WISH FOR A PONY 1947, THE SUMMER OF THE GREAT SECRET 1948, THE MIDNIGHT HORSE 1949, THE WHITE RIDERS 1950, CARGO OF HORSES 1951, HIDDEN IN A DREAM 1952, NO ENTRY 1954, THE NIGHTBIRD 1955, STORM AHEAD 1953, STRANGER TO THE MARSH 1957, OPERATION SEABIRD 1957, NO GOING BACK 1960. *Collins*. The Romney Marsh stories. Illustrated by Geoffrey Whittam.

*Edwards, Monica. NO MISTAKING CORKER 1947, BLACK HUNTING WHIP 1950, illustrated by Geoffrey Whittam. PUNCHBOWL MIDNIGHT 1951, illustrated by Charles Tunnicliffe. THE SPIRIT OF PUNCHBOWL FARM 1952, THE WANDERER 1953, PUNCHBOWL HARVEST 1954, illustrated by Joan Wanklyn. FRENCHMAN'S SECRET 1956, THE COWNAPPERS 1958, illustrated by Geoffrey Whittam. *Collins*. The Punchbowl Farm stories.

Edwards, Monica. THE UNSOUGHT FARM (Autobiography). *Michael Joseph* 1954.

Gray, Patsey. CHALLENGER (1959 U.S.A.). *Dent* 1960. Illustrated by Sam Savitt.

Girl helps grandfather to train horses and riders in California, and becomes show rider. Character and technical details equally good.

Phipson, Joan. GOOD LUCK TO THE RIDER. *Angus & Robertson* 1953. Illustrated by Margaret Horder. Australian homestead and various events with horses: cheerful, good-hearted tale.

Pullein-Thompson, Christine. A DAY TO GO HUNTING. *Collins* 1956. Illustrated by Sheila Rose. Good use of the one-day formula.

Pullein-Thompson, Christine. THE HORSE SALE. *Collins* 1960. Illustrated by Sheila Rose. One-day formula again, a number of sharply-drawn people; more mature attitude to riding and horses than in earlier books.

*Pullein-Thompson, Diana. I WANTED A PONY. *Collins* 1946. Illustrated by Anne Bullen.

*Stafford, Ann. FIVE PROUD RIDERS. *Hamish Hamilton* 1937.

Stanford, Don. THE HORSEMASTERS (1957 U.S.A.). *Harrap* 1958. Illustrated by Michael Lyne. Fascinating story of intensive training in advanced riding school: good characterization.

*Treadgold, Mary. WE COULDN'T LEAVE DINAH 1941, illustrated by Stuart Tresilian. NO PONIES 1946, illustrated by Ruth Gervis. *Cape*.

Wait, Mrs Peter. THE WANTED MAN. *Methuen* 1956. Illustrated by Mary Gernat. Escaped convict, stolen necklace, missing pony: an improbable but entirely readable tale.

West, Joyce. DROVER'S ROAD. *Dent* 1953. Illustrated by the author. The friendliest and most unorthodox horse-story I know, set on a New Zealand sheep-station.

3.*Ballet, stage, circus and music*

*Barne, Kitty. SHE SHALL HAVE MUSIC 1938, MUSICAL HONOURS 1939. *Dent*. Illustrated by Ruth Gervis.

*Benary, Margot. CASTLE ON THE BORDER. *Macmillan* 1957.

*Brown, Pamela. THE SWISH OF THE CURTAIN 1941, MADDY ALONE 1945, GOLDEN PAVEMENTS 1947, BLUE DOOR VENTURE 1949, MADDY AGAIN 1956. *Nelson*. The Blue Door Books. Illustrated by Newton Whittaker.

*Brown, Pamela. HARLEQUIN CORNER 1953, illustrated by Marcia Lane-Foster. UNDERSTUDY 1958, illustrated by Drake Brookshaw. *Nelson*.

*Brown, Pamela. SHOWBOAT SUMMER. *Brockhampton* 1957.

*Dane, Clemence. BROOME STAGES. *Heinemann* (1931) 1960.

Fitzroy, Olivia. WAGONS AND HORSES. *Collins* 1955. Illustrated by Mary Gernat. Lively story of circus families tenting about England, and in particular two children with their lions and horses.

Haskell, Arnold. FELICITY DANCES. *Nelson* 1937. An early ballet story based on fact and with emphasis on ballet technique and training.

Hewitt, Hilda. PANTOMIME CHRISTMAS. *Dent* 1955. Illustrated by Terence Freeman. An ordinary child involved in pantomime excitement but deciding not to go on the stage permanently in spite of success; refreshingly sane.

*Moore, George. EVELYN INNES (1898). *Benn* 1929.

*Spring, Howard. SAMPSON'S CIRCUS 1936, TUMBLEDOWN DICK 1939. *Faber*. Illustrated by Steven Spurrier.

*Streatfeild, Noel. BALLET SHOES. *Dent* 1936. *Penguin* (Puffin Story Books) 1949. Illustrated by Ruth Gervis. THE CIRCUS IS COMING, illustrated by Clarke Hutton. *Dent* (1938) 1948 (revised edition).

*Streatfeild, Noel. WHITE BOOTS 1951, WINTLE'S WONDERS 1957. *Collins*. Illustrated by Richard Kennedy.

Ure, Jean. DANCE FOR TWO. *Harrap* 1960. Illustrated by Richard Kennedy. Two children of different countries and social background make friends during ballet career. Interesting character studies.

*Vipont, Elfrida. THE LARK IN THE MORN 1948, THE LARK ON THE WING 1950, THE SPRING OF THE YEAR 1957, illustrated by T. R. Freeman. FLOWERING SPRING 1960, illustrated by Shirley Hughes. *O.U.P.*

Drawing by T. R. Freeman for Elfrida Vipont's LARK ON THE WING (O.U.P.)

Chapter 11 | *Good Chaps and Bad Chaps*

So far I have not felt it a disadvantage to be an adult commenting on children's books. In the realms of fantasy, adult and child read in the same way and look for the same things: the difference is one of degree only. The books I have discussed in the last chapter (success stories about schools or ponies or the theatrical world) perhaps offer less to adults than some other kinds, but they are interesting as a guide to what young people want and the clues they give are very definite. We come now to adventure stories, which adults must read in two different ways. If I am rereading a tale which I knew as a child, so that the suspense element is absent, or lessened, I find I am free to notice the characters and the background as I never did before; and I demand more from these than a child would. If I pick up an adventure story that is new to me, I try to read it (and am often compelled to) as a child reads, purely for the story—for 'what happens next'. The story, if it is a good one, carries me away: afterwards, I can consider the characters, the whole technique.

Obviously, action must come first. We must have a plot. We must, equally, have a background. Events must happen somewhere, and more often than not, background and plot have evolved together. Africa and KING SOLOMON'S MINES, Mississippi and HUCKLE-BERRY FINN, Arizona and Zane Grey's WILDFIRE, South America and THE TAKING OF THE GRY—you cannot separate the two elements. But what about character?

Dominating the adventure story is the formula of good chap versus bad chap. We are not to look for changes of heart, as a rule; complexity in character might slow down the action. The most interesting thing about adventure stories is the way character, persistent as weeds or woodworm, pokes up its head when you think it is dead, says its say in the middle of the banging and crashing. The force of an interesting character comes stealing upon you, making a gradual but permanent impression. Though you may have been aware only of an exciting sequence of events, you realize in the end that character has been at the bottom of it all.

It may be there for a very simple reason. Most of us, young or old, have dreams of a life more exciting than the one we lead. The gangs that children form for their own aggrandizement are repeated in another form in the stories about Bulldog Drummond, or Biggles and his pals, or the adventure-prone trio, Colt and Co., in J. Macdonnell's Australian tale. People like this do not have to look for adventure. It comes to them, and they take us with them into a world which we accept whole-heartedly in all its violent improbability. Because this is so, we can excuse the fascist outlook and the near-cruelty of the Drummond tales or the facetiousness of Biggles. They are still good yarns that carry us along. They satisfy us, whatever age we are, because, in them, action and motive are clear-cut, free from the confusions and divagations of real life. They make us feel that we too could act freely and courageously in exciting circumstances.

What happens next matters to us very much in this kind of book. In the case of a writer of Buchan's calibre it matters even when we know it already. THE THREE HOSTAGES is just as compelling at a tenth reading as it is at the first. Perhaps there is such a thing as a 'born story-teller'. It is certainly a way of saying that one writer can make you believe in the simple exploits of his characters where another, far more sensational, merely bores you. But a good narrative is a matter of craftsmanship—an adventure story particularly. You can read it again and again because when the element of surprise has gone, suspense remains, and motive, and authenticity. It is easy to parody Buchan, because the ingredients of his plots (disguise and escape) are elementary. But he wins his readers by the skill with which he holds off revelation till the last possible moment, by the vitality behind his villains and villainous places, and by the heroes he gives his readers—strong, sensitive and sensible, the unmistakable heroes of a dream-world.

The people in this dream-world are of first importance. If, in an adventure story, we see action concentrated and energized, in its characters we see people like ourselves, but larger, more upstanding, more vital. In THE SPANISH CAVE by Geoffrey Household, a really spectacular adventure story for children, the writer leads on from point to point, holding attention partly by the extraordinary events he describes, partly by his characters. This is the most superbly improbable plot I have come across for a long time, and I must not spoil it for those who do not know it. Part of the pleasure in reading it is in asking questions. Why is the cave on the Asturian coast dreaded by the villagers? For how many centuries has its mystery existed? The author lets out the secret grudgingly and expertly. All the time he avoids too much pressure on credulity by bringing first one character and then another into the foreground—the eager young English boy, Dick Garland; Lolita, the young countess, brave and tomboyish; the Basque shipwright, Echegaray, with his inheritance of magical lore; Pablo, the faithful fisherman. Lightly sketched, but sketched in action, they are so real that they make it impossible to doubt the adventure; only these people, you feel, would have embarked on such an enterprise and come out alive.

Another masterpiece of craftsmanship, which goes more deeply into character, is Masefield's DEAD NED. This is the story of a man who was hanged for murder and brought to life again. But this happening is not so much the climax of the story as the resolution of it. The climax is the murder itself, discovered only after the reader has been almost unbearably expecting it through the events of a long summer's day in a village near London, in the late eighteenth century. The old Admiral who is murdered is friend and benefactor to young Ned Mansell, a medical student near the end of his apprenticeship. The first part of the book establishes place and characters, deliberately and with superb timing; it establishes Ned's innocence and enlists your active sympathy for him as he tells his story. From the Admiral's house, centre of the action, which you come to know and to visualize in great detail, you move out to the surrounding country, beyond that to the alleys of London town, and further still, to glimpses of the French and English courts. The background gives the story breadth: the foreground is established with circumstantial detail that has great interest of its own. Every detail, every person has a place in the slow accumulation of events. Even the minor characters—like Jane Jollycok in her pedlar's stall at the fair, or Dick Copshrews who has cost his father so much money, or pretty Polly, daughter of the Admiral's housekeeper—in some way affect the chances and catastrophes of the dreadful day that takes Ned to

Newgate. Fate is against Ned, but so is his temperament. Events follow their pattern because he has an affectionate, intuitive nature; because the Admiral is crusty and secretive; because Dennis Rackage is too mean-spirited to bear his step-brother's prosperity.

DEAD NED is a novel, an historical novel brilliantly done. But it is also very much an adventure story, and one conceived in so classic a pattern, with such a fine technique, that I would offer it to children, first because they will enjoy it, and then because they will understand, eventually, how much goes to the making of a good yarn. They will not, if they read this book at fourteen or so, see all the subtlety and wisdom of the character-drawing, but it will have been the characters, and the way they are integrated with the action, that has held them through the compelling story.

Most writers of adventure stories are content with a rather more simple combination of character and action than this. Certain subjects, indeed, may seem to demand the good chap/bad chap formula and nothing more. E. S. Turner has put it in a nutshell. In his splendid history of boys' literature, BOYS WILL BE BOYS, discussing the scientific magazine story, he says:

> That attempt by Venus to steal the Moon was only one illustration of a failing which characterized the inhabitants of other planets: they were not sporting. Time after time, in stories of planetary adventure, this deficiency was stressed. The dwellers on alien stars might be, and usually were, ahead of us technically; they might have robots working for them as slaves; they might have attained the twin goals of perpetual motion and perpetual life; but they had no more sense of fair play than Neanderthal Man.
>
> E. S. Turner. BOYS WILL BE BOYS (Michael Joseph, 1948) p. 189.

Scientific tales are a special case, of course. For one thing, while scientific teaching lags behind in girls' schools, they will be less interested in technical plots, and if a writer can ignore girls when he is writing, he will have less need to allow for flexibility of character. But do the science stories of the last three decades offer enough even for boys, who are more ready to accept broadly drawn characters? I think not.

Space is the stage for science stories. As a subject it is superb, but few books nowadays have the force and excitement of those old-fashioned practitioners, Jules Verne and H. G. Wells. Inspiration is notably lacking, and so is enterprise. Curious limitations seem to have been imposed. In a great many space stories, the writer con-centrates on the *journey*, which is easier to describe than worlds different from our own. Certainly there should be as much scope for drama in the preparation for a journey into space as in the actual arrival; but, again, many writers concentrate on technical detail and leave out the clash of character which alone could enliven it.

Many space stories, in fact, are stories about machinery. The monotonous exploits of Dan Dare are varied only by changes in technique, and the popular Kemlo books of E. C. Eliott often give me the same impression. In KEMLO AND THE END OF TIME, for instance, the theme is the discovery of a Sphere of Sound where radio programmes and conversations from Earth have been trapped and frozen, forming a rich historical deposit for the people of outer space to study. People from space finding a vessel preserved in space from centuries back—what might they not feel about the past, what might they not be allowed to discover? But no; Kemlo and his friend Kerowski, two space-boys, are impressed, momentarily, but soon rush on to more exciting things—and things, incidentally, which are far easier to describe. When they make contact with space-officers on Earth, you can almost hear the sigh of relief as the author steps back on to known ground. Small wonder that he gives far too many pages to a description of a meteoric storm in space from which the boys rescue a fleet of earth-vessels. The storm itself, the explanation of it, the squaring up for the rescue of the vessels, all take up a good many words. When at last we reach the crisis, what noise, what agitation—and what complete lack of excitement:

The first two ships were about to hit the holding rays when Kemlo yelled:

'Calling all centre ships in formation! Lower holding rays to half distance!'

As Kemlo gave this order, Kerowski manipulated their own holding rays, and at the same moment all the ships around them, except those on the outside edges, brought down their holding rays. In this way the first two of the nine ships were lowered; then the next three, and before the last four could descend farther but were below the height of the outside circle of rays Kemlo almost screamed into the speaker pad, so tense was he:

'They're gathered! Now sweep them away! Full power—twenty degrees right—forty degrees hull incline. Full blast—NOW!' He shouted the last word urgently because no mistake must occur at this moment.

E. C. Eliott. KEMLO AND THE END OF TIME (Nelson, 1957) pp. 166-7.

You have only to compare this passage with one of the really fine descriptions of urgent action (for instance, the dismasting of the *Hurrying Angel* in Masefield's VICTORIOUS TROY, or the fight between Curtis and Twala in KING SOLOMON'S MINES) to see where the trouble lies. Imagination is lacking, and the action never comes to life.

Without imagination—strong, vigorous, free-ranging imagination—it is no use writing space-stories for children except for their very temporary enjoyment, and there the field has been fully exploited. No boys' comic or magazine is complete without its space story. No publisher's list is complete without at least one writer who knows how to get into a space-suit. But the really vital writers for children in this sphere are as scarce as inhabited planets. If boys over twelve really want to be stirred by exploration in space, by the feeling of alien worlds, I can only suggest they give up children's books at once and turn to writers like Arthur Clarke and James Blish. Let these guide them into space and the mysteries of science, for their speculation, conceived in adult terms, has the force of questioning youth. No writer of space stories can afford to be limited by what young readers can understand. Which of us can, after all, understand space? But we want, and children want, the feeling of the unknown. No writer who is still mentally tied to the quadrangle and the officer's mess can give us this.

So we come back to the good chaps and bad chaps. Take Dan Dare, for instance. How monotonous, how mechanical, how limited the adventures of this big, bronzed tailor's dummy of a hero! What matters in the Dan Dare stories? First, the machinery—but does it matter? These gravity rays, these streamlined vessels, these mysterious gases—are they really very new? Or does it matter that Dan should conquer all the planets whose inhabitants are so suspiciously like the nigs and wogs of adventure stories forty years back? No, there is nothing stimulating here. This is where we came in:

Once more Dan made a tour of the area . . . The skeleton defences of Tony's battle patrol were thickened and deepened; outposts and O.P.s were set up miles out in the Martian desert, to control the long-range atomic artillery and the batteries of guided H-missiles; the latest forms of anti-spacecraft defence, borrowed from Treens and Therons, were sited in the area, and all around it. When the operation was complete, the helenium mines were powerfully defended on all sides. And when Dan finally handed over command and responsibility to Major Crawford he was satisfied that the area was as near impregnable as human resources could make it.

Basil Dawson. DAN DARE ON MARS (Hulton Eagle Novels, 1956) pp. 83-4.

The books about Dan Dare and the similar space stories by W. E. Johns are full of this brashly imperialistic flavour, this crude reduction of human beings to two camps. Of course every good adventure story has in it the element of conflict as well as of discovery. But even if a space story is conceived in the all too familiar terms of warfare, need it be confined to the struggle of two earth powers to dominate space, or the equally distasteful theme of imperialist conquest? Will no writer go deep enough to show children a conflict with worlds that are really different—as Donald Suddaby almost does in his unusually enterprising PRISONERS OF SATURN? There seems no reason why boys should not be asked to make some imaginative effort, to try to appreciate the possible existence of points of view other than their own; yet in book after book the author makes his space people no more than physically modified versions of ourselves, bad chaps for our good chaps to fight, or good chaps to be taken on the strength.

Of course it is natural that bad chaps, in outer space, should be seen as power-mad, tyrannical, rigid in mind—natural that they should reflect our own present fears.

Equally, the nobler races from other planets can be used to comment on the problems of our times. In TO WORLDS UNKNOWN, by Captain Johns, Rolto, a space-pilot, feels that Earth should be destroyed before her inhabitants have wrecked the universe by their war-mongering; and there are other writers who make this a subject for interplanetary discussion. The idea of an international spysatellite, put forward by the Americans in October of 1959, may be found in Patrick Moore's WHEEL IN SPACE, published in 1956. E. C. Eliott's KEMLO AND THE CRAZY PLANET contains a moving plea that the race of Zanians, still not fully evolved as humans from their web-footed ancestors, should be left alone by men of Earth and Space to work out their own destiny.

In discussing such moral questions, writers of space-fiction have been more, or less, successful according to the force of their imagination.

Donald Suddaby's PRISONER OF SATURN (like many other stories) is based on fear of oppression; but he has really tried to imagine personality and power in extra-human terms. The Will of the Saturnians is expressed, as far as the visiting Earthmen are concerned, in terms of cosmic rays allied to an invincible intelligence. For the benefit of men, a physical appearance is formed to communicate with them. This being, built up rather lumpily of congealed cloud, they nickname Alpha, and it is presented at first in a partly humorous way:

Eyes and mouth might have been playfully designed with a pair of compasses; the nose was beaked, he had no finger-nails, no hair on the fuzzy head, and his chest and back and arms and legs looked as though they were made of discoloured wheat-husks.

'Here!' exclaimed Jonah after a time, somewhat nobly stripping himself of his jacket. 'Put this on.'

In spite of himself he had kept glancing back at the worrying figure and suddenly decided to humanize it a little more. Alpha, of course, had no notion of how to wear clothes, so plain Fred Jones and I had to dress him—lifting the queer, heavy arms and thrusting them into sleeves, buttoning him across the chest, pulling the tweed down properly behind.

'I'll be hanged if I'm giving him my trousers,' said Jonah, standing back half angry, half laughing, to gauge the general effect. 'But you look a trifle better now.'

'*It is an act of what you call kindness,*' the eerie figure pronounced, and we all noticed that his intonation was much more human, a proof of quick learning. '*Spasíbo. Thank you. If it causes you to accept me more easily, it is good.*'

Donald Suddaby. PRISONERS OF SATURN (Bodley Head, 1957) p. 115.

But in later descriptions of this being, and of the glass cities where thought has a local habitation, there is real force and originality. The author has tried to take us to Saturn, not only geographically, but also psychologically. Patrick Moore, from whom we are surely entitled to expect a great deal, has somehow failed to do either. With all the energy and skill he has spent on the invention of supremely terrifying death-rays and ultra-ingenious machines, the planets he describes are really only the same old pantomime backcloth that comes out each year for the next conflict of Demon King and Fairy Queen. There is no feeling that we are in a mysterious unknown world. The characters are almost always men of the familiar pattern, representing either the good British or the evil foreigners. There are, it is true, some Martians, but their thought-processes seem very much like our own: they are out to win land, power, or wealth of some kind and to do down their rivals. Patrick Moore's stories are most exciting, but children will be more permanently satisfied, I am sure, with something like David Craigie's artless tale, THE VOYAGE OF THE LUNA I, where he tells of a boy and girl unexpectedly rocketed to the Moon; for here, together with a generous allowance of bat-like, spider-like and jelly-like creatures (which are *really* frightening), the young reader can follow the adventures of a hero and heroine who are not hard-boiled and invincible, but timorous and brave by turns, sensible and then frantic, one minute longing for Earth and the next minute observing eagerly an entirely new world.

What I miss more than anything else in children's space stories is the element of discovery, that priceless element in any adventure story. What other real excuse can there be for using space as a setting?

In the long run, no child demands that other worlds should be *described*. We have to be made to believe in them by the force of suggestion, by arrangement of significant details; by the glancing, poetic descriptions, for instance, in Paul Berna's THRESHOLD OF THE STARS and its sequel CONTINENT IN THE SKY. His stand-point is expressed by M. Wertz, a school teacher in the sealed experimental station where space-vessels are launched to circle the Moon:

'The Moon may well seem to you to be another living, friendly planet like our Earth. Do not believe it: it is a dangerous world burnt out alternately by roasting heat and freezing cold, in which nothing is on a human scale. My first lesson in lunar geography may perhaps disabuse you of that inclination towards the marvellous which is only natural at your age. You have this consolation, children—soon you will come to agree with me that scientific fact is just as enthralling as legendary fiction.'

What followed swept from our heads all the pretty pictures that had amused past generations. None the less this strictly scientific viewpoint which he substituted left a door through which the imagination could range, and I think many of us felt the poetry that shone from the dead planet.

Paul Berna. THRESHOLD OF THE STARS. Translated by John Buchanan-Brown. (Bodley Head, 1958) pp. 32-3.

And what child would not find his mind suddenly racing after reading the test-pilot's description of the crystalline formations on Copernicus which, when the sun catches them, look like 'fields of dazzling roses', or the impressionist picture of a journey through a canyon on the Moon (in CONTINENT IN THE SKY) where a 'sheer wall of delicately tinted lava, like an immense stained-glass window . . . glowed an instant and then was swallowed up in darkness behind us.'

Ultimately, though, Paul Berna's space stories are valuable for their characters. The details of the use of space ships, for instance, which can be wearisome even to the most scientifically-minded boy, are floated from time to time on an agreeable personal humour, as in Dimoto's description of the flight of the *Agnes*:

'The newspaper men who were there . . . got together straight away and called the new craft the *flying saucepan* and declared that its first flight would be its last! I gave them forty seconds to laugh their fill and then took off with all eight jets at full power. The roar soon stopped their chatter! I was ordered to go through some set manœuvres at high altitude; that was a piece of cake, then I treated myself to a few low level aerobatics right under the noses of the stupid asses, finishing with a burst of speed that nearly blew out their eardrums . . . Then I brought my flying saucepan down plumb on the launching platform, two hundred yards from the observation post, as neatly as an egg in an egg-cup. The observers who weren't flat on their faces with their hands over their ears fell over backwards to see ten tons of deadweight touch down as gently as a toy balloon.' Ibid., p. 15.

More deeply, the books are concerned with the *effect* of discovery— on the boy Michael Jouffre (who tells the stories), on Captain Bouscart the bully and the mutinous lieutenant Yves, and the Commander himself, who wants power and achievement for his country's sake but who wants scientific discovery far more. There are good chaps and bad chaps here, but something more besides.

Children have a right to that 'something more', and this brings me to the question of the hero in adventure stories. Who is he? And who should he be?

Now adventure—danger and discovery, national or personal conflict—must to some extent be adapted for children. They should be given real dangers, real wounds, but, for them, dead bodies should not lie in the horrifying and soul-cringing postures of bodies in police photographs. There is no room for the sordid in adventure stories, though plenty of room for the disgraceful. Crooks must be wicked: they should not be perverted. Heroes, even if they show cynicism or self-doubt, must have the brightness of the stars somewhere about them. Adventure stories are a form of romance. To this extent they are limited, but they need not be unreal. They must reflect an active world, even if it is a world that no longer exists (like Rider Haggard's Africa, or Masefield's oceans crowded with clipper ships).

This is primarily an adult world, and is best presented, as a rule, with adult or near-adult heroes. The scuffling investigations of children can rarely hold up a tale of great danger, great disaster, great enterprise. That is why the great adventure stories of the past, like ROBBERY UNDER ARMS or LORNA DOONE or KING SOLOMON'S MINES, go on flowering while lesser and more recent books have wilted away; and that is why children have appropriated many modern writers who do not write for them—among the most obvious, Buchan, Masefield, Hammond Innes, C. S. Forester and Nevil Shute.

We have our hero, then, an ardent youth or an active pioneer keeping middle age at bay. What are his adventures to be? Above all, they must have an ideal behind them. The hero must be concerned for a cause, a great love, a treasure-hunt whose end is mystery as well as gain. When we read adventure stories, at any age, we want the power to disengage ourselves from the affairs of this world and to follow by proxy a course of action not wholly materialistic. Allan Quatermain is paid a salary for some of his exploits, but even for a child reader his desiccated and matter-of-fact exterior conceals a romantic heart. Quatermain is a complex character. His superb skill as a hunter is enough for children at their first reading. It is later that they will notice the fears and doubts behind that skill. As a hero, he probably appeals to boys more for what he does than what he is, and yet, rereading the Quatermain stories, I am struck by the way his character dominates these brilliant, exciting tales of elephants and witches, treasure and betrayal.

In much the same way Andrew Balfour's magnificent African travelogue, THE GOLDEN KINGDOM,* can be read simply for such dramatic scenes as the crossing of the perilous swamp or the shooting at the papegai, but in fact the book stands and falls by the character of Corkran the Coxswain, who drags the unwilling narrator, Doctor Mortimer, from his comfortable village practice with the lure of untold riches. Here, as with Alan Quatermain, we have, not a good chap nor a bad chap, but a fascinating amalgam of worthy and unworthy, heroic and unheroic.

Africa, that secret and fabulous land, has always been a mine for adventure stories, most of them conceived as adult novels. There is Buchan's PRESTER JOHN, with its earnest, determined young hero, and its fantastic treasure-house. There is Masefield's LIVE AND KICKING NED, with its vivid descriptions of attack and defence in a Guinea village. There is FLAMINGO FEATHER, by Laurens van der Post, a thriller so compelling that you seem to tread in the footsteps of fugitive and tracker. Against these adult stories, how does the boy hero look, in the story written for boys?

Such stories are most likely to be good if they accept and exploit their limitations; almost certain to fail if they try to pretend that they are not limited. Obviously children can be brave and their adventures can be exciting and dangerous; but they do not often, in real life, meet a villain on his own terms and defeat him, and it is not easy to believe in a story that makes them do this. Nor is the attitude of children to danger usually romantic. It is desperate and direction-

---

* (THE GOLDEN KINGDOM, first published in 1903, has been out of print for many years. It is long-winded in parts, occasionally tedious, but it is still one of the best African adventure stories ever written.)

less, sometimes cunning, sometimes futile and mistaken. So that a writer who embroils a hero of twelve in a serious matter like a native uprising, as Frances Greenall does, for instance, in THE ULENDO DETECTIVES, is asking for trouble. It is true that this author does confine the activities of her young characters to nosing around, tracking and other matters suitable to their years, and keeps them a longish way away from danger. All the same, the telegram that comes to them as a reward for their detective work does suggest what dangerous ground she is treading. It reads like an abstract of a whole class of adventure stories:

'The Brightstones Diamond Corporation expresses its sincere thanks to four young detectives who exposed illicit diamond route from Tanganyika. Present successful operations against smugglers entirely due to information received from you stop. Brightstones arranging one hundred and fifty pounds reward to each detective whose aid they hope to enlist again in future.'
Frances Greenall. THE ULENDO DETECTIVES (Bell, 1956) p. 188.

Far better, I believe, to put your young hero and heroine a little off centre, and give them attendant adults who can at moments of crisis produce commonsense or pistols as required, while the children face danger in their own way. In Masefield's boys' story MARTIN HYDE, a woman spy (who has been outwitted by the young hero) remarks 'a boy is so unexpected, there's no beating a boy, except with a good birch rod.' Any writer who wants to make the best of a boy hero would do well to take this as his motto.

Patrick O'Brian has done so in THE ROAD TO SAMARCAND, a superb picaresque story. Young Derrick does the fantastic journey across the Gobi desert and through Himalayan passes with the support of his tough uncle and the tougher Mr Ross, of Professor Ayrton, whose absent-mindedness is more apparent than real, of Li-Han the Chinese cook and Olaf, the thick-headed Swedish sailor. A good deal of what he does, in fact, is planned for him; but his wits and his powers of endurance are often called upon, and he comes out of the adventure older and wiser. The magnificent adventure, BIG TIGER AND LITTLE CHRISTIAN, by Fritz Muhlenweg, has the same plan. The two boys, one English and one Oriental, are mixed up in Chinese guerilla warfare and they survive because of good luck, because of the kindness of adults, and, often, because of their own resourcefulness, and their boyish talent for turning up unexpectedly at the wrong moment for the villain.

The story-telling magic works best, of course, when the reader can identify himself with the hero, and this may sometimes be easier (though not always so satisfying) when that hero is a boy. One of the best African stories written for children is Roy Fuller's SAVAGE GOLD, a casual, sophisticated tale about the clash of rival mining interests in Kenya, with two boy heroes and two adult supporters. The adults (Mr Craig the District Commissioner and Mr Brown the anthropologist) are pleasantly lazy and like to keep out of danger. The two boys, Charles Craig and Robert Brown, are presented crisply as interesting individuals, Robert with his know-all front, Charles with his affectation of insouciance. Conversations like these are not easy to find in children's stories:

'Makala is boring,' said Charles, as they prepared for bed the first night, 'but if you really want to see them I'll take you round and show you the sights—such as they are.'

'After my experiences on the ship and in Mombasa,' said Robert, a little sententiously, 'I should hesitate before I called anywhere boring.'

'Yes,' said Charles, with a lethargic air, 'I must say you have been involved in a bit of blood and thunder. But nothing like that ever happens to me. I don't think I want it to.'

'Well, then,' asked Robert, with the seriousness of one who imagines he is just beginning to see what life is about, 'what do you want out of existence?'

Charles turned round from an experiment he was conducting at the mirror of introducing carbolic soap with a needle into a pimple on his chin. 'Detachment,' he said. 'The opportunity to observe. To make scientific observations like this.' He wagged the needle.

Robert laughed amiably. The ice between them was broken.

'I must say, Brown,' said Charles, with interest, 'you are one of a very few persons who laugh at me.'

Roy Fuller. SAVAGE GOLD (Penguin, 1957. First published 1946) p. 32.

This naturalness, and the refreshing attitude to adventure, make it easy to believe in the way the boys tackle situations of real danger, as boys and not as imitation adults. Robert, when he is kidnapped

Frontispiece by Robert Medley for Roy Fuller's SAVAGE GOLD (Penguin).
Sets the sophisticated tone of the story

in a brutal fashion, is worried, alarmed, despondent, even tearful.
His plot to circumvent the villain by pouring away all the whisky
intended to bribe the native king is more a hindrance than a help.
The boys react to the war between the king and his usurping half-
brother in a typical way. Charles comments at one point:

'There seemed to be so few of them . . . And the villages were
burning so casually. And then we came along so accidentally. I
had imagined a war to be very different. There is such a lot of
space where the war *isn't*.'
Ibid., p. 123.

And after William, their negro servant, is killed by the enemy, the author touches the event with delicacy and truth:

'The poor fellow's dead.' The Major's hat was in his hand, and he did not know where to look.

'Oh, Father!' said Robert, turning aside and wanting to run away over the huge green country which lay before him, from the ugly body and the warriors standing silently round it. But it was not until William was lifted and being borne back to the guest huts and he saw the dangling arms and the lightish undersides of the bare feet that the full sense of loss was brought home to him. He started painfully and silently to cry.
Ibid., p. 170.

In fact, Roy Fuller has had the courage to show a boy behaving in adventure as we can believe he really might behave, skirting danger and not at all sure if he likes it. Stories like this say something about their characters which is well worth saying.

Adventure flourishes at its simplest and most striking in tales of the sea. An apprenticeship in sail or in steam has always given opportunity for the young to show their gifts, though these have more often been gifts of endurance and patience than anything more dramatic. Here we have a special version of the hero, the apprentice seaman or junior officer of seventeen or eighteen, a boy free from the dependencies of schooldays but not yet cast in the mould of a man; a boy with plenty to learn but with the right equipment for learning, with the ardour and curiosity and energy of his age. Such heroes we find in Masefield's VICTORIOUS TROY and THE BIRD OF DAWNING. These are not children's books—that is, they are not sold by the publisher for children, and they present adventure in a serious adult manner. All the same, no child with any feeling for adventure can afford to miss them. In both stories (they are founded on fact) a young man is suddenly burdened with overwhelming responsibility. 'Cruiser' Trewsbury, a young officer, hero of THE BIRD OF DAWNING, is twenty-two when he meets with the adventure of the drifting, mysteriously empty clipper ship. We can well believe in his skill and enterprise and we are chiefly interested in how he will use his experience. But in VICTORIOUS TROY we are dealing with a lad, Dick Pomfret, senior apprentice of the *Hurrying Angel*. When the ship is caught in a cyclone in the South Pacific, with Mate and

Second Mate dead and the Captain disabled, Dick is taken unawares. He is a worrier, a boy who likes to chew over dangers and approach them slowly. Somehow, with a courage that is blind and muddled and infinitely touching, he collects his thoughts and makes plans for putting over a sea-anchor, cutting away the wreckage of the masts, rigging emergency sails. Some of his plans succeed, others fail. At the burial of the elderly Mate, whom he had liked in an exasperated fashion, he blunders through the few words he can remember of the service, confusedly and in misery, Always, at the back of his mind, he thinks about the support of someone older:

> Crawling away from where he was he thought, 'Why, the officers may be in the half-deck. They may have been swept down here . . . They may have brought Newbarn here . . . Of course: why haven't I thought of that before? That is where they will be . . . waiting for someone to help—Captain Cobb, old Duck, and good old Dudley Mac, that glorious Scot, and Newbarn, saddle-sore from the boom.' Dick was still a boy. Though the sea had given him man-hood before his years, he still hoped as a boy. 'Oh God,' he prayed, 'please let them all be there.'
> John Masefield. VICTORIOUS TROY (Heinemann, 1935) p. 97.

Yet, as the storm rages on, Dick changes. Confidence comes, slowly: he takes courage to assert himself with the Old Man, and even, in a burst of fury at the fate of his fellows, to criticize him. When they are hailed at last by a passing steamer, Dick speaks to its captain as a man. He knows that if he can borrow tools and supplies he can rig the ship and get her to a Cape port. Courage in him has met and responded to the endeavour of the old ship. The spirit of courage and endeavour, victorious Troy, the defeated rising again, this is the theme of the book, expressed in the behaviour of a boy in time of danger; a boy in years and a boy in temperament, so that no young person reading the book could fail to understand and follow his feelings and actions.

With Masefield, as with Conrad, it is endeavour that matters, the motives and the potentialities of the people who behave heroic-ally. The hero is a symbol of the best in man, as well as an individual meeting danger in his own way and in nobody else's. This splendid theme is not easy to use in children's books, where heroism is taken for granted, not analysed. In adult stories, adventure is something that can be real and strong and impressive and yet suffer the indignities and malignities of real life. We can see a hero in the making, whereas, in stories for children, the boy hero usually has his courage already, as an accepted quality, at the outset of the story. Adventure shapes him: he does not shape adventure.

Armstrong Sperry's THE BOY WHO WAS AFRAID is a notable exception. It tells briefly and lyrically the story of a Polynesian boy, Mafatu, who was wrecked as a baby and is haunted by fear of the sea. It is with a boy's limitations that he takes a canoe and pushes off into unknown waters, sails through a storm and lives for a time, in some danger, on a *tapu* island. The theme, the conquest of fear, is studied seriously, in regard to this particular boy. But in another of Sperry's stories, DANGER TO WINDWARD, we have the more familiar externalized adventure story. Our young hero, Hugh Dewar, involved in a family feud, is impressed on to the whaler *Good Intent*. In his adventures on shipboard and on the island of Tongareva he is supported by the young ship's doctor; and in the end he defeats his enemies, white and black, and wins back his inheritance. This is a good adventure story, tough, thrilling, vivid and fast, but it is limited. Action comes first, character second. The two are never, really, interdependent. The majority of children's adventure tales are externalized, and use the formal distinction between good chaps and bad chaps. Given a good story (which is not as easy to find as you would think), these simple characters will do very well; but the story must be especially convincing. Among sea stories, Captain Frank Knight's tales of the great age of sailing ships are outstanding in this respect. THE GOLDEN MONKEY has a boy as hero, seeking for a father lost in the early Australian gold-rush. VOYAGE TO BENGAL has for nominal hero a lad of seventeen working as a foremast hand on an East Indiaman; but in fact this is a spirited contest of good chaps and knaves, rounded off by a romance with the captain's daughter. CLIPPERS TO CHINA, with its tea-race plot, is a straight fight between the ship's apprentice and the sinister First Officer Pengold. Background and action carry these stories through; only the simplest typed characters are needed.

It is no accident that the best stories of adventure at sea are historical in setting and subject. It is far more difficult to make a successful story out of a trawler, a steamship or a dinghy with an outboard motor. The bad chaps of a century ago can be dressed up to suit the author's needs. Their evil deeds wear the gloss of antiquity. But let the writer move from the deck of a sailing ship to a modern steam yacht and he moves at once into hazard. He has got to create modern crooks and here we shall be hampered by reality—for, however imperfectly they understand, his younger readers do study newspapers and have their own ideas about crime. Besides, modern communications have affected the sea story. Anything might happen on a voyage of five or ten weeks; but today, ships being as accessible as any other environment, crooks are merely visitors or refugees— no longer inhabitants of an enclosed and extraordinary world. The sea itself has become a mere background, having no effect on character, mood or action.

Not for all writers, luckily. Allan McLean has sited the adventure of THE MASTER OF MORGANA, most successfully, in a working trawler; and Richard Armstrong, in SEA CHANGE, THE LAME DUCK and NO TIME FOR TANKERS, presents his dirty modern vessels in as exciting a light as even Masefield shed on clipper ships. I was stirred by Armstrong's books, not because Cam Renton's adventures in South America or Greg Harris's in the Persian Gulf were particularly original, but because the purpose of the stories was not, ultimately, adventure. They are stories full of thrills and surprises and chases, but what matters all the way through is the development of character, the making of a man out of the changeable, uncouth elements of a boy.

It is obvious, of course, that a story of adventure *can* only last because of its characters, and this is not contradicted by the paramount necessity of a good story. For it is the characters who make the story move. It is Allan Quatermain who makes KING SOLOMON'S MINES outstanding among innumerable searches for lost tribes and treasure in the African interior. It is the perplexities of Armstrong's young heroes which light up his stories, unoriginal as to plot, of crooks at sea. There are only a few stock adventures on which the writer must exercise his ingenuity—and the illustrator, too, though I myself often find him out of place. Certainly no boy who is eagerly following a fight in his imagination wishes to see one moment of it frozen in a drawing on the opposite page. Scenes of action could only be adequately illustrated by *moving* pictures. Failing these, the author can only hope that his illustrator will try to interpret the mood of his story and create the right atmosphere for him. One

Drawing by Michael Leszczynski for Richard Armstrong's DANGER ROCK (Dent)
Below: Drawing by Edward Osmond for Richard Armstrong's THE LOST SHIP (Dent)

sailing ship, one tanker, is much like another, but an artist with a sure line and a personal vision can make it seem the one and only; and since at the present time illustration seems to be the rule in adventure stories, this is what we must look for.

But the sea is not only a place of transit for crooks and would-be heroes. It is the road to that most romantic subject of adventure stories—buried treasure.

There are few of us who are unmoved by the lure of a desert island which offers privacy and adventure at the same time, few of us who do not feel excited at the thought of hidden treasure. In TREASURE ISLAND, Stevenson welded the Robinsonnade and the treasure hunt together once and for all. This splendid adventure story, written to please his thirteen-year-old stepson, first serialized in a boys' magazine, is built upon *character*; on the opportunism, the sheer nosiness of Jim Hawkins, a boy meeting danger as a boy; and on the bad chap with a heart of gold, Long John Silver, loud-mouthed, sinister, with an intermittent yearning for the good. Barrie's caricature of him, in Captain Hook, only emphasized what children have been discovering for more than a century, that Long John Silver is the most convincing, as well as the most exaggerated, of all story book villains.* The ambivalence of his character is not allowed to upset the balance of the story. Stevenson accepted, like all his descendants, the formula of good chaps and bad chaps. The good chap, by definition, is the chap who has a right to the treasure; the bad chap is trying to take it from him or to get there first. The good chap's right may only be in fact a priority. It may be a matter of sheer good luck, the fact that he is the first to see the map or hear the legend. But we know from the start which side we are on. Just as, in a space story, we accept the author's assumption (not always cheerfully and easily) that Earthmen have a right to colonize Mars or Saturn, regard-

---

* In 1936 Black's of London published a sequel to TREASURE ISLAND by H. A. Calhoun, BACK TO TREASURE ISLAND, which follows up hints for a sequel which the author believes were left deliberately by Stevenson. It is a good swashbuckling tale, with Jim Hawkins and Silver once more opposed on the beach and in the stockade; the language is a tolerably good imitation of Stevenson's; what is missing is the subtlety of character, especially in the case of Silver, who has become an out-and-out villain.

Mention must also be made of THE ADVENTURES OF BENN GUNN by R. F. Delderfield (Hodder & Stoughton, 1956), an ingenious attempt to explain Gunn's presence on the island.

less of the wishes of the inhabitants, so in treasure tales we turn a deaf ear to any possible claim the bad chaps may have.

In a good yarn by Richard Armstrong, THE LOST SHIP, two boys feel it their duty to beat Bull and Mac to the gold on the wrecked *Drachenfels*. The author makes it clear that Shorty and Nick are good chaps and that Bull and Mac are a couple of crooks, and yet it is Bull and Mac who first knew of the treasure and nobody has more right to it than they have. Of course no one is going to question the author, because this is a story, and everybody expects the good chaps to get the treasure. The claim of young David and his uncle is just as dubious in Ian Serraillier's South Sea tale, THEY RACED FOR TREASURE; and in THE TAMBAI TREASURE by R. S. Porteous, the thirteen-year-old hero learns by eavesdropping the secret of a syndicate of Australian businessmen who are after a sunk Spanish galleon.

In a book that turned on character, all this would matter very much. But these are stories of action which, based on apparently concrete facts of place and time and event, belong, really, to an unreal world governed by the strictest conventions. The traditional morality of the cowboy tale sometimes cuts right across the morals of civilized communities. It grows from an environment where violent means may be justified by their ends. It prescribes that the good chap shall always win, no matter what he does in the process. Now this is fair enough so long as we *are* dealing with good *chaps* and not with good *boys*. In the true cowboy story, it is a case of 'children (and women) should be seen and not heard'. This is probably, in part, because the Western story grew up alongside the Western film. Tom Mix and Buck Jones, those cowboy heroes of the 'twenties, belong to the Zane Grey period. Hopalong Cassidy rose to international fame simultaneously in print and on the screen. The exploits of Buffalo Bill and Wyatt Earp were always chronicled both in comics and in films. Where our eyes, as well as our minds, are filled with the picture of a young man leaping on to his horse, we are affronted by the sight of a lad in cut-down breeches doing the same.

This is why Rex Dixon has failed in his attempt to introduce a boy into a man's world. Pocomoto, hero of a series of boys' stories, is an orphan brought up by two old-timers and admirably equipped for outdoor adventure; but he invariably stands on one side of the action. In POCOMOTO—BUFFALO HUNTER, the action is almost all in flash-back, with the boy a ready listener. In POCOMOTO—PONY-EXPRESS RIDER, he has one exciting ride in dangerous circumstances, but he rides as an imitation cowboy, and he is far more interesting as a boy trying to settle down in a respectable household. I would rather prescribe for boys the rattling yarns of John Robb, like SIOUX ARROW and TEN GUNS FOR SHELBY, where the central character is a man. Young Ray Milroy plays a useful part in the stories, but any boy reader will at once identify himself with the enigmatic, tough Captain Shelby. Again, Rutherford Montgomery's Golden Stallion stories have a young hero, still at school though he enters fully into the life of his father's ranch. But although the Golden Stallion's adventures involve men—stockmen, oil-prospectors, dudes visiting the ranch, bad chaps of various kinds—it is really the band of wild horses that chiefly concerns us, and the tang of the open air, in blinding sun or whirling snow, is more impressive than the rather limited clashes of character, the rather perfunctory plots.

In Rutherford Montgomery's tales we are still out West, but the cowboy of today is moving his range, and perhaps in the future the climate of Australia may suit him better than that of Texas or Arizona. Frank Dalby Davison's fine story of a red calf, MAN-SHY, has its cowboys, but they resemble the traditional cowboy only in their monosyllabic names. They are drawn from the life—tough, enduring, speaking only when they have to and then little. This is not a story of conflict between men. Theirs is a geographical problem. How are they to keep their herds separate from the scrubber gangs that roam the waste lands, the rogues and outlaws and escaped beasts whose brands have grown over?

The old energetic life of the Westerns seems to have been transferred. Perhaps the Western as such is finished. Certainly it has dwindled, except in the hands of a few writers, to a meaningless series of fights. These are not in themselves bad for children, in my opinion. They are entirely formalized. The hero and the villain will settle their differences with stereotyped punches, one-two-one-two, and the hero always wins; or there will be a shooting match in which, even if the good chaps and bad chaps get mixed in the reader's mind, he has the comfortable certainty that the good chaps are bound to come out best. There can be nothing either frightening nor misleading in a morality so absolute. What *is* wrong is that the motives of violence, in cowboy stories and in films of today, are so often superficial. The writer will put his best efforts into the action of a story, letting character take its chance. The child reader is bound to gather that cowboys only fight over money or water-holes or such material objects, that personal enmity counts for nothing. There is no room for the real conflict of character which is what he should be persuaded, now and then, to contemplate.

I am sure, anyhow, that every boy and girl should know the traditional cowboy as he once was, and for this he must go to the adult bookshelf. Here he will find stories where men are men and yet may also be mixed, interesting human beings. Among modern writers, there is H. L. Davis, difficult to read, but infinitely rewarding, with pioneer tales like WINDS OF MORNING and THE DISTANT MUSIC. There is Jack Schaefer, with stories like THE BIG RANGE and, above all, SHANE; for Schaefer can put across the man of mystery, the outlaw with a secret, the cryptic hero, as nobody else can at the present time. There is Max Brand's DESTRY RIDES AGAIN, with its magnificent hero-villain. And there is Zane Grey, with his gallery of heroes as dashing as Rupert Rassendyll himself, as tormented as Captain Nemo, as adult as you could wish but with a youthful flame of courage and idealism burning in them.

Nothing is ever simple with Zane Grey. The arresting, brooding peculiarities of the Mormons make gang-warfare seem quite new in THE HERITAGE OF THE DESERT and the superb RIDERS OF THE PURPLE SAGE, and, in this last book, there is Lassiter, one of the most mysterious and compelling of all adventure heroes. There is the historical, pioneering background of FIGHTING CARAVANS or THE THUNDERING HERD. There is the fascination of horse-breaking, the pure breath of the open spaces, in WILDFIRE, and, besides, the romantic force of the character of Slone. There is everything here for the boy or girl who will take a chance on occasionally wearisome passages. For, if Zane Grey's style is sometimes slow, at other times it moves faster than a wild mustang. He has the two priceless gifts for a writer of adventure stories—he can describe action and he can create character. It is the duty of the writer to isolate the moment of action from the hours of inaction, to prove that life is exciting. And he can only do this if, even as he sweeps his reader right away from the ordinary world, he takes with him into the unknown parts of sea or land or air, not good chaps and bad chaps, but men.

Reading List

1.*Space stories*

*Berna, Paul. THRESHOLD OF THE STARS (1954 France) 1958, illustrated
by Geraldine Spence. CONTINENT IN THE SKY (1955 France) 1959,
illustrated by Janet Duchesne. *Bodley Head*. Translated by John
Buchanan-Brown.

*Craigie, David. THE VOYAGE OF THE 'LUNA I'. *Eyre & Spottiswoode* 1948.
Illustrated by Dorothy Craigie.

Cross, John Keir. THE ANGRY PLANET 1945, S.O.S. FROM MARS 1954. *Hutchinson*. Mock-veracious accounts of expeditions, startling and exciting.

*Dawson, Basil. DAN DARE ON MARS. *Hulton* (Eagle Novel) 1956.

*Eliott, E. C. KEMLO AND THE CRAZY PLANET 1954, KEMLO AND THE END
OF TIME 1957. *Nelson*. Many other titles. Illustrated by Bruce Cornwall.

*Johns, Capt. W. E. TO WORLDS UNKNOWN. *Hodder & Stoughton* 1960.
Illustrated by Stead.

*Moore, Patrick. THE MASTER OF THE MOON 1952, THE FROZEN PLANET
1954. *Museum Press*. WHEEL IN SPACE. *Lutterworth* 1956. RAIDERS OF
MARS 1959, CAPTIVES OF THE MOON 1960. *Burke*.

*Suddaby, Donald. PRISONERS OF SATURN. *Bodley Head* 1957. Illustrated
by Harold Jones.

Walters, Hugh. BLAST OFF AT WOOMERA 1957, THE DOMES OF PICO 1958,
OPERATION COLUMBUS 1960. *Faber*. Contest of British and an enemy power
on the Moon. Good example of imperialistic type of space-story, with little
time for describing space and rather bloodthirsty emphasis on violence and
physical suffering.

2.*African adventure*

*Balfour, Andrew. THE GOLDEN KINGDOM (1903). *Nelson* (1916) 1920.

*Buchan, John. PRESTER JOHN. *Nelson* 1910. *Penguin* 1956.

*Fuller, Roy. SAVAGE GOLD. *John Lehmann* 1946. *Penguin* (Puffin Story Books)
1957. Illustrated by Robert Medley.

*Greenall, Frances. THE ULENDO DETECTIVES. *Bell* 1956. Illustrated by Michael
Ross.

Guillot, René. ELEPHANT ROAD (1957 France). *Bodley Head* 1959. Translated
by Richard Graves. Illustrated by Don Higgins. Ivory Coast, boy seeking
father in the jungle; background of film-making among animals in the wild.

Guillot, René. THE WHITE SHADOW (1948 France). *O.U.P.* 1959. Translated by Brian Rhys. Illustrated by Faith Jaques. French West Africa, mysterious bond between French girl and African orphan. Wonderful atmosphere and background.

*Haggard, H. Rider. KING SOLOMON'S MINES (1885). *Penguin* (Puffin Story Books) 1958. ALLAN QUATERMAIN (1887). *Macdonald* 1949. NADA THE LILY (1892). *Dent* (1933) 1959. THE IVORY CHILD (1916) *Cassell* 1926. THE HOLY FLOWER (1915). *Macdonald* 1954. ALLAN AND THE ICE GODS. *Hutchinson* 1927. ALLAN'S WIFE AND OTHER TALES (1889). *Macdonald* 1951.

*Masefield, John. LIVE AND KICKING NED. *Heinemann* 1939.

*Post, Laurens van der. FLAMINGO FEATHER. *Hogarth Press* 1955.

3.*The Sea and Treasure Islands*

*Armstrong, Richard. SEA CHANGE 1948, DANGER ROCK 1955, illustrated by Michel Leszczynski. THE LOST SHIP 1956, illustrated by Edward Osmond. NO TIME FOR TANKERS 1958, illustrated by Reginald Gray. THE LAME DUCK 1959, illustrated by D. G. Valentine. *Dent.*

Armstrong, Richard. HORSESHOE REEF. *Dent* 1960. Illustrated by D. G. Valentine. Wrecking on remote island in North Sea: two boy heroes.

Catherall, Arthur. DANGEROUS CARGO. *Dent* 1960. Illustrated by Geoffrey Whittam. Contest between honest and crooked tug-masters over wrecked ship in Java Sea which carried illicit arms.

*Knight, Captain F. THE GOLDEN MONKEY 1953, illustrated by J. S. Goodall. VOYAGE TO BENGAL 1954, CLIPPERS TO CHINA 1955, illustrated by Patrick Jobson. *Macmillan.*

*Masefield, John. THE BIRD OF DAWNING 1933, VICTORIOUS TROY 1935. *Heinemann.*

Masefield, John. THE TAKING OF THE GRY. *Heinemann* 1934. Two young men stealing Dutch ship from Santa Barbara harbour in time of revolution; incomparable mixture of meticulous detail and suspense.

*McLean, Allan. THE MASTER OF THE MORGANA. *Collins* 1960.

*Porteous, R. S. THE TAMBAI TREASURE. *Angus & Robertson* 1958. Illustrated by Wal Stackpool.

*Serraillier, Ian. THEY RACED FOR TREASURE. *Cape* 1946. Illustrated by C. Walter Hodges.

*Sperry, Armstrong. THE BOY WHO WAS AFRAID. *Bodley Head* 1942. Illustrated by the author. Published in U.S.A. in 1940 as CALL IT COURAGE.

*Sperry, Armstrong. DANGER TO WINDWARD (1947 U.S.A.). *Bodley Head* 1952. Illustrated by the author.

*Stevenson, R. L. TREASURE ISLAND (1883). *Dent* (Children's Illustrated Classics) 1948. Illustrated by S. Van Abbé. *Penguin* (Puffin Story Books) 1946.

4.*Cowboy stories*
*Brand, Max. DESTRY RIDES AGAIN (1930). *Pan* 1950.
*Davis, H. L. WINDS OF MORNING. *Cassell* 1952. THE DISTANT MUSIC. *Gollancz* 1957.
*Davison, Frank Dalby. MAN-SHY: A STORY OF MEN AND CATTLE. *Angus & Robertson* (1931) 1947. *Penguin* (Puffin Story Books) 1956. Also published as THE RED HEIFER. *Eyre & Spottiswoode* 1949.
*Dixon, Rex. POCOMOTO—PONY-EXPRESS RIDER 1953, POCOMOTO—BUFFALO-HUNTER 1954. *Nelson*. Many other titles. Illustrated by Jack Harman.
*Grey, Zane. RIDERS OF THE PURPLE SAGE (1912 U.S.A.) 1954, THE HERITAGE OF THE DESERT (1910 U.S.A.) 1956, WILDFIRE (1917 U.S.A.) 1920. *Nelson*.
Grey, Zane. THE THUNDERING HERD (1925 U.S.A.) 1958, FIGHTING CARAVANS (1929 U.S.A.) 1930. *Hodder & Stoughton*. Many other titles available in paper-back editions.
*Montgomery, Rutherford. THE CAPTURE OF THE GOLDEN STALLION 1954, THE GOLDEN STALLION'S REVENGE 1955, THE GOLDEN STALLION TO THE RESCUE 1956. *Hodder & Stoughton*. Illustrated by George Giguere.
*Robb, John. SIOUX ARROW 1956, TEN GUNS FOR SHELBY 1958. *Hutchinson*.
*Schaefer, Jack. SHANE 1954, THE BIG RANGE 1955. *Deutsch*.

5.*Miscellaneous adventure stories*
*Buchan, John. THE THREE HOSTAGES. *Hodder & Stoughton* 1924. *Penguin* 1953.
Catherall, Arthur. LAPLAND OUTLAW. *Dent* 1960. Illustrated by Fred Wood. Threat to private herd by crooked syndicate: fine action and local colour.
Dillon, Eilís. THE SAN SEBASTIAN. *Faber* 1951. Illustrated by Richard Kennedy. Boy discovers galleon off Connemara coast: adventures with Norwegian sailors and discovery of treasure.
Durrell, Lawrence. WHITE EAGLES OVER SERBIA. *Faber* 1957. Secret service agent in Yugoslavian mountains. The effort, boredom and fatigue of guerilla warfare are excellently conveyed.
*Household, Geoffrey. THE SPANISH CAVE (1936). *Bodley Head* 1960.
*Johns, Capt. W. E. BIGGLES SWEEPS THE DESERT 1942 (Sahara), BIGGLES

BREAKS SILENCE 1949 (Antarctic), BIGGLES GOES HOME 1960 (India). *Hodder & Stoughton*. Illustrated by Stead.

Johns, Capt. W. E. BIGGLES TAKES CHARGE 1956 (Southern France), BIGGLES BURIES A HATCHET (N. Russia). *Brockhampton* 1958. Illustrated by Stead. A selection from innumerable titles.

*Macdonnell, J. COLT AND CO. IN THE VALLEY OF GOLD. *Dent* 1960.

*Masefield, John. DEAD NED. *Heinemann* 1938.

*Mühlenweg. Fritz. BIG TIGER AND LITTLE CHRISTIAN (1950 Germany). *Cape* 1954. Translated by Isabel and Florence McHugh. Illustrated by Rafaello Busoni.

*O'Brian, Patrick. THE ROAD TO SAMARCAND. *Hart-Davis* 1954.

'Sapper'. BULLDOG DRUMMOND. *Hodder & Stoughton* (1920) 1953. Many other titles about this hero.

Drawing by Faith Jaques for René Guillot's THE WHITE SHADOW (*O.U.P.*)

Chapter 12 | *Truth and Ginger-bread Dragoons*

Adventure here and now, adventure in the past—whichever we are dealing with, problems of balance will have to be faced. Character, setting, plot—the importance of each must be decided. But when we come to the historical story we must ask another question. How is fact to be balanced with fiction? The journey into the past gives an *impression*, whole and vivid; it depends on atmosphere; fact is subordinated to fantasy. The writer of a straight historical story has got to deal far more directly with the stuff of history, and here lies his difficulty.

For the more fact he has to deal with, the more imagination he will need to carry it off. It is not enough to be a scholar, essential though this is. Without imagination and enthusiasm, the most learned and well-documented story will leave the young reader cold, where it should set him on fire. Stevenson, writing of a child's imagination,* says that 'he cares no more for what you call truth, than you for a ginger-bread dragoon.' As adults, if we do not care for ginger-bread dragoons, we enjoy them in fancy-dress very much; but we read historical stories with a conscious suspension of belief, aware all the time that we are reading a story. With children, fact and fiction fuse, or should fuse, into a warm, exciting whole. Historical fact should not strike them as fact at all; it should live in the story.

How many people of my generation must have had the historical sense stirred in them for the first time by stories like Kipling's THE KNIGHTS OF THE JOYOUS VENTURE, or by the superb purple passages in Van Loon's HISTORY OF MANKIND, or by the dashing romances of Dumas? Now it would not be possible to write an essay on early explorations of Africa based on Kipling's story; to rely on

* R. L. Stevenson. TRAVELS AND ESSAYS (Scribner, New York, 1898) vol. 3, pp. 147–8.

Van Loon's prehistory today would be to make many false statements; to take Dumas's Buckingham as the whole man, or even as a reasonably accurate portrait, would be a mistake. Yet these books gave us a priceless feeling of the past. They may have taught us very little accurate history; but they made us *want* to learn more. Imagination must come first. This is not to say that we do not, always, need accuracy. But we need boldness as well, and better a few mistakes made in the heat of writing, a few omissions, a few prejudices, than a book that is still-born in a superfluity of facts.

Thirty-four years ago M. G. Bonner, in a critical book on children's reading,* said that once you had mentioned Buchan and Masefield, 'the forecast for historical romances is not very bright.' Today, historical stories for children are sure sellers from any publishing house and the standard of style, documentation and narrative is very high. Still, there are relatively few stories that will swing and startle and electrify a child into real imaginative experience; we must find and hold fast those writers, past and present, who can provide such stories.

A child's imagination will often be more easily roused if he is reading about a character like himself, whose feelings and actions he can understand even if they are conspicuously different from his own. Historical writers of today often present their story in terms of the modern world, as an eye-witness account, often a first person account. The modernization of history can be successful even at its most extreme. Roger Lancelyn Green used mythological history boldly in MYSTERY AT MYCENAE, when he told the story of Helen of Troy as a modern detective-story, with Ulysses (naturally) as chief detective. His vivid story of the Argonauts and their journey from Colchis with the Golden Fleece, THE LAND BEYOND THE NORTH, reads like a thriller by Hammond Innes. John Masefield's two stories of the Eastern Roman Empire, BASILISSA and CONQUER, with their pattern of social revolution, their colloquial dialogue and wholly contemporary feeling, achieve a special liveliness by this kind of presentation. (These last two are adult novels, but I warmly recommend them to older schoolchildren.)

It is in dialogue that we see most clearly the way historical stories have changed during the present century. You can write historical dialogue in two ways. You can work out an approximation of the

* M. G. Bonner. PARENTS' GUIDE (Funk & Wagnall, 1926) pp. 64–5.

language of your period. At its worst this method degenerates into a ludicrous pishtushery, and those writers are fortunate who have chosen a period for which an approximation is impossible. At its best, archaic or antique idiom is supremely well suited to moments of lofty importance, and many present-day writers use it like this, occasionally and with effect—among them Hilda Lewis and Jane Oliver. This is a welcome change from the clotted and jewelled language which was in vogue two generations ago, and the tense or dramatic moments of history stand out in relief if the rest of the dialogue is simple and everyday, as we know it. In Pauline Clarke's novel of Henry V's times, THE BOY WITH THE ERPINGHAM HOOD, we have, as it were, an eye-witness account, not only of Norwich with its monastic houses, its markets and festivities, but also of Harfleur and Agincourt. The Londoners discuss the war which they can fore-tell from the piling up of supplies and the building of new ships. The dialogue is colloquial, designed to give an immediate, vivid picture; for instance, in this description of the Norwich wrestlers waiting to perform at Windsor before the King:

> A man in motley leaped out of a tree into the middle of the nervous men, making them jump and curse before they laughed.
> 'Scram! Scatter! Pass along from the clearing please! No standing about 'ere, his Grace is to watch some half-baked, rough wrestlers from a little village called Norridge who will tear each other to pieces with their Norfolk outplay.'
> He laid about him with a blown-up bladder on the end of a stick, hitting whoever was in his way.
> 'You fool, we *are* the wrestlers,' William Thweyt snapped. 'From the city of Norwich.'
> The fool smiled slyly, he knew this perfectly well. He somer-saulted out of the way, making faces at them through his legs each time and tripping over his balloon. They roared with laughter, and felt better.
> Pauline Clarke. THE BOY WITH THE ERPINGHAM HOOD (Faber, 1956) p. 37.

The battle of Agincourt is dealt with in the same practical vein. We are conscious of the weather, the men's fatigue and hopelessness, the details of strategy, the camp-fire and the tending of weapons. But there is a slight heightening of tension, an echo of Shakespeare's grand manner, to isolate the end of the description of Agincourt:

The king had raised his hand. He looked pale and exhausted, but his eyes glittered with triumph. It had begun to rain again.

'Fellows,' he said. 'We thank you. England thanks you. To-day is the feast of Saints Crispin and Crispian. It will never dawn, but Englishmen will remember this field. Now let not any man take himself the glory which is God's alone. Sing you therefore his praises and keep you yourselves in his grace, through whom he has laid this host in the dust.'

Ibid., p. 127.

Some writers today compromise by using a neutral style, with a sprinkling of period words—as indeed did Scott and Charles Reade a long time ago. Rhoda Power carries her scholarship easily in the language of REDCAP RUNS AWAY, a story of the late Middle Ages. Cynthia Harnett uses historical technical terms with great skill, but she has given herself an extra aid by using line-drawings to do some of the work for her. Carola Oman, a better historian than any of these, is defeated by erudition. Here are two children discussing a troupe of wandering jongleurs, in the time of King John:

'Like those that came and performed in the Great Hall last Martinmas,' agreed Ferry. 'There was a singing damsel with them no taller than you, though, judging by her face, a little older may-hap. She was a jocund little piece, as rosy and brown as a robin. I saw her afterwards in the stables, together with a whole parcel of our fellows, very merry, slaying fleas and drinking ale. One of our fellows accollared her and kissed her, whereat one of the fellows that had come with her smacked her face and knocked him down. There was a great bru all amongst the burning straw (for they had overturned a torch), some of our hounds joining in . . .'

Carola Oman. FERRY THE FEARLESS (Penguin, 1945) p. 38.

This is a stilted way of describing a domestic episode.

If you can modernize historical dialogue, you can also, of course, modernize characters. What boy or girl could not find a parallel among their acquaintance for Sir Fulk de Grandmesnil, one of the knights in Ronald Welch's KNIGHT CRUSADER ? Here he is holding forth about the iniquity of an Arab doctor:

'Do you know what he had the infernal impudence to tell me? . . .

Told me that the best treatment for sword wounds was clean bandages and fresh air. To me, who've been wounded scores of times! Everyone knows the only thing to do is to tie the wound up, keep the air out, and let the blood and pus sort themselves out. If they don't, then it shows your blood is unhealthy, and that's the end of you.'
Ronald Welch. KNIGHT CRUSADER (O.U.P., 1954) p. 47.

Jack Lindsay used this method of presenting character a quarter of a century ago, when, in RUNAWAY, he told simply and racily the story of Brennos, a Britain, and Maron from Thrace, slaves who escaped from their master and joined in the rebellion of Spartacus against the Roman legions. We might easily meet the kind of people he puts into this book, just as we might meet the characters in Geoffrey Trease's more recent WORD TO CAESAR, set in the second century A.D. Calvus, king of the Roman underworld, with spies operating all over the Empire, is the modern gangster in fancy-dress. For roadside cafés we have wayside taverns, for chases in car and aeroplane, wild horseback rides. The racy dialogue reflects easily, but in a scholarly fashion, the Roman scene. Here is Manlius, the chariot-racer, talking to young Paul on their arrival at Ostia:

'Somewhere to stay?' he echoed, looking thoughtful. 'I'd steer clear of the inns if I were you—Roman inns are no place for a decent boy to sleep in. Why not get a room for the time being, and buy your food as you want it?'
'I'd sooner do that.'
'Rooms take some finding. The city's shockingly overcrowded, and you don't want to land yourself in a slum. Let me see now ... I know—' He frowned, then gave me a name and address in the Clivus Palatinus. 'They're a very respectable family—one of our drivers, retired now. Mention my name, and they'll let you have one of their rooms. Top floor, I'm afraid, but you won't mind the stairs at your age. Anyhow, it's a good solid building, it won't collapse under you in the middle of the night.'
'Is that usual?' I laughed.
'Happens more often than you think! Too much cheap building —and they stick on too many storeys for the foundations to carry. But this block is sound enough. You needn't worry.'
Geoffrey Trease. WORD TO CAESAR (Macmillan, 1955) p. 163.

How does this work when we leave fictitious characters for historical figures? Understatement is the prevailing tone today. Familiar characters are treated in a deliberately off-hand manner, for the author tries to get behind their historical reputation to see them as ordinary men and women of their time. This, again, has to be carefully done.

In COLUMBUS SAILS, Walter Hodges looks at the explorer's career first through the eyes of an old monk who had seen him when he was a novice, secondly through the eyes of one of Columbus's own seamen. The explorer is presented casually, as a contemporary *would* present him. His ambitions are summarized when a group of sailors sign on for a voyage and are brought up short by the forceful criticism of an old salt:

> 'All right, then, here's what you don't know. Along comes this Admiral Christopher Columbus that nobody's ever heard of, and he enlists a crew for an expedition. He doesn't say where he's going, but he says we'll find gold, and he offers four months' pay in advance, so all we here sign on. And then what do we find? . . . Believe it or not, he says he's going to sail that way, Westwards, to India! India, if you please! When every man with a sound head on his shoulders knows that India lies East, and always will! And that, my lads, . . . is the voyage you've signed on for, and I hope you like it.'
>
> C. Walter Hodges. COLUMBUS SAILS (Bell, 1939) p. 44.

Again, in RED MAN'S COUNTRY, Philip Rush draws a fine picture of Captain John Smith of Virginia. We first see the Captain when he rescues the young Lincolnshire boy who becomes his protégé; we see Smith not with foreknowledge but as simply as young John Brookes did:

> If he was a Willoughby man, he could be trusted and John said he would tell a secret. 'I am running away. It was my school satchel and books I sold.'
>
> The response was unexpected. The gentleman doubled up and slapped his bulky thighs in delight.
>
> John saw nothing to laugh at. 'My aunt says it's vulgar to slap your thighs when you laugh!' he said sharply.
>
> 'Is that why you're running away? No, boy, I'm not laughing

at you, but do you know I did the self-same thing as a boy?'

'Did you now! What luck did it bring you?'

'They tied me to a desk at Lynn! But they couldn't lime me for long. I got clear and jogged around the world a little. I'm not much older than yourself. I was born in 1580, the year Frankie Drake sailed round the world.'

Philip Rush. RED MAN'S COUNTRY (Collins, 1957) p. 27.

Sensible writers use this device sparingly, for it can easily become absurd—as I think it is in this extract from the adventures of a girl in eighteenth-century London:

Prue was not offended. 'Oh please, Mr Johnson', she exclaimed, 'may I see The Dictionary?' She contrived to give it capital letters as if she had been Great-Aunt Penelope.

Johnson looked flattered. 'But that is dull matter for young eyes', he objected half-heartedly.

'No, really, sir, I do want to see how you do it, for I can't imagine how it's possible', said Prue in awestruck tones. 'To list all the words in the English language! And to give their meaning! I hope it will be ready soon, for father has promised to buy a copy, and it will be such a help with my spelling.'

'Females', pronounced Mr Johnson, 'seldom possess the ability to spell or the knowledge of what words to use if they had the power of spelling them!'

Joyce Reason. TO CAPTURE THE KING! (Phoenix House, 1956) p. 125.

All the same, it is sound sense to create a fictitious boy or girl and involve them in affairs of state or with historical characters, so long as the young reader can really believe in this involvement. Philip Rush is particularly ingenious and successful here. In QUEEN'S TREASON, for example, he very naturally combines the story of Edward II, his favourites and his embittered Queen with the fortunes of two boys—Alan Blount, son of a warder in the Tower, and Nicolas, a journeyman stone-mason. Alan is training as a surgeon with John Arderne, himself a servant of Hugh Despenser, the current favourite, so the boy is brought up against matters of state most convincingly; at the same time the real meat of the story lies in the domestic and social background, the London homes of the boys, their work and their play. You can find the same ease of manner in KING OF THE CASTLE, which puts a young squire in the thick of Wat Tyler's rebellion, and in A CAGE OF FALCONS, where Roger Crispin, son of a shoemaker, and an aspiring artist, watches as a Londoner the contest between Henry VI and the Yorkist rival Edward. This is an author who can always make history live for his readers, especially when he is writing of London and Westminster, whose medieval streets and buildings and customs are obviously as real to him as the city of today.

It is easy for children to identify themselves with the past while they are reading Philip Rush's stories. He chooses the kind of situation which they can appreciate—spying, overhearing, fighting— and his details of food, clothes, games, weapons and so on are congenial and interesting. His books are, however, rather light emotionally. He only occasionally shows what adventure *means* to his heroes in terms of emotional strain and inspiration. Children who want to go deeper will appreciate Masefield's stories for boys, JIM DAVIS and MARTIN HYDE, written many years ago, which combine lucid and exciting plots with some fine character drawing. Young Martin Hyde does not like adventure, although at the outset of the story he thinks he does, and all through the West Country campaign of Monmouth against James II, in which Martin acts as messenger for the rebels, we see how events change his attitude. There is a sad note of expected failure in the book which comes from the gradual opening of his eyes to the unromantic side of great causes.

The story starts in a fine, open, active style. Martin, newly come to London from Suffolk to live with his uncle, is leaning on a parapet, looking at the river, when he notices an intriguing passenger being rowed past, intriguing because a sudden puff of wind reveals that he has a false beard. The passenger is an agent for Monmouth and, through his inquisitiveness, Martin is drawn into treasonable activities. Offered far more kicks than ha'pence in the plotting trade, he begins to see adventure less like a heedless boy and more like a sensible youth. His first thought, that he would soon become a General and return to his uncle splendidly dressed ('I thought that life was always like that to the adventurous man') gives place to this view:

You don't know what an adventurous life is. I will tell you. It is a

life of sordid unquiet, pursued without plan, like the life of an animal. Have you seen a dog trying to cross a busy street? There is the adventurer. Or the rabbit on the cliff, in his state of continual panic; he, too, lives the adventurous life.
John Masefield. MARTIN HYDE (Wells Gardner, Darton, 1949) p. 106. (First published 1910).

And through Martin we see, too, exactly what happens in history (or what might be reasonably assumed to have happened). What child does not long to be told exactly what a battle or a siege was like; but how seldom does a writer go beyond the obvious details. Here is Martin's impression of the battle of Sedgemoor:

That morning's work is all very confused to me. I remember seeing men cut down as they ran. I remember a fine horse coming past me lurching, clattering his stirrups, before leaping into the river. I remember the stink of powder over all the field; the strange look on the faces of the dead; the body of a trumpeter, kneeling against a gorse bush, shot through the heart, with his trumpet raised to his lips, the litter everywhere, burnt cartridges, clothes, belts, shot, all the waste of war.
Ibid., p. 187.

The tension and confusion of battle, the different tension of single combat—these are extraordinarily real in Masefield's books.

Present-day writers are doing nothing new, of course, when they cut the cloth of history to fit the form of their own time. Shakespeare's view of Richard III was essentially a Tudor view. Scott wrote in the mood of eighteenth-century Gothic romanticism. Geoffrey Trease, in BOWS AGAINST THE BARONS (published in 1934), presented Robin Hood under the shadow of hammer and sickle, as a revolutionary trying to inspire an oppressed and stupefied peasantry. His book was written in the spirit of the 'thirties and now seems an exaggerated piece of propaganda, as he would be the first to admit.* L. A. G. Strong's study of Wat Tyler's

---

* In an article, 'Why write for children?' (in *The School Librarian*, Vol. 10, No. 2, July 1960, p. 107), he says: '*Silver Guard* was an attempt to correct the romantic royalist vision most children have of the Civil War: if I had written it ten years earlier it would have been a fervent piece of Roundhead propaganda, but by 1947 I was attempting a more objective approach.'

rebellion, KING RICHARD'S LAND, published three years after
BOWS AGAINST THE BARONS, gave a more all-round picture of
feudal tyranny. Nor was Trease the first to present the case for the
ordinary man. Scott had been aware of it and so had Marjorie
Bowen and Herbert Strang in the 'twenties. Trease's effect upon
children, and upon the course of historical writing for children, has
all the same been far greater than that of earlier writers, because of
his gift for choosing his subject so as to show that past and present
are comparable, interacting, interdependent. He applies Marxism
to history with real genius, and, in his later books, very easily. In
THE HILLS OF VARNA, which is set in the early sixteenth century,
he links the Renaissance with the atmosphere of discovery in our
own times, and CUE FOR TREASON, a spy story of Tudor times,
draws a parallel with modern secret service methods.

Interpretation of history has somehow to be reconciled with historical truth, if, indeed, there is such a thing. Obviously it must always be partial truth. We cannot know, even with the fullest use of
contemporary documents, just what a past age was like or how its
people thought and felt. We can only feel towards an approximation
of the truth. This is no reason to condemn historical stories, either
for adults or for children, even if they are prejudiced by the writer's
own ideas. Children's stories in particular must be prejudiced, as a
rule, so that they may be simple. Academic history is a matter of
adjustment, of reservations, of constant parenthesis; but in a story for
children the issues must be clear-cut. A sensible child adjusts his
ideas of history as he grows older, discarding parts of stories he has
read, keeping others. In a book like Hilda Lewis's HERE COMES
HARRY, he may find all kinds of hints which will mean more to him
later—hints about Gloucester's character, his heroic and his ignoble
side, hints about the mental instability of the young Henry VI; but
he will be caught first by the sympathetic portrait of the boy king
and, by contrast, the enmity and ambition of Gloucester (no Crook-
back but, for the purposes of the story, a villain). The author has
decided on an interpretation of historical fact, and her young readers
are all the better for this.

An historical story must have a point of view, though this may
sometimes become a prejudice. Geoffrey Trease recalls how the
BBC declined to serialize one of his stories in Children's Hour because it was 'anti-Cavalier.' He comments:

... it was an attempt to present my own belief that, in every ten people during the Civil War, there were approximately one Cavalier, one Roundhead, and eight others just longing for it to stop.
Geoffrey Trease. 'The Problems of the Historical Story Teller.' *Junior Bookshelf*, vol. 15, 1951; pp. 263-4.

True as this may be, children expect to be on one side or the other. An impartial tale of the Civil War might well be confusing and it would certainly be dull. Trease's own series about this period (SILVER GUARD, THE GREY ADVENTURER and TRUMPETS IN THE WEST) is written from the Puritan point of view, though he deals fairly with the Cavaliers. By contrast, in THE CHILDREN OF THE NEW FOREST, Marryat endears the Cavalier Beverlys to readers of all time, whether they live in a reactionary or a progressive age; all the same, the Roundheads in his story are ordinary, unexaggerated people with their own rights. Rosemary Sutcliff's SIMON has two heroes, one on each side of the war, friends divided by politics but not in heart. This conflict of loyalties makes the book moving and mature, but, in the long run, most readers will plump for the Roundheads, because the author is chiefly interested in them. There is still room, too, for the romantic point of view, if it is fresh and original. Two writers have used brilliantly the story of Charles II's flight after the battle of Worcester. In HUNT ROYAL, David Scott Daniell concentrates on the chase itself; this is a rousing adventure story in which we are on the king's side as a matter of course, not because we really see him as a person at all. Laurence Meynell has taken a more interesting line. Charles's flight, in THE HUNTED KING, is not a national but a local event. In a preface, Meynell explains:

Shortly after World War I when I was an articled pupil in land agency (the Giffards' estate at Chillington was amongst the ones we managed) a man came into the office and said without explanation or preamble: 'My name is John Penderel and I have come for the money for saving the King.' He was in fact a lineal descendant of the Penderels who befriended Charles, and I paid out the requisite annuity to him.

That incident, a piece of live history if ever there was one, started my interest in the astonishing story of Boscobel and the King's secret journey to the coast.

In my version of it the only real invention is the one character Philip; apart from him it is historically true, and it will always surely remain the most colourful and romantic episode in England's long story.
Laurence Meynell. THE HUNTED KING (Bodley Head, 1959).

Philip, the only fictional character, is most important; he and the king are young men in company with older and more experienced people, and this contrast helps to throw into relief the character of the king—innately melancholy, courageous and debonair—and to make history most moving.

We need not be too much afraid of a partisan approach to history. We must allow children some intelligence in these matters. If they read IVANHOE and feel a fine sympathy for the poor Saxons persecuted by the brutish Normans, they will redress the balance by reading a story like Meriol Trevor's MERLIN'S RING, where it is the Romanized Britons who are persecuted by the brutish Saxons. Against a picture of marauding Norsemen they can set Joyce Reason's THE SECRET FORTRESS or Rosemary Sutcliff's THE SHIELD RING, where the Norsemen in Cumberland make a wonderful stand against the settled invaders, the Normans. The invader of today becomes the besieged of tomorrow. The author must choose a period and a point of view and make an honest job of it. This is specially necessary in the case of ancient history, where the background is less familiar to most of us. Here, too, if anywhere, an author must have an imagination well stored and well exercised. This is the moment to speak in detail of Rosemary Sutcliff, whose books are waking as many children to the special delight of Roman Britain as Kipling's did in my day.

The feelings and thoughts of her characters are universal. The hero of OUTCAST is Beric, Roman-born but brought up by Britons, sold as a slave to a Roman senator, serving a spell in a galley, finally returning to Britain to work on the draining of Romney Marsh. The feeling of exile is common to any period, but in this book it is always expressed in terms of a Roman, not of a young man of the present day. The Roman strength, reticence, lack of imagination—all are here. There is no introspection, no sentimentality, no over-subtle motives. The same is true of THE EAGLE OF THE NINTH and THE LANTERN BEARERS, the first dealing with the last years of Roman rule in Britain, the second with the vexed days of Arthur and Vortigern. There is nothing in these books that is incompatible with known fact, historical or archæological, but no detail, likewise, that is not illuminated by a passionate, tense realization of the past, communicated in a very pictorial manner. This glimpse of Arthur in battle is a characteristic example:

It was like Artos to sweep his men into action with the gay notes of a hunting-horn. The sound rose above the battle din, high and sweet and shining as the song of the storm-cock in the whitethorn tree. A great warning cry went up from the nearest ranks of the enemy, and snatching one glance over his shoulder, Aquila saw the flower of the British cavalry sweeping towards them along the tawny slope. There was a swelling thunder of hooves in his ears, and the wild, high song of the hunting-horn as the great arrow-head of wild riders hurtled down upon the battle. At the shining point of the arrow-head, Artos swept by, his great white horse turned for a flashing moment to silver by the burst of sunlight that came scudding down the valley to meet him, the silver mane streaming over his bridle arm, and the sods flying like birds from the great round hooves.

Rosemary Sutcliff. THE LANTERN BEARERS (O. U. P., 1959) p. 216.

Rosemary Sutcliff shows a Britain completely unlike anything we know now, small, claustrophobic, dark, lit up with passionate conflict and passionate loyalties; and the illustrations of her books,

Drawing by Charles Keeping for Rosemary Sutcliff's THE LANTERN BEARERS (O.U.P.)

particularly Charles Keeping's strange drawings for THE LANTERN BEARERS, with their hatching of thick lines, echo this impression.

Very far from our own times, yet all these books will take children back to the past easily because of their vividness. Prehistoric times present greater difficulty. It is by no means easy for anyone to put himself in the place of a tribesman of the New Stone Age, for instance, when that tribesman (as Henry Treece points out) is probably nearer to the natives of Australia or New Guinea than to us. To bring prehistoric times to life, the writer must make a bold attempt to give his characters something to say, something to ponder over, although their processes of thought can only really be guessed at. But most of all, he must interpret history in a rather special way, by the careful selection of details; for in early times it was the means of existence (fire, food, predators, weather) that determined tribal rules and patterns of thought. Henry Treece's MEN OF THE HILLS, a study of the Cattle Folk of the Bronze Age moving in on the Stone Age natives of Britain, is distinguished by this synthesis of domestic life and thought. Here is a description of the men of the flint settlement going out on a wolf hunt:

> The twenty warriors loped on, their thin, delicately featured brown faces streaked with white ochre in a tribal sign, the bear-claw necklaces clacking about their necks, their shiny black hair knotted with bone pins on top of their long heads, or pushed down into white tubes of bone from which the marrow had been sucked. They were in quest of their enemy and must take no chances; so each man wore a broad belt of tough cowhide about his middle and wide bracelets of leather up to his elbows. Old Hair the wolf must not be allowed to sink his yellow fangs into body or arm, for the wounds he made seldom healed, however carefully one covered them with cobwebs or let the good cow milk curdle into them, however many times the Old Man of the tribe, the chieftain, said his spells. Old Hair was a dangerous one to hunt, and a man must be ready for him, always.
>
> Henry Treece. MEN OF THE HILLS (Bodley Head, 1957) p. 10.

Christine Price has drawn for this story pictures which with their bold, simple lines emphasize the contrast between the two races.

Archæological research in the last decade has opened new sources of material for illustrators, and in many of the best stories of early

Drawing by Malcolm Pride for Jane Oliver's THE EAGLET AND THE ANGRY DOVE (Macmillan)

communities (like Kurt Schmeltzer's THE AXE OF BRONZE and Rosemary Sutcliff's WARRIOR SCARLET) verbal descriptions and drawings complement each other admirably. Action is still best described in words; but pictures can give the *feel* of action, its emotional content. The description of the king-making in WARRIOR SCARLET, extremely vivid in the text, is completed by Charles Keeping's magnificent decoration. Again, THE EAGLET AND THE ANGRY DOVE contrasts Druidical belief with Columba's early Christian teaching. Jane Oliver's dramatic analysis of these beliefs is helped by Malcolm Pride's drawings. For periods remote from our own, this impressionistic, poetic method of illustration is supremely well suited.

A more practical, informative style is more often used for stories which are concerned with a technique—a good basis for an historical study of any period. What child ever forgets the detail of how the Beverlys made the stockade, in THE CHILDREN OF THE NEW FOREST. That glorious, multi-coloured jumble, THE CLOISTER AND THE HEARTH, is fascinating most of all because it tells you *how* people do things. In THE BOMBARD, Henry Treece makes the invention of the first cannon the centre of a rousing story of Crecy and its aftermath. Patrick O'Brian's matchless tale, THE GOLDEN OCEAN, is completely instructive, in the most readable way, about the way sailors worked on Anson's frigate in the eighteenth century. Ursula Moray Williams bases THE NOBLE HAWKS on falconry in the fourteenth century, and her book shows what can be done with a domestic subject. Details of a craft must necessarily lead to questions of rank and status, and there is a chance here to cover the social ground without bringing in any political bias. THE NOBLE HAWKS offers not an adventure but a situation—the rivalry between Dickon (who, as a yeoman's son, has the right only to a goshawk) and young Gareth, heir to a Welsh earl, whose skill falls short of his birth.

Cynthia Harnett's domestic stories give the same clear, precise social picture. THE LOAD OF UNICORN, for instance (an uncommonly good story), has for its theme the introduction of printing. Bendy, the boy hero, is the son of a scrivener, who sits in St Paul's writing letters for his fellow-citizens while his sons run the family business of manuscript chapbooks. Bendy, with his father's consent —for John Goodrich feels and responds to the renaissance in learning—goes as apprentice to Caxton, who is newly arrived in London, and it is Bendy who tracks down the paper thieves who are trying to put his master out of business, secures for Caxton an unknown Malory manuscript, and, to crown his efforts, reveals a spy-ring sending information out of England to Henry Tudor. Exciting this plot may be, but behind adventures with spies and robbers, the daily life of Bendy's family is meticulously described. The spy-plot of RING OUT BOW BELLS, set in the reign of Henry V, has the same mercantile setting, while in THE WOOL-PACK (a Carnegie medal award, and deservedly so) we are in the middle of the Cotswold wool trade in the time of Chaucer. Major historical events are kept in the distance in these books. There is no probing of character and only the simplest statements about motives. But there is a sure handling of innumerable details which, like pieces in a mosaic, add up to an accurate and lively panorama of everyday history.

This panorama is mirrored in the author's representational drawings. As a rule she is concerned less with illustrating actual scenes in her story than with annotating it with insets of clothes and weapons, buildings, ships, anything germane to her period. But there is no suggestion of the textbook here, for each object she draws has its place in the story. Bendy's doings, in THE LOAD OF UNICORN, are all the more real because we can see his father's desk and ink-well, the composing-frame he learns to use, and many other tools of his trade.

Costume is one of the easiest ways of setting an historical period on paper, but many artists allow it to become an end in itself. Those of us who first met Jane Austen's characters in the edition illustrated by Hugh Thomson will remember how disappointing were those insipid faces which looked out above the carefully drawn Regency clothes. No illustrator can afford to use his characters as tailor's dummies. If he is going to draw people, they must be people. William Stobbs's gallery of late eighteenth-century types, in Frederick Grice's AIDAN AND THE STROLLERS, shows how faces can be used to bring out points from the text, and in David Scott Daniell's

HIDEAWAY JOHNNY, a Regency story for younger children, Biro's slighter portraits similarly echo the period language.

Clothes, utensils, dwellings—the background of life at any point of historical time—are more interesting as we approach our own times and can better appreciate details of domestic life. Here the keynote is familiarity, and writers and illustrators alike play upon it. Domestic stories written from living memory—Tales of a Grandfather, you might call them—have a particular authenticity and charm, and I am always surprised that more writers do not exploit the tales that are current in their own locality. John Niven's GYPSY IN SCARLET tells of a young man who learns the logging trade on an East Scottish river and then leaves his home to fight in the Crimean War. This does not read like a tale invented or reconstructed. It has the sound of hearsay, almost of gossip. It might have been passed on to the author by an aged relative. Henry Garnett's stories of the Severn barge traffic at the same period (ROUGH WATER BROWN and SECRET OF THE ROCKS) also have the special vividness of localized history.

Barbara Ker Wilson's novels of the recent past gain much from their illustrations. In PATH-THROUGH-THE-WOODS, the story of a girl fighting her way to a medical career in the late Victorian era, each section of the story is marked by a vignette with a family-album flavour, by Charles Stewart, and THE LOVELY SUMMER, a tale of the suffragette movement, is decorated by Marina Hoffer with daintily framed idealizations of the time. The key to these drawings is the phrase 'family album'; they tantalize the memory as well as the imagination.

Among American writers, Lois Lenski is most important as a recorder of social history. To collect material for tales like CORN-FARM BOY, BOOM-TOWN BOY, BAYOU SUZETTE and STRAW-BERRY GIRL, she visited isolated communities in Iowa, Oklahoma, Louisiana and Florida, she talked to old people and noted their idiom, looked at family documents, got the feel of localities whose special character may well be wiped out soon by the standardizing of civilization.

Most vivid of all American tales of this kind are those by Laura Ingalls Wilder, in which she relives her childhood in pioneering days. Her books reflect sincerely the point of view of a child living through difficult and dangerous times, protected by trust in her parents, understanding part of what she sees and observing much more. Here is Laura's impression of her first night on the great Kansas plain:

On the other side of the canvas, Pet and Patty were eating their corn. When Patty whooshed into the feed-box, the whoosh was right at Laura's ear. There were little scurrying sounds in the grass. In the trees by the creek an owl called, 'Who-oo? who-oo?' Farther away another owl answered, 'Oo-oo, oo-oo.' Far away on the prairie the wolves howled, and under the wagon Jack growled low in his chest. In the wagon everything was safe and snug.

Thickly in front of the open wagon-top hung the large, glittering stars. Pa could reach them, Laura thought. She wished he would pick the largest one from the thread on which it hung from the sky, and give it to her. She was wide awake, she was not sleepy at all, but suddenly she was very much surprised. The large star winked at her!

Then she was waking up, next morning.

Laura Ingalls Wilder. LITTLE HOUSE ON THE PRAIRIE (Methuen, 1957) p. 24.

And here is a deeper note out of the memory of the past:

Laura was not exactly scared, but that sound made her feel funny. It was the sound of quite a lot of Indians, chopping with their voices. It was something like the sound of an axe chopping, and something like a dog barking, and it was something like a song, but not like any song that Laura had ever heard. It was a wild, fierce sound, but it didn't seem angry.

Ibid., p. 164.

For a thoughtful child, history personalized in this way has an irresistible attraction, and there is great scope here for British writers.

Fact used imaginatively—this is what children look for in historical stories—a good story and a full, even a crowded background. A quarter of a century ago we used to get these things, in profusion, from historical romances which were not, in fact, intended for children. They suited the taste of older schoolgirls, in particular, very well. Perhaps they still do, those glorious, long-winded, partisan tales of the French Revolution and the Regency. But though

Baroness Orczy and Georgette Heyer are still read and enjoyed by girls (and Jeffrey Farnol, Rafael Sabatini and Stanley Weyman could be, too, if they knew about them), the wind has changed. Our children cannot think only in terms of the dashing Scaramouche or the intrepid Pimpernel. They know too much about the other side. Their eyes have been opened to the less romantic side of these periods of history by C. S. Forester's tales of Captain Hornblower, with their subtle deflating of the pomp and circumstance of war, or by David Scott Daniell's matter-of-fact dealings with the Napoleonic wars through that lively couple, Polly and Oliver. L. A. G. Strong's vigorous story, MR SHERIDAN'S UMBRELLA, has taken them out of the stuffy atmosphere of court life to the Regency Brighton the ordinary tradesman saw.

Those bygone romances may be collecting dust on our shelves now, but many other historical novels will be borrowed from us by our children, for different generations may easily share them. The themes of history are ageless and for no special age. Lost causes, the din of battle, the breaking and making of laws, the founding of dynasties and the tribulations of the common man—all these subjects can be appreciated by children in their full strength. They will pick up their parents' books and have no feeling of inadequacy if the writers who cater specially for them have given them the right diet beforehand. The transition from junior to adult novels will be easy if history has been presented to them, in stories strong rather than sentimental, pictorial and not vague, pointed and not trivial. The best historical stories for children have little or nothing of the juvenile in them.

Reading List

Ashton, Agnes. WATER FOR LONDON. *Epworth* 1956. Illustrated by Monica Walker. Sir Hugh Middleton's scheme of 1609: clever combination of fact and fictional adventure.

Baumann, Hans. THE BARQUE OF THE BROTHERS (1956 Germany). *O.U.P.* 1958. Translated by Isabel and Florence McHugh. Illustrated by Ulrik Schramm. Two brothers exploring west coast of Africa with Henry the Navigator. Distinguished style, packed with interesting detail.

Brink, Carol Ryrie. CADDIE WOODLAWN. *Macmillan of New York* 1947. Illustrated by Kate Seredy. A child in Wisconsin in the 1860's: Indians, school and the delights of home life.

*Clarke, Pauline. THE BOY WITH THE ERPINGHAM HOOD. *Faber* 1956. Illustrated by Cecil Leslie.

Dallow, Mark. THE HEIR OF CHARLECOTE. *Cassell* 1938. *Penguin* (Puffin Story Books) 1955. Illustrated by Arthur Hall. Two boys travel from Stratford to London, ending in Burbage's company. Free, natural narrative, suitable for younger children.

Daniell, David Scott. THE BOY THEY MADE KING. *Cape* 1959. Illustrated by William Stobbs. Perkin Warbeck's tale told in domestic vein, chiefly set in Oxford. Class differences especially well done.

*Daniell, David Scott. MISSION FOR OLIVER 1953, POLLY AND OLIVER 1954, POLLY AND OLIVER AT SEA 1960. *Cape.* Illustrated by William Stobbs.

*Daniell, David Scott. HUNT ROYAL. *Cape* 1958. Illustrated by William Stobbs.

*Daniell, David Scott. HIDEAWAY JOHNNY. *Brockhampton* 1959. Illustrated by Biro.

Fabricius, Johan. JAVA HO! (1926 Holland). *Methuen* 1933. Abridged and translated by M. C. Darnton. Rousing tale of four boys on voyage to the East in the seventeenth century; uncompromising attitude to danger and death.

Forbes, Esther. JOHNNY TREMAIN (1943 U.S.A.). *Constable* 1958. Illustrated by Lynd Ward. Boston at opening of War of Independence: one of the most human and interesting stories about this period.

*Forester, C. S. THE HAPPY RETURN 1937, FLYING COLOURS 1938, A SHIP OF THE LINE 1938, LORD HORNBLOWER 1946, MR MIDSHIPMAN HORN-BLOWER 1950, LIEUTENANT HORNBLOWER 1952, HORNBLOWER AND THE ATROPOS 1953. *Michael Joseph.* Cadet editions, selected by G. P. Griggs. *Michael Joseph* 1954. Illustrated by Geoffrey Whittam.

*Garnett, Henry. THIRTEEN BANNERS. *Bodley Head* 1956. Illustrated by Peter Jackson. Rebellion of Simon de Montfort: emphasis on feudal system and threats to it.

*Garnett, Henry. ROUGH WATER BROWN 1955, illustrated by Sheila Findlay. SECRET OF THE ROCKS 1958, illustrated by Peter Jackson. *Bodley Head.*

Gray, Elizabeth Janet. ADAM OF THE ROAD. *Black* 1943. Illustrated by Robert Lawson. Journey of minstrel's son from London to Winchester and back; panorama of English medieval life.

*Green, Roger Lancelyn. MYSTERY AT MYCENAE 1957, illustrated by Margery Gill. THE LAND BEYOND THE NORTH 1958, illustrated by Douglas Hall. *Bodley Head.*

*Grice, Frederick. AIDAN AND THE STROLLERS. *Cape* 1960. Illustrated by William Stobbs.

Grice, Frederick. THE BONNY PIT LADDIE. *O.U.P.* 1960. Illustrated by Brian Wildsmith. Brilliant evocation of Durham mining village a century ago: fine characterization and a sturdy narrative style.

Guillot, Rene. RIDERS OF THE WIND (1953 France). *Methuen* 1960. Translated by Geo. H. Bell. Illustrated by Richard Kennedy. Boy from river gang, seventeenth century, and his adventures in North Africa. Superb feeling for place and event.

*Harnett, Cynthia. THE WOOL-PACK 1951, RING OUT BOW BELLS! 1953, THE LOAD OF UNICORN 1959. *Methuen*. Illustrated by the author.

*Hodges, C. Walter. COLUMBUS SAILS. *Bell* 1939. Illustrated by the author.

Howard, Elizabeth. NORTH WINDS BLOW FREE (1949 U.S.A.). *Bodley Head* 1953. Michigan in time of Fugitive Slave Law: family helping with underground railway and Freedom Settlement in Canada.

Keith, Harold. RIFLES FOR WATIE (1957 U.S.A.). *O.U.P.* 1960. Civil War in Oklahoma and neighbouring states: Northern point of view. A vigorous and varied tale.

*Kipling, Rudyard. PUCK OF POOK'S HILL, REWARDS AND FAIRIES. (see Chap. 6).

*Lenski, Lois. BAYOU SUZETTE 1943, STRAWBERRY GIRL 1945, BOOM-TOWN BOY 1948, CORN-FARM BOY 1954. *J. B. Lippincott*, Philadelphia and New York. Illustrated by the author.

Lenski, Lois. PRAIRIE SCHOOL (1951 U.S.A.). *O.U.P.* 1959. Illustrated by the author. Based on facts of winters 1948–9 and 1949–50, in South Dakota: a fine example of living history and a good story.

*Lewis, Hilda. HERE COMES HARRY. *O.U.P.* 1960. Illustrated by William Stobbs.

Lewis, Hilda. THE GENTLE FALCON. *O.U.P.* 1952. Illustrated by Evelyn Gibbs. Richard II and Isabella of France: a touching story told by a woman.

*Lindsay, Jack. RUNAWAY. *O.U.P.* 1935.

Lowndes, Joan Selby. MAIL COACH. *Collins* 1945. Illustrated by the author. Light-hearted tale of two children adventuring to London: glimpses of Astley's Circus.

Lowndes, Joan Selby. ROYAL CHASE. *Collins* 1947. Illustrated by the author. Dissolution of monasteries. Set in North Bucks. Excellent background and detail.

Manning-Sanders, Ruth. CIRCUS BOY. *O.U.P.* 1960. Illustrated by Annette Macarthur-Onslow. Boy training with Bright's Circus, tenting through Ireland during Orangeman troubles. Lively mixture of adventure and period detail.

*Marryat, Captain. THE CHILDREN OF THE NEW FOREST (1847). *Dent* (Children's Illustrated Classics) 1955. Illustrated by Lionel Edwards.

*Masefield, John. MARTIN HYDE 1910, JIM DAVIS 1911. *Wells Gardner.*

*Masefield, John. BASILISSA 1940, CONQUER 1941. *Heinemann.*

Masefield, John. LOST ENDEAVOUR. *Nelson* (1910) 1923. Pirates and treasure in Virginia, late seventeenth century.

*Meynell, Laurence. THE HUNTED KING. *Bodley Head* 1959.

Mitchison, Naomi. THE LAND THE RAVENS FOUND. *Collins* 1955. Illustrated by Brian Alldridge. Practical and moving story of colonization of Iceland by the Vikings, ninth and tenth centuries.

*Niven, John. GYPSY IN SCARLET. *Faber* 1954. Illustrated by Richard Kennedy.

*O'Brian, Patrick. THE GOLDEN OCEAN. *Hart-Davis* 1956.

O'Faoláin, Eileen. HIGH SANG THE SWORD. *O.U.P.* 1959. Illustrated by Brian Wildsmith. Eleventh century, Brian Boru and his attempt to unite Ireland against the Norsemen. Exciting and carefully documented with fascinating drawings.

*Oliver, Jane. THE EAGLET AND THE ANGRY DOVE. *Macmillan* 1957. Illustrated by Malcolm Pride.

*Oman, Carola. FERRY THE FEARLESS. *Pitman* 1935.

Parker, Richard. THE THREE PEBBLES. *Collins* 1954. Illustrated by Prudence Seward. Three French boys in new settlement in Florida, sixteenth century: practical and realistic.

Polland, Madeline. CHILDREN OF THE RED KING. *Constable* 1959. Illustrated by Annette Macarthur-Onslow. Thirteenth century, guerilla war against Norman castles in Ireland, with boy and girl heroes.

*Power, Rhoda. REDCAP RUNS AWAY. *Cape* 1952. Illustrated by C. Walter Hodges.

*Reade, Charles. THE CLOISTER AND THE HEARTH (1861). *Dent* (Everyman) 1955.

*Reason, Joyce. TO CAPTURE THE KING! *Phoenix House* 1956. Illustrated by David Walsh.

*Reason, Joyce. THE SECRET FORTRESS. *Dent* (1946) 1950. Illustrated by S. van Abbé.

*Rush, Philip. QUEEN'S TREASON 1954, A CAGE OF FALCONS 1954, KING OF THE CASTLE 1956, illustrated by Martin Thomas. RED MAN'S COUNTRY 1957, illustrated by Brian Keogh. *Collins.*

Rush, Philip. APPRENTICE AT ARMS. *Collins* 1960. Illustrated by Christopher Brooker. Rising of Sir Thomas Wyatt seen by a boy who joined him in march from Kent to London.

*Schmeltzer, Kurt. THE AXE OF BRONZE. *Constable* 1958. Illustrated by M. A. Charlton.

Snell, J. B. JENNIE. *Nelson* 1958. Illustrated by G. K. Sewell. Story of a narrow-gauge railway in Wales and the life of a nineteenth-century family that ran parallel with it.

Sperry, Armstrong. WAGONS WESTWARD (1936 U.S.A.). *Bodley Head* 1948. Illustrated by the author. Vivid tale of pioneering in America in the 1840's.

Strang, Herbert. DICKON OF THE CHASE. *O.U.P.* 1931. Local Robin Hood at end of Wars of the Roses.

*Strong, L. A. G. KING RICHARD'S LAND. *Dent* 1938.

Strong, L. A. G. MR SHERIDAN'S UMBRELLA 1935. *Penguin* (Puffin Story Books) 1949.

*Sutcliff, Rosemary. SIMON 1953, illustrated by Richard Kennedy. THE EAGLE OF THE NINTH 1954, illustrated by C. Walter Hodges. OUTCAST 1955, illustrated by Richard Kennedy. THE SHIELD RING 1956, illustrated by C. Walter Hodges. WARRIOR SCARLET 1958, THE LANTERN BEARERS 1959, KNIGHT'S FEE 1960, illustrated by Charles Keeping. *O.U.P.*

Sutcliff, Rosemary. BROTHER DUSTY-FEET. *O.U.P.* 1952. Illustrated by C. Walter Hodges. Boy travelling South Country with strolling players in reign of Elizabeth.

Swift, Hildegard Hoyt. THE RAILROAD TO FREEDOM (1932 U.S.A.). *Bodley Head* 1960. Illustrated by James Daugherty. Fictional version of story of Harriet Tubman, negro slave and indefatigable rescuer of slaves from South. A sincere and moving book.

Syme, Ronald. RIVER OF NO RETURN. *Hodder & Stoughton* 1958. Illustrated by William Stobbs. Spanish exploration of Amazon after Pizarro's expedition: detailed picture of a terrible journey.

Syme, Ronald. THE FOREST FIGHTERS. *Hodder & Stoughton* 1958. Illustrated by William Stobbs. Two English boys involved in War of Independence. Local interest, a very immediate picture of war.

*Trease, Geoffrey. BOWS AGAINST THE BARONS. *Martin Lawrence* (1934) 1948.

*Trease, Geoffrey. CUE FOR TREASON 1940, THE GREY ADVENTURER 1942, illustrated by Beatrice Goldsmith. TRUMPETS IN THE WEST 1947, SILVER GUARD 1948, illustrated by Alan Blyth. *Blackwell.*

*Trease, Geoffrey. THE HILLS OF VARNA 1948, illustrated by Treyer Evans. WORD TO CAESAR 1955, illustrated by Geoffrey Whittam. *Macmillan.*

Trease, Geoffrey. COMRADES FOR THE CHARTER. *Martin Lawrence* 1934. Vigorous story of the Chartists with strong social moral.

*Treece, Henry. MEN OF THE HILLS 1957, THE BOMBARD 1959. *Bodley Head.*
Illustrated by Christine Price.

Treece, Henry. THE EAGLES HAVE FLOWN. *Bodley Head* 1954. Illustrated by
Christine Price. Britain after departure of the Romans: study of Arthur.

Treece, Henry. LEGIONS OF THE EAGLES. *Bodley Head* 1954. Illustrated by
Christine Price. Roman invasion of Britain; leadership of Caratacus.

*Trevor, Meriol. MERLIN'S RING. *Collins* 1957. Illustrated by Martin Thomas.

*Welch, Ronald. KNIGHT CRUSADER. *O.U.P.* 1954. Illustrated by William
Stobbs.

Wibberley, Leonard. THE WOUND OF PETER WAYNE (1955 U.S.A.). *Faber*
1957. Illustrated by Douglas Gorsline. Southern point of view in Civil War:
boy trying to recover and run his estate after war is over.

*Wilder, Laura Ingalls. LITTLE HOUSE IN THE BIG WOODS (1932 U.S.A.) 1956,
LITTLE HOUSE ON THE PRAIRIE (1935 U.S.A.) 1957, ON THE BANKS OF
PLUM CREEK (1937 U.S.A.) 1958. *Methuen.* BY THE SHORES OF SILVER
LAKE (1939 U.S.A.) 1953, THE LONG WINTER (1940 U.S.A.) 1953, LITTLE
TOWN ON THE PRAIRIE (1941 U.S.A.) 1953, THESE HAPPY GOLDEN YEARS
(1943 U.S.A.) 1953. *Harper*, New York. Illustrated by Garth Williams.

*Williams, Ursula Moray. THE NOBLE HAWKS. *Hamish Hamilton* 1959.

*Wilson, Barbara Ker. PATH-THROUGH-THE-WOODS 1958, illustrated by
Charles Stewart. THE LOVELY SUMMER 1960, illustrated by Marina Hoffer.
Constable.

Worth, Kathryn. THEY LOVED TO LAUGH. *Doubleday*, New York 1942.
Illustrated by Marguerite De Angeli. North Carolina in the 1830's,
Quaker family and their pioneering life.

Worth, Kathryn. THE MIDDLE BUTTON. *Doubleday*, New York 1950. Illustrated
by Dorothy Bayley. North Carolina in the 1880's: girl fighting for the right to
study medicine.

Adult Historical Fiction recommended for older children

Bowen, Marjorie. DICKON. *Hodder & Stoughton* 1929. Still the best sympathetic
study of Richard III.

Bullett, Gerald. THE ALDERMAN'S SON. *Michael Joseph* 1954. Sensible and
lively version of Shakespeare's early life at Stratford.

Daniell, David Scott. FIFTY POUNDS FOR A DEAD PARSON. *Cape* 1960. Napoleonic period, 1806, in an English village.

Duggan, Alfred. KNIGHT WITH ARMOUR 1950. *Penguin* 1959. First Crusade.

Duggan, Alfred. LEOPARDS AND LILIES. *Faber* 1954. Thirteenth century.
Noble lady marries mercenary captain under King John and follows the army.

Duggan Alfred. WINTER QUARTERS. *Faber* 1956. Late Roman Empire. All
Duggan's books are distinguished by his dry sense of humour and extraordinarily actual presentations of the ordinary in the past.

Garnett, David. POCAHONTAS. *Chatto* 1933. Captain John Smith in Virginia,
seventeenth century. Beautifully written and a fascinating story.

Graves, Ralph. THE LOST EAGLES. *Faber* 1956. Roman Legions in Germany.

Graves, Robert. I CLAUDIUS (1934) 1941, CLAUDIUS THE GOD (1934) 1954.
Penguin. Classic study of Roman Imperial rule from the inside.

Heyer, Georgette, THE TOLLGATE. *Heinemann* 1954. Regency adventure,
romantic and exciting.

Irwin, Margaret. ROYAL FLUSH. *Chatto* 1932. Story of Minette, daughter of
Charles I. Touching and wonderfully thorough study of royal family.

Jefferis, Barbara. BELOVED LADY. *Dent* 1956. Masterly use of Paston Letters
to show ordinary people in Wars of the Roses.

Le May, Alan. THE SEARCHERS. *Collins* 1955. American frontier, Texas. Moving
and vivid.

Lofts, Norah. SCENT OF CLOVES. *Hutchinson* 1959. Indonesia, seventeenth
century. Exotic and romantic.

Lofts, Norah. THE TOWN HOUSE. *Hutchinson* 1959. Story of a family and a house
fourteenth and fifteenth centuries.

Masefield, John. BADON PARCHMENTS. *Heinemann* 1947. Superb version of
story of King Arthur and battle of Mount Badon.

O'Brian, Patrick. THE UNKNOWN SHORE. *Hart-Davis* 1959. Long account of
the disastrous experiences of the crew of *Wager*, separated from Anson's
squadron, late eighteenth century, struggling round Cape Horn and to Chile.

Oldenbourg, Zöe. THE CORNERSTONE. *Gollancz* 1954. Long, intricate, fascinating study of Crusades in Europe.

Onions, Oliver. THE STORY OF RAGGED ROBYN 1945. *Penguin* 1954. Seventeenth-
century panorama, domestic.

Prescott, H. F. M. THE MAN WITH THE DONKEY. *Eyre & Spottiswoode*
(1952) 1956. Henry VIII and the dissolution of the monasteries.

Sutcliff, Rosemary. THE RIDER OF THE WHITE HORSE. *Hodder & Stoughton*
1959. Civil War from the point of view of Fairfax.

Chapter 13 | *Innocents in the Underworld*

Adventure stories rest on a delicate balance of fantasy with circumstantial detail, and I am never quite sure how far children notice this balance. From good nature, laziness, ignorance or the pure joy of reading, they may accept story after story without question, but now and then something will stir their critical sense; and this is most likely to be when they are reading about children running into danger in a contemporary setting.

Even then it is probably some factual detail they will question, rather than the general concept of the happy ending, the young hero triumphing against the crook, penknife against pistol, innocent curiosity against experienced lawlessness. They like this formula because it offers them a preview of what they feel sure life is like. It is up to the writer to make up his mind, every time he begins a story, whether it is to be reasonable or not. In this kind of writing, I believe that adult criticism must give a lead to the hit-and-miss opinions of children.

Every author has his own way of approaching this business of probability. Some, like E. W. Hildick and Erich Kästner, choose plots which are easily related to everyday life. Others, like Mary Fitt, put over tall stories by sheer virtuosity. Others, like J. M. Scott and John Verney, carry their readers along because of the liveliness of their characters. Others, like Eilís Dillon and Elisabeth Kyle, rely on authentic backgrounds to carry off their mysteries. One of the best methods, perhaps, is to give your adventure to a gang of children, for hazard will then be shared, wits and resources pooled and the chances of success multiplied.

The ancestor of the gang-story is probably Erich Kästner's EMIL AND THE DETECTIVES, which reached England in translation in 1931 (it was published in Germany in 1929). It did not set a fashion straightaway. In fact it was not for nearly twenty years that the same relaxed, slangy, casual note was heard again in this country, in Cecil Day Lewis's masterpiece, THE OTTERBURY INCIDENT. A few of the episodes in this book were modelled on the film *Nous les Gosses*, and the general idea of making money to pay for damage was taken from it. The characters have little or no relation to those in the film, and the dialogue is the author's own. Kästner had the advantage of an unselfconscious approach to class-distinction. At a time when, in England, adventure stories were still largely middle-class, Kästner could write as a matter of course of a very mixed Berlin street-gang, in which one member has a father working as night-watchman in an hotel and another belongs to a professional family; while Emil, whose journey to the city to stay with his grand-mother sparks off the whole comical business, lives with a widowed mother who takes in washing. The adventure rises naturally out of this very background. Emil goes to Berlin by train, with an envelope in his pocket containing his money. For safety he pins the notes to his jacket, and it is the pin-marks which finally convict smooth Mr Grundeis, who has stolen the notes while Emil is asleep in the car-riage. Nothing was ever more convincing than that Emil should awake just in time to see his chatty companion hurriedly leaving a station, and should be able to keep him in sight until the happy accident of his meeting with the gang of street boys. Nothing was ever more utterly lifelike than the swift, efficient deploying of the gang—one to stand by for telephone reports, one to lurk in the hotel where Grundeis has taken refuge, others to shadow him until the triumphant moment when they all close in on him at the bank with the cry, 'Stop him. That is stolen money.' Kästner has not once had to go beyond probability, and yet here are all the requirements of the adventure-story—tension, speed, surprise.

The course of such stories in England might have been happier if more writers had taken note of Kästner's technique; his brilliant selection of detail, his crisp, utterly unpadded narrative, broken up with racy dialogue; his strict attention to character. For if his crook, shady and meagre, is horrifyingly real, his boys are too, each one set in his proper environment. We know who they were, what they were like, where they lived and how they lived. The crowning touch of realism comes with the reaction of Emil's mother to the publicity the 'boy-detective' receives. I would have her words learnt by heart by anyone who wants to write crook stories for children:

'Emil's a clever boy, and works hard. He's always top of his class. But supposing something had gone wrong! It makes my hair stand on end to think of it, though I know it is all over now, and everything has really turned out all right. I'll never let him go away alone again, that's certain. I'd die of fright, wondering what was happening to him.'
Erich Kästner. EMIL AND THE DETECTIVES. Translated by Eileen Hall. (Penguin, 1959) p. 121.

together with Grandma's trenchant reminder of the lesson *she* has learned from all the fuss—'Money should always be sent through the post.'

Kästner, then, chose a probable plot and a probable crook. In THE OTTERBURY INCIDENT the gang is up against a tougher proposition, black marketeers who have also tried and abandoned the idea of coining. We are led towards this by such gradual stages that it is impossible even to consider doubting whether it could all have happened. The setting, a country town, is superbly described, not in set pieces but emerging through the activities of Ted's gang and Toppy's gang as they carry on a sporadic war on the bomb site known as The Incident. When the story begins a campaign is in progress:

Just then, Toppy blew his whistle, and all his men who weren't casualties began streaming back towards the tank. In the heat of the battle, the enemy hadn't yet realised that their tank was captured. As they shot past behind the tank, Nick leant out and bopped one after another of them on the head with his football, yelling out: 'You're dead! *You're* dead! *You're* dead!' He got four of them like that, and at last he got Toppy himself.

'What the hell are you playing at?' shouted Toppy.

'Lie down,' I said. 'Don't you know when you're dead?'

'*And* we've destroyed the tank,' said Charlie. 'We've put five sticky bombs on it, honest. Look.'

'Oh, you have, have you?' Toppy said, when he'd examined the side of the tank, and underneath it. 'Yes, that's O.K. Five bombs. The tank's blown to smithereens. And so are you two fools in it. And therefore Nick couldn't have conked anyone with his football. And *therefore* I'm *not* dead.'

C. Day Lewis. THE OTTERBURY INCIDENT (Putnam, 1948) pp.12–13.

But a treaty drawn up by the narrator (one of those brainy boys who can usually be found in a gang) gives them space to plan a more useful campaign, for they have to earn enough money to pay for a window broken in the fight. Ted keeps the money in a box; it disappears; the gang is divided into those who suspect Ted and those who want to investigate the unsavoury Johnny Sharp, a local lounger. And so we move naturally from the streets to Skinner's yard and then into his cellar. The boys have no easy job when they tackle Skinner and his associates. Ted, who is caught in the cellar, is in real danger and is rescued by the police only just in time. And the police, far from congratulating the boys on their detective skill, as many inferior authors would have allowed them to do, temper their praise with severe warnings against interfering with police routine.

It is in the relation of boys to grown-ups that the author shows his quality. The boys succeed because of virtues typically their own—blind courage, inquisitiveness, intelligence—plus a certain amount of luck. When they learn that Ted is caught in the cellar, they send a message to the police and wade in at once to attack the warehouse:

> An odd thing, worth recording, is that it never occurred to any of them to enlist the aid of one or two grown-ups who came along the lane while they were making their plans. Rickie had to admit, though, when we told him the whole story later, that they were probably right: either these passers-by wouldn't have believed them, or else they'd have said, 'Wait for the police,' grown-ups being a bit windy about winkling out gangs of desperate criminals.
> Ibid., p. 130.

and when they are chasing the wounded Johnny Sharp through the town, their status as tiresome boys is unchanged:

> The rest of them passed on down the street, and spread out across the allotments, where one ancient man leant on a fork and shook his fist at them for treading all over his vegetables.
> Ibid., p. 139.

A beautiful sense of proportion, allied to a smooth, flexible style, make this a jewel among children's stories.

This is, above all, a story of action. The characters are neatly sketched, not complex; for you see them all, in action and in talk, through the eyes of George, who is one of them. But two stories by Richard Church are written first and foremost as studies of character. At the beginning of THE CAVE we are introduced formally to the members of the Tomahawk Club. There is John Walters, on holiday with an uncle and aunt; Meaty, son of a butcher, oafish and good-hearted; Harold Soames, called Lightning, 'a tiny little chap who was always in front of time and in a desperate hurry'; Alan Hobbs, self-appointed leader, and George Reynolds, quiet and reserved because of an unhappy home. The story is a simple one. John finds by accident the entrance to a limestone cave. The boys decide to explore it, prepare systematically for the expedition, venture into a network of passages and vaults, and, in circumstances of some doubt and danger, get out again by way of an underground river. What happens in the cave is far less important (and even less exciting) than what happens to the boys themselves. They do not come out just as they went in. John overcomes some fear of the dark; Alan loses his ascendancy and is revealed as a coward; George, in a crisis, accepts responsibility and deserves it. The author is quite unconcerned with what his readers can or cannot appreciate in the realm of human feelings, and this is as it should be. Everything he says in this and in the vigorous sequel, DOWN RIVER, is genuine, straightforward, undiluted.

Here is an author who can describe a fight so that it can be followed blow by blow. It is not this that will keep his readers, though, but his psychology, and the same is true of Paul Berna, whose plots, unlike Church's, are pretty unlikely. A HUNDRED MILLION FRANCS, one of the liveliest children's stories I know, supposes that a gang of children in a French suburb could really, behind the backs of long-suffering and overworked policemen, round up several thieves and recover a huge sum of money stolen from the Paris-Ventimiglia express. I defy anyone to disbelieve one detail of this logical craziness, from the moment we meet the children riding their headless horse perilously down the hill to the moment when, with the cockiness of children who have got more than they deserve, they bid farewell to weary Inspector Sinet, with an offer of a turn on their battered steed. Their characters show in every word they say, every drawing of their exploits. At one point we see them engaging in a pitched battle with the crooks in a factory full of carnival novelties; but their barricading is a matter of hasty discipline, and they have first of all been behaving with the wild irresponsibility of their age:

> The younger ones were calmly trying on wigs and false beards
> in the store-room at the end, standing round Zidore, who was
> dressed up as a demon; Tatave had already broken a dozen
> gazookas; Berthe and Mélie were hurling paper streamers furi-
> ously at each other; and Criquet, decked out in a three-cornered
> hat, was having a row of medals pinned on his chest . . .
> Paul Berna. A HUNDRED MILLION FRANCS. Translated by
> John Buchanan-Brown (Bodley Head, 1957) pp. 113-4.

We know these children—Monica, the tomboy, with her attendant
dogs collected from all over the town; Gaby, terrified of growing
out of the gang; Criquet, the negro boy, grinning and alert; Bonbon,
the youngest, who serves as mascot; and all the rest of the crew.
Their appearance, their talk, their homes and their hide-outs, all are
as real as they can be, and they are just as much so in a sequel, THE
STREET MUSICIAN.

Authenticity, that is the secret, as in Anne Barrett's SONGBERD'S
GROVE. Here is a story which turns out pat, involving half a dozen
startling coincidences by which the Singer family is left in peace to
enjoy a new home, a spiv is given new hope for the future, an ageing
dancer is restored to slimness, and a row of Georgian houses is
revealed in its former elegance. An improbable plot, but in every
other respect the book is so real that most children will accept
what happens without question. You can imagine right from the
start the slummy London street, and Number Seven, and the
Singers as they move in—quiet father, a factory worker, and his
plump wife, relaxing after a trying stay with her sister-in-law;
and spectacled, determined Martin:

> Clutching his parcels to him and glaring at them from behind the
> blinding shields of his glasses, on which the afternoon sun was now
> shining, Martin strode past them and up to the front door, where
> his mother had already rung the appropriate bell. The paint had
> once been red but was now darkened and peeling; there was a
> fanlight above with the number seven painted on it in black, with
> a thin gold edge. For the first time a touch of sympathy with the
> house stirred in Martin. It was a good seven.
> Footsteps sounded from inside and an old man, frail and

pinkish, stood blinking in front of them, as though he had suddenly been recalled from very far away. He was in his shirt-sleeves and slippers and wore a curious sort of tapestry waistcoat, from whose pocket the end of a measure-tape was trailing; all over him, as though he had been sleeping inside a mattress, small bits of cloth and thread and horsehair were clinging, and a pad stuck full of pins was attached to one of his wrists.
Anne Barrett. SONGBERD'S GROVE (Collins, 1957) p. 8.

The author wisely spends a long time establishing the scene, describing the down-at-heel houses and the urchins, loitering and spiteful, and the spoiled only child, Lennie, Number One of the street gang.

As a gang leader, Lennie is a failure. He soon collapses under the practical opposition of Martin and his ally, and the sensible way the author shows up this petty spiv and explains his background makes up for the sensational happy ending. Lennie is the kind of boy who *does* develop into a crook, and who can very suitably be used in a story, and so is Red Hendy, the young spiv in JO AND THE SKIFFLE

Drawing by Richard Kennedy for Paul Berna's A HUNDRED MILLION FRANCS (Bodley Head)

GROUP by Valerie Hastings, another story with the true atmosphere of London back streets. The crooks are kept in proportion; here is an impression of one of them, delivered with scorn by the sensible Don:

> Monkey approached the place with exaggerated caution. Then he flattened himself against a wall, with his hands thrust in his pockets, and looked both ways along the street. Satisfied that he wasn't observed, he made a dash for the door, stumbling up the low step in his haste.
> Don chuckled. 'Not so hot at the cloak and dagger stuff, is he? Sticks out a mile that he's up to no good. You know, if it wasn't for their outbreaks of real viciousness Red's gang could be dismissed with a good laugh. They're a ham bunch.'

Valerie Hastings. JO AND THE SKIFFLE GROUP (Parrish, 1958) p. 86.

This is salutary, I suppose, from the moral point of view, and it is certainly a more satisfactory basis for a story than the idea that a crook with an international connection can be floored by a pack of kids. It is perfectly likely, in fact, that children on their own ground, in streets or fields which they know inside-out, should be able to run rings round crooks who underestimate the opposition out of sheer stupidity. From this point of view the crook story of today, set as a rule in a familiar background, has a chance of being more convincing than the spy and treasure tales of the 'twenties, with their exotic backgrounds in Egypt, South America or Afghanistan. If you use a background which your readers are likely to know, you have to be scrupulous about detail and the balance of your story must be absolutely true. What Peter Fleming calls 'with-Harry-it-was-the-work-of-a-moment adventure stories', are far less common today, thank goodness, than they used to be; in their place we have tales like E. W. Hildick's recent thriller, THE BOY AT THE WINDOW, where a crime is attempted, and stopped by a bedridden boy and his two friends—an idea handled by the author composedly and with absolute success.

Amateur detection, too, is all the better for a familiar setting and for situations which boys and girls could naturally cope with. Anthony Wilson's clever pair, Norman and Henry Bones, for example, solve all their cases by fair means, by pertinacity or simple deduction or observation or memory, and they tackle nothing outside their range. If these are not stories to read often, they provide for younger readers (say from eight or nine) an introduction to the traditions and formulas of the detective story which will probably remain a permanent part of their diet; and Malcolm Saville's clever tales of Susan and Bill serve the same purpose. These children (they are nine and eleven and not particularly clever or precocious) solve mysteries suitable to their capacity, tracing a long-lost legacy for an old lady, stopping a back-door snooper from taking the farmer's wife's treasures, disclosing the secrets of some fairly innocuous smugglers.

In fact, the amateur detective had better not be up against anything too tough. Linda Carroll, Winifred Donald's schoolgirl detective, who is consulted officially even by adults, is far more convincing when she is following up clues leading to a legacy (in LINDA IN CAMBRIDGE) than when she is hunting down, with foolhardy courage, an American kidnapper (LINDA IN NEW YORK) or a seller of national secrets (LINDA AND THE SILVER GREYHOUNDS). She is sixteen when she goes in for this kind of case, and when you get to this point I should have thought it was better to go over to adventures where adults take control and the young merely stand by. Stories like P. H. Newby's THE LOOT RUNNERS, or Rex Warner's drug-smuggling thriller, THE KITE, or Henry Treece's brilliant series ASK FOR KING BILLY, HUNTER HUNTED, and DON'T EXPECT ANY MERCY, deal with serious crime in a suitably serious manner.

You can't have it both ways, in fact. If you want to write about real danger, you can't really have children as your main characters. If you want children, your plot must be cut to fit them, or you get an awkward compromise that satisfies nobody. Yet how many children in fiction launch themselves into the country, on to the moors, to the seaside, to old ruined mansions, meeting on their arrival (or even on the journey) some ferocious challenge from the underworld. The formula is easily recognized:

A lively family rather reluctantly go to spend the Easter holidays with a hitherto unknown grandfather. The prospect of any fun coming their way seems slim; but even before they leave London they find they have become involved in a mystery.
Blurb for SECRET OF THE SANDHILLS by Kitty Barne. (Nelson, 1955).

Suppose we accept the premise that children on holiday are likely to stumble on a spy, a smuggler or a jewel thief—what follows? Another premise, that the grown-ups will allow them to run their heads into danger. In R. J. McGregor's story, THE SECRET OF DEAD MAN'S COVE, Mr Mackenzie remarks that he hopes his children will allow *this* holiday to be peaceful; the year before he had been recalled from Scotland to Cornwall to learn that they had stopped a gang from stealing a new, secret explosive (see THE YOUNG DETECTIVES). This understandable attitude lasts for two chapters; after that he cheerfully backs up the recommendation of the local police inspector that they should 'watch out for a little man with very ruddy cheeks who has a glass eye' and pass on all they see. Mr Mackenzie is in fact working for the government and has, rather casually, brought a top secret paper down to work at. It is true that he has taken the precaution of bolting down the window-seat which conceals a secret way to the beach, but this year's batch of crooks manages very well elsewhere.

It is obviously best to ditch the parents at the start, and most fiction writers do this expertly. I am always prepared to accept a major operation on Mother or a sudden business trip to China, other things being equal; among these 'other things' are character-drawing and a good setting. It is hard to accept literally the coincidences and convenient endings in Elisabeth Kyle's stories, but nobody draws old cities as well as she does, nobody can suggest as she does the mystery of a small object (a musical-box or a model ship or a jewel) which crystallizes the feeling of past and present. Edinburgh in the incomparable story, THE HOUSE OF THE PELICAN; Glasgow in CAROLINE HOUSE; London in THE SEVEN SAPPHIRES and RUN TO EARTH; the Outer Isles in VANISHING ISLAND; all these places *make* the story.

Elisabeth Kyle stands head and shoulders above most writers of this kind of topographical thriller because her characters are as variable and interesting as her backgrounds. Two other writers must be mentioned who dig deep into motive and whose criminals, such as they are, are fallible human beings, not just lay figures providing a focal point for action. Allan McLean's three excellent stories for boys are set in Skye. The first (perhaps the best), THE HILL OF THE RED FOX, with its Buchanesque crypto-villain, its plot of the kidnapping of scientists by foreign powers, has a firm domestic basis.

The hero, young Alastair Cameron, is not in fact a hero; he is a boy, at first intrigued by an odd encounter in the train, then frightened when he realizes he is out of his depth in villainy:

> I had read many adventure stories, and I used to play a game, imagining myself to be the hero facing dreadful perils with cool courage. But this was no game, and now that I knew my life to be in danger I was afraid. None of the heroes in my stories was ever afraid. Sword in hand, they fought off half a score of attackers with a smile on their lips. But this was different. A whispered word, spoken in the darkness of the night, could be far more frightening than a dozen sword blades.
> Allan McLean. THE HILL OF THE RED FOX (Collins, 1955) pp. 81–2.

Alastair and the solitary crofter, Duncan Mor, who helps him, blunder to success through a number of mistakes (one of which costs Duncan his life) and the head of M.I.5 makes a familiar but appropriate remark at the end—'it has always been the amateurs who have pulled us through.' In other words, Alastair is an ordinary boy who fights with the weapons at his disposal, who is often in extreme danger, whose ultimate fate you can't take for granted, although you can be sure he will fight to the last gasp. THE MAN OF THE HOUSE, with its tale of theft and intrigue, and THE MASTER OF MORGANA, which skilfully mixes salmon-fishing and the search for a wrecked galleon, offer, too, so much that is sound and real about ordinary people that their melodramatic scenes seem entirely natural too.

What Allan McLean has done for Skye, Eilís Dillon is doing for remote Irish seaboards. Here are no crooks in the story-book sense, but people gone wrong. In THE ISLAND OF HORSES it is a local dealer who has turned thief to bolster up his self-importance. In THE SINGING CAVE it is an egotistical recluse who covets the Viking found in the sand. In THE HOUSE ON THE SHORE it is an old man warped by his wife's death. With the free emotional swing of Irish tales, the motives of these very individual criminals are laid bare to us. Here is Jim O'Malley's Uncle Martin gloating over the church plate which he has kept hidden in his derelict house for years:

'I was a young man when I found them first. They have been wife and child to me ever since. I never wanted to leave them. I never went away from my house without taking leave of them first. I have loved them and watched over them for twenty years. See how they gleam in the light. That's because I always kept them polished—'

'God save us from such a curse!' said Roddy in my ear. 'Look at the miserly face of him! Look at the greedy paws of him! The devil has a hold of that man, for certain sure!'

Uncle Martin's hands were opening and shutting and rubbing each other, over the gold vessels, as if they had a life of their own. He certainly looked like a man that had an evil spirit in him, which now seemed to fill the little house to suffocation.

Eilís Dillon. THE HOUSE ON THE SHORE (Faber, 1955) p. 173.

And behind the people is the Irish scene, superbly described; the hidden valley where the wild horses wheel and stamp, the cave with the pieces of the wolf-game lying beside the Viking skeleton, old Martin's tree-house, peat bogs and mountains and crofts. To find crime in everyday life, to find real motives for it, and to fuse detail into an imaginative whole—Eilís Dillon has done this, and has raised the standard of the adventure story in doing it.

Oddly enough, the most fantastic kind of plot may also be the nearest to the events of real life. The adventures of a spy are as exciting in fact as in fiction, and can provide excellent plots. Unfortunately, writers for children often leave out the essential element, the reasons for spying. John Buchan, ancestor of the spy-story writers, knew better than this. His international agents, his monomaniacs seeking world power, are formidable indeed, yet nothing in their motives or their circumstances is beyond the understanding of a schoolboy. Though Buchan did not write for children, he is still, and always will be, popular with them, because he gives them character as well as action, whereas many writers today, realizing the complexity of the spy or the traitor, take him for granted and concentrate on the adventure. M. Pardoe's Bunkle, chattering his way past enemy agents of all nationalities, Bertram Edwards's schoolboys tackling enemy agents during a half-term holiday, John Pudney's boy heroes helping or hindering Uncle George—none of these youthful heroes has much idea of what is going on in the minds of their adversaries, or, indeed, what they are really trying to do. It is true that John

Verney's children, in FRIDAY'S TUNNEL, have some idea what they are up against, but their father is a roving correspondent who detects in his spare time, and they know enough about the secret mineral of Capria to make themselves useful in his absence. In J. M. Scott's romantic adventure, THE BRIGHT EYES OF DANGER, the children who foil Communist elements on a Ruritanian island in the Aegean have been brought up in diplomatic circles and make the most of what they have picked up. But I know only one story, written for children, which really examines the mind of a spy. THE MARLOWS AND THE TRAITOR, by Antonia Forest, involves the twins, Nicola and Lawrie (whom we have already met in two first-class school-stories) and their brother Peter, with Ralph Foley, one of Peter's instructors at Dartmouth, who is selling secrets to the Germans in wartime. To the end of the story, the children are not sure what they think of Foley. They like him, a good deal of the time, even when he has given them a bad time in a lonely lighthouse; they are puzzled by his behaviour and by his odd lack of apology for being a traitor; they hover uneasily between the accidental perceptiveness of children and the orthodox views they have learned from grown-up people. This story, with its warmth, its courage in character-drawing, its narrative skill, deserves to outlast hundreds of tales which may seem, at first reading, to be just as exciting.

It is not easy to put spies into stories for children because of the complexity of their motives and of political and national affairs as a whole. Geoffrey Trease was one of the first to try to give children an honest version of war. THE CALL TO ARMS, which was published twenty-five years ago, is no tale of honour and glory; it is a business of secret arrangements, vested interests, confusion, discomfort and death. This is very much a book of the 'thirties, and parts of it (like the strike in the South American town, and the triumph of the People's Army) are more doctrinaire than anything this author is writing today; his theories stand out like gaunt signposts pointing to a new world, rather than being related to the characters. He must be respected always for his consistent belief that children are not given enough of the truth in their stories.

Writers who have an axe to grind must often be blamed unfairly for deafening us with the sound. Certainly reviewers will be on the look-out for tendentiousness in a writer whose political views are well known. In any case, children will not stand for principle if it holds up action. It is all the more to the credit of Naomi Mitchison that she has kept a well-informed and progressive point of view in the forefront of stories which are exceptionally readable, for old or young. JUDY AND LAKSHMI, a story of modern India, has a good deal of political theory in it, but it is primarily a touching story of the friendship of two girls with dissimilar backgrounds. THE FAR HARBOUR, with its uncompromising picture of fishermen in the Western Highlands, stands and falls by its characters, and so does THE RIB OF THE GREEN UMBRELLA, which is set in an Italian town in the Second World War. All the dangers of the underground movement are here, all the social structures of the place, but what we shall remember is the two lively boys who carry messages, laughing and playing through danger. Again, among many recent stories for children which touch on African problems, the one that impressed me most was ASHANTI BOY by Akosua Abbs, because its knowledgeable picture of Ghana on the eve of independence was enlivened by the brilliant characters of schoolboys, boys aspiring to school life, teachers, preachers, native chiefs and many others.

Perhaps it is not surprising that books like these are in the minority, for they have cut loose from the prevailing belief that stories for children must adopt a youthful tone. For every book of the calibre of THE SILVER SWORD, Ian Serraillier's story of children in war-shattered Poland, with its crystal-clear sincerity, there are half-a-dozen which romanticize war into a matter of chases and excitement, with danger nothing more than a word. Until we return to the Victorian custom of treating children as embryo adults (at least in their reading matter), they are not likely to get many books which give them enough to think about without being laboured or priggish. We are not likely, for this and other reasons, to get many books like DOG TOBY, Richard Church's clear-headed, sympathetic story showing up the causes of war.

Here we are in a Central European country, looking over the frontier into another country on the brink of war. Between the two a tunnel carries a railway, through which patrol-trains run, their staff keyed-up and nervous. The Brown children, Maria and Jan, and their friend Fritz, plan an all-day outing to the frontier, to the delectable hillsides where they have been forbidden to play. In the sunshine, they relax and wonder about the tension among the grown-ups. Then their puppy runs into the tunnel. They follow, are caught by the guards, help to avert a collision with an international express, and the whole stupid, inevitable, indefensible deadlock is summed up in the farewell of the rival parties, now on friendly terms after the homely incident:

Dog Toby shook a paw with him, and accepted a biscuit from another of the Northern Guards. Mitzi also came forward and was suitably rewarded for the part she had played in the tunnel; not a very heroic part but worth a biscuit.

'Well!' said the once-grumpy Northern officer, when all the fraternizing was complete and people had begun to look at each other with that 'what comes next?' shyness in their eyes. 'Time we got going! What do we do with the prisoners?'

This was indeed a problem, almost an international situation. 'Hang 'em!' said a voice, the kindest voice in the whole party. 'Hang 'em from that strand of ivy over the tunnel-mouth.'

Laughter! Slapping of backs, patting of dogs; handing round of biscuits and cigarettes.

'You can't do that. It is strung with bells,' said another.

More laughter, more congratulations, as though a heavy weight had been lifted from all hearts; as though a good spirit had come down out of the Northern and the Southern sky and whispered to these men: 'No more suspicions; no more barbed wire! Let the Transcontinental run; let the children wander over the hills where their fathers used to wander when *they* were children!'

And so it was. The guards shook hands once more, but surely not for the last time; shook hands and separated into their two patrols, making for the trains, mounting the trucks, blowing the whistles, and setting off.

Richard Church. DOG TOBY: a frontier tale (Hutchinson, 1954) pp. 170–1.

This is a fine book, humorous and moving. Aiming at the truth, because he believes children should have no less, Richard Church has climbed the heights, leaving most of his fellow-writers panting on the foothills.

Reading List

1. *Children and Crooks*

Aldous, Allan. THE TENDRILLS IN AUSTRALIA. *Chatto* 1959. Nuclear physics and cattle-rustling combine in a good story.

Ballantyne, Joan. KIDNAPPERS AT COOMBE. *Nelson* 1960. Illustrated by Edward Ardizzone. Children of Balkan Prime Minister, at holiday home, threatened by kidnappers; older children do some effective and convincing detective work.

*Barne, Kitty. THE SECRET OF THE SANDHILLS. *Nelson* 1955. Previously published as THE EASTER HOLIDAYS. *Heinemann* 1935. Illustrated by Joan Kiddell-Monroe.

*Barrett, Anne. SONGBERD'S GROVE. *Collins* 1957. Illustrated by David Knight.

*Berna, Paul. A HUNDRED MILLION FRANCS (1955 France) 1957, THE STREET MUSICIAN (1956 France) 1960. *Bodley Head.* Translated by John Buchanan-Brown. Illustrated by Richard Kennedy.

*Church, Richard. THE CAVE. *Dent* (1950) 1953 (revised edition). Illustrated by Geoffrey Whittam.

Church, Richard, DOWN RIVER. *Heinemann* 1958. Illustrated by Laurence Irving.

Clarke, Pauline. THE WHITE ELEPHANT. *Faber* 1952. Illustrated by Richard Kennedy. Jewel-thieves in London streets: convincing because of speed and authentic background.

Clarke, Pauline. SMITH'S HOARD. *Faber* 1955. Illustrated by Cecil Leslie. Sophisticated tale of children in East Anglia saving Iron Age hoard from thieves.

Cross, John Keir. THE SIXPENNY YEAR. *Hutchinson* 1957. Agreeably adult and sensible tale of town children staying on Devon farm, involved with sheep stealer.

*Dillon, Eilís. THE SAN SEBASTIAN 1953 (see also Chap. 11), THE HOUSE ON THE SHORE 1955, THE ISLAND OF HORSES 1956, THE SINGING CAVE 1959. *Faber.* Illustrated by Richard Kennedy.

*Donald, Winifred. LINDA AND THE SILVER GREYHOUNDS 1952, LINDA IN CAMBRIDGE 1955, LINDA IN NEW YORK 1956. *Hutchinson.*

*Edwards, Bertram. MIDNIGHT ON BARROWMEAD HILL 1957, STRANGE TRAFFIC 1959. *Brockhampton.* Illustrated by Richard Kennedy.

Finlay, Winifred. PERIL IN LAKELAND 1953, COTSWOLD HOLIDAY 1954, STORM OVER CHEVIOT 1955, THE LOST SILVER OF LANGDON 1955, CANAL

HOLIDAY 1957, THE CRUISE OF THE 'SUSAN' 1958. *Harrap.* Adventure stories, with crooks or treasure or both, unusually convincing because rational and unexaggerated. Excellent backgrounds in Border country, the Lakes, the Cotswolds and Northamptonshire.

*Fitt, Mary. THE ISLAND CASTLE 1953, ANNABELLA AT THE LIGHTHOUSE 1955, POMEROY'S POSTSCRIPT 1955, THE TURNIP WATCH 1956, THE SHIFTING SANDS 1958. *Nelson.*

*Forest, Antonia. THE MARLOWS AND THE TRAITOR. *Faber* 1953. Illustrated by Doritie Kettlewell.

Gunn, John. THE HUMPY IN THE HILLS. *Lutterworth* 1960. Illustrated by Noella Young. Australian setting: boys join with educated tramp to foil the last member of a gang of thieves.

*Hastings, Valerie. JO AND THE SKIFFLE GROUP 1958, JO AND CONEY'S CAVERN 1959. *Parrish.*

*Hildick, E. W. THE BOY AT THE WINDOW. *Chatto* 1960.

*Kästner, Erich. EMIL AND THE DETECTIVES (1929 Germany). *Cape* 1931. Translated by Eileen Hall. *Penguin* (Puffin Story Books) 1959. Also EMIL, comprising EMIL AND THE DETECTIVES, EMIL AND THE THREE TWINS and THE THIRTY-FIFTH OF MAY. *Cape* 1949. Illustrated by Walter Trier.

*Kyle, Elisabeth. THE HOUSE OF THE PELICAN 1954, illustrated by Peggy Fortnum. CAROLINE HOUSE 1955, illustrated by Robert Hodgson. VANISHING ISLAND (1942) 1956, THE SEVEN SAPPHIRES (1944) 1957, illustrated by Leslie Atkinson. RUN TO EARTH 1957, illustrated by Mary Shillabeer. *Nelson.*

*Lewis, C. Day. THE OTTERBURY INCIDENT. *Putman* (1948) 1958. Illustrated by Edward Ardizzone.

*McGregor, R. J. THE YOUNG DETECTIVES 1934, THE SECRET OF DEAD MAN'S COVE 1937. *Burns Oates.*

*McLean, Allan. THE HILL OF THE RED FOX 1955, THE MAN OF THE HOUSE 1956, THE MASTER OF MORGANA (see Chap. 11). *Collins.*

*Newby, P. H. THE LOOT RUNNERS. *John Lehmann* 1949.

*Pardoe, M. FOUR PLUS BUNKLE. *Routledge* 1939. And many other titles.

*Pudney, John. SATURDAY ADVENTURE 1950, SUNDAY ADVENTURE 1951. *Bodley Head.* Illustrated by Ley Kenyon.

*Pudney, John. MONDAY ADVENTURE 1952, TUESDAY ADVENTURE 1953, WEDNESDAY ADVENTURE 1954, THURSDAY ADVENTURE 1955. *Evans.* Illustrated by Ley Kenyon.

*Saville, Malcolm. SUSAN, BILL AND THE WOLF DOG 1954, SUSAN, BILL AND THE IVY-CLAD OAK 1954, SUSAN, BILL AND THE VANISHING BOY 1955,

SUSAN, BILL AND THE GOLDEN CLOCK 1955, SUSAN, BILL AND THE DARK STRANGER 1956, SUSAN, BILL AND THE SAUCY KATE 1956, illustrated by Ernest Shepard. SUSAN, BILL AND THE BRIGHT STAR CIRCUS 1960, illustrated by T. R. Freeman. *Nelson.*

*Scott, J. M. THE BRIGHT EYES OF DANGER. *Hodder & Stoughton* 1950.

Treadgold, Mary. THE POLLY HARRIS. *Cape* 1949. Illustrated by Pat Marriott. London riverside adventure with smugglers: good characterization and setting.

*Treece, Henry. ASK FOR KING BILLY 1955, HUNTER HUNTED 1957, DON'T EXPECT ANY MERCY 1958. *Faber.* Illustrated by Richard Kennedy.

*Verney, John. FRIDAY'S TUNNEL. *Collins* 1959. Illustrated by the author.

*Warner, Rex. THE KITE. *Blackwell* 1936.

Westlake, Veronica. THE INTRUDERS. *Routledge* 1954. Illustrated by Sheila Rose. Schoolboy inherits manor and comes up against crooked lawyer: natural, easy style and convincing direction of story.

*Wilson, Anthony. NORMAN BONES, DETECTIVE 1949, NORMAN AND HENRY BONES, THE BOY DETECTIVES 1952, NORMAN AND HENRY BONES INVESTIGATE 1953, illustrated by Kenneth Beauchamp. NORMAN AND HENRY SOLVE THE PROBLEM 1957, illustrated by Elizabeth Andrewes. NORMAN AND HENRY FOLLOW THE TRAIL 1959, illustrated by Margery Gill. *Methuen.*

*Wilson, Anthony. FOUR MYSTERIES SOLVED BY NORMAN AND HENRY BONES. *Penguin* (Puffin Story Books) 1957. Illustrated by Elizabeth Andrewes.

2. *War and its aftermath*

*Abbs, Akosua. ASHANTI BOY. *Collins* 1959.

Barne, Kitty. WE'LL MEET IN ENGLAND. *Hamish Hamilton* 1942. Illustrated by Steven Spurrier. Norwegian family escaping from Nazi occupation.

Barne, Kitty. VISITORS FROM LONDON. *Dent* 1940. Illustrated by Ruth Gervis. Good-humoured and realistic tale of evacuees.

Benary, Margot. THE ARK 1954, ROWAN FARM 1955. *Macmillan.* German family fighting back to reasonable life after Second World War.

Benary, Margot. THE LONG WAY HOME. *Macmillan* 1960. Orphan in Eastern Zone escapes to new life in America: a distinguished and mature book for older children.

*Church, Richard. DOG TOBY. *Hutchinson* 1954. Illustrated by Laurence Irving.

Gleit, Maria. CHILD OF CHINA (1948 Germany). *O.U.P.* 1960. Translated by E. F. Peeler. Illustrated by Walter Holtz. Girl sold into slavery, her courage in Japanese attack on Chinese city: superbly real and moving.

Jong, Meindert De. THE HOUSE OF SIXTY FATHERS (1956 U.S.A.). *Lutterworth*

1958. Illustrated by Maurice Sendak. Chinese boy and family pig hiding from Japanese and helping American airman.

Kemp, Rouse. YOU CAN'T FIGHT WITH CATTIES. *Methuen* 1959. Illustrated by William Randell. Kenya before Mau-Mau riots: unrest seen through adventures of a group of children camping. Simple, direct and vigorous.

Loeff, Rutgers van der. AVALANCHE (1954 Holland). *U.L.P.* 1957. Translated by Dora Round. Illustrated by Alie Evers. Exciting and human story of a village in danger: aspects of Pestalozzi international village.

*Mitchison, Naomi. THE FAR HARBOUR 1957, illustrated by Martin Thomas. JUDY AND LAKSHMI 1959, illustrated by Arinash Chandra. THE RIB OF THE GREEN UMBRELLA 1960, illustrated by Edward Ardizzone. *Collins.*

*Serraillier, Ian. THE SILVER SWORD. *Cape* 1956. Illustrated by C. Walter Hodges.

*Trease, Geoffrey. THE CALL TO ARMS. *Martin Lawrence* 1935.

Watson, Sally. TO BUILD A LAND. *Hutchinson* 1959. Jewish refugee children settling in a new community in Israel.

Chapter 14 | *Little Birds in their Nests Agree*

When the sandhills and the moors are deserted, when the streets are empty and the children of fiction are safe at home, we might then expect a greater measure of realism in stories; but family stories are often as unreal as the most far-fetched adventure yarn. The convenient label turns out to be misleading, for, far from being in a family, children are left on their own quite as much as they are in stories of gangsters and smugglers. Their parents are barely glimpsed in the background.

There is one type of story where this is essential, the story about the solitary child, where everything and everybody else becomes background, to be seen through her eyes. We are concerned here with the poetry of living, a single, private affair. Among the riotous family chronicles of Elizabeth Enright, two books stand out for their concentration of atmosphere. THIMBLE SUMMER is the story of a few months in the life of Garnet Linden, a nine-year-old girl on a farm in the Middle West. Garnet is not a recluse. She works in the harvest field, she goes to a country fair, she helps in the house and the farmyard. All the same, the book is a record of private pleasures, of an enchanted summer. Here is a child seeing familiar surroundings with the fresh vision of her age. In THE SEA IS ALL AROUND, Mab Kendall opens sharp eyes and ears to an unfamiliar world, an island she is visiting off the New England coast, with the noise of the sea, the oddness of the people, the delight of new objects, all to discover. This kind of story cannot be written to order. It must come from a mind recollecting in tranquillity the joys of childhood. This is the impetus behind that exquisite, sharp picture of the English countryside, THE TRUANTS by J. C. Badcock, with its lovely decorative drawings, and behind a good deal of Elizabeth Coatsworth's work. ALICE-ALL-BY-HERSELF, for instance, sets a little girl plumb in the middle of her home in Maine, observing, listening, saying very little; watching old Miss Abby in her house full of pot-plants, watching an old man making figureheads, watching the stall-holders at the fair, always watching, and reflecting on her impressions, as she does about the wonderful fair:

Alice drank root beer. A man went by quarrelling with his wife. When Alice stopped near the booths she could not help seeing how worn and dirty the cloth was, though it looked so gay at a distance. And hardly any of the people in them had nice eyes.
. . . But that night as she lay quietly in bed, with the square of moonlight showing in her open window and the smell of salt water drifting to her from the river, she saw the fair again in her mind's eye. She was standing watching Mr Dunbar and his big oxen, and the bright horses flashing by in the outer ring, and beyond them were the roundabouts, foreign-feeling and mysterious in spite of their shabbiness. Where would they all be to-morrow? How did they live? She felt again her first excitement in the crowd; her sense of the known and the unknown all stirring together, of eyes that looked at her which had come from far-away places, of the music beating and beating, and the balloon which had floated up against the blue sky.
Elizabeth Coatsworth. ALICE-ALL-BY-HERSELF (Harrap, 1959. First published 1938) pp. 69-70.

Stories like this do not challenge the attention with action; their characters have, at first sight, little definition, there is no 'story'. Adults will read them for their nostalgic quality: children, more often, for the details of childhood pleasures. The feeling of getting inside a child's mind, the imaginative reconstruction, will steal on a thoughtful young reader unawares.

Children hardly analyse their own desire for privacy, but they recognize it in fictional children, and they recognize, too, their natural desire for independence. This accounts for the popularity of stories about running away—about children on their own. We do not want realism here, in the strict sense. After his wanderings, the child must get home again. The place for the lost child, the homeless, the unwanted, is in adult fiction, through which older boys and girls may widen their experience; not in stories for schoolchildren, which must assure their readers of safety in the end, no matter what hazards they describe first.

But we should demand realism in one way. It is no fun reading about a child on his own unless you feel he really *is* on his own, unless he meets some difficulties and has some doubts in the course of his adventure. Every writer has his own kind of probability. When I first read THE JOURNEY OF JOHNNY REW, I felt things were made too easy for the hero. Anne Barrett sends him off from London to the West Country in search of his long-lost father with no better clue than his surname and a letter with two geographical details. Certainly Johnny is taken for a burglar, early in his travels, but before this can worry him too much, he wanders to Miss Merrament's house and has her kindness and good sense to rely on. When I reread the story, I forgot these niggling doubts because I was interested in the characters, in Johnny himself, reflective and determined, and in the odd and exciting people he met.

This is one way of establishing the veracity of a story. Another is to accumulate domestic detail, to make the journey, wherever or whatever it is, seem exact in every particular. This is what Marjorie Fischer does in STREET FAIR, a gay and utterly believable story about two American children, Anna and John, on holiday in Paris, who are whisked away by accident in a train to the Riviera. You know exactly how much money they had between them and what they spent it on, what they eat, where they sleep and who they talk to. Above all, you know how they feel; you realize how irresponsible they are, as they casually plan that sometime they will try to get in touch with Mother (who is at Cannes); you notice when they begin to find independence a little frightening. They deal with emergencies as they arise. When John splits his shorts, they bribe a small English girl (with ice-cream) to steal a pair of her brother's trousers for him:

At last they saw the little girl turn the corner and John stood up to see what she was carrying over her arm, and it was plainly long trousers. He was so excited that he told Anna.

'She's got longs!' he said.

'Something like mine, I expect,' said Anna. 'Only not sailor.'

'Of course not,' said John. 'Regular long trousers.'

'Well, I don't see anything to get so excited about,' said Anna.

'And you'd better sit down till she comes. You look funny.'
Marjorie Fischer. STREET FAIR (Penguin, 1949. First published
1935) pp. 150-51.

The whole essence of a child's view of life is summed up in this small
exchange. Richard Parker's story, MORE SNAKES THAN LADDERS,
has the same glancing eye over a child's world, the same telling use
of small details; and his tale of a boy and girl making their way
(again, quite without plan) from Kent to Weymouth fulfils its title,
for nothing is as easy as the two of them had expected.

Beside children travelling, there are the equally popular young
heroes and heroines who escape from parental control and establish
a home of their own. A story like Eleanor Graham's THE CHILDREN
WHO LIVED IN A BARN is the logical extension of all the books for
small children about dolls' houses and rabbit burrows, the older
child's version of the housekeeping of Golliwogg and his Dutch
dolls, or of the bachelor life of Pooh. The reader is ready now for
a sterner view of responsibility than Pooh's. Eleanor Graham has
not made housekeeping easy or romantic for Sue and her family.
Removing their parents (rather violently, in a air-crash), she then
leaves them in a serious dilemma, for their unpleasant landlord has
decided to terminate their lease, and the only shelter that offers is
Farmer Pearl's barn. Picnic delights soon pall—at least for thirteen-
year-old Sue, who feels she must keep the twins and little Alice clean
and well-fed, but does not know how to set about it or how to persuade Bob to pull his weight. Bad weather, an interfering District-
Visitor, Alice's tantrums, problems of washing and cooking and
funds—all these are faced squarely, and not always cheerfully, until
the wonderful moment when the parents are found to be alive after
all, and the children realize what home really means to them.

The children in Nan Chauncy's THEY FOUND A CAVE have the
same lesson to learn, though they start with a better understanding
of what it means to be homeless. Their extended picnic in a cave on a
Tasmanian hillside begins on a sensible note:

'We've decided everything, but first we're going to make one rule.
We won't grumble. However things turn out we won't grumble,
but we will work hard. Is that agreed, you blokes? We don't expect
it to be all jam, do we? There won't be any jam as a matter of
fact . . .'

Nan Chauncy. THEY FOUND A CAVE. (Oxford University Press 1948) p. 49.

For all their common-sense, they have not been able to foresee boredom and the exasperating effect of continued lack of comfort; and for Cherry at least the responsibility becomes very hard before their aunt comes back from hospital to rescue them from the unpleasant married couple who are trying to persuade them from their eyrie.

There is something more in these two books than an adventure entertaining and spiced with discomfort; there is something more than the entrancing details of housekeeping with a difference. There is a feeling for character, for the behaviour of the various members of a family when faced by a crisis. Let children enjoy the ninety-nine readable but undistinguished holiday adventures which merge into one jumble of caravanning, toffee-making and stamp-collecting. The story with characters in it, the hundredth story, is the one I am concerned with; the book that children will read till its pages fall out. And that hundredth book may well be by the pioneer in the field of holiday stories, Arthur Ransome.

Now with Ransome the rule is 'Grown-ups not admitted unless accompanied by a child.' The Blackett and Walker parents know their place; they stay tactfully at home and act as ship's chandlers. Uncle Jim can approach a little nearer when he is needed as a pirate or a mining expert or a ship's captain, but even he is some distance away from the centre of action—like Ransome himself, who watches, with evident delight, the important exploits of his creations, and lets them express themselves (even in the illustrations).

And they *are* important. Ransome's children always have something on hand—bird-watching, gold-mining, astronomy, tracking, innumerable outdoor projects, involving (usually) no serious expense of emotion but a great deal of energy and technical skill. As he never writes about anything unless he knows it from A to Z, his books have an accuracy and precision much appreciated by his readers. If they followed his clear indications they could probably become as accomplished as the Swallows and Amazons. And they will want to imitate Ransome's children all the more because he never cheats. He never makes things too easy. When, in PIGEON POST, Dick has built his kiln to extract gold (as he hopes) from the pile of stone they have collected, he feels triumphant, but then comes the reaction:

> The miners looked at each other and at the stone furnace that was far too hot to touch. They were suddenly tired. It was as if the string of a necklace had snapped and the beads were rolling all ways on the floor. The work that had kept them all awake was at an end. With no bellows to work or furnace to feed they were no longer a team, and each one separately was wondering how it had been possible to keep awake so long.
>
> Arthur Ransome. PIGEON POST. (Cape, 1936) p. 32.

It is the writer who understands children who thus alters the pace of their schemes and their achievements. The stories of Lois Lamplugh and Tyler Whittle, two authors who write in the Ransome tradition, are immensely spirited and readable, but they have this flaw, that the children are seldom anything but energetic and successful. Certainly these writers communicate the enthusiasm of the young and their casual erudition on subjects that interest them, and these subjects (bird-watching, archæology, amateur building) are highly topical. All this is worth a great deal. But it is interesting to compare their versions of young adventure with books written by young holiday adventurers themselves.

In the remarkable stories written by Katharine Hull and Pamela Whitlock (the first of them, THE FAR-DISTANT OXUS, when they were schoolgirls of fifteen and sixteen respectively), there is a convincing variety of pace. These are outdoor stories, set on Exmoor, and the children are on their own by choice (as one title, ESCAPE TO PERSIA, emphatically suggests). They camp in their own log-hut very much as children would. They get bored from time to time because meals do not produce themselves, though they will put endless effort into a special feast. There are moments of slackness, even moments when they feel uneasy at the absence of authority. All these off-moments are faithfully recorded, and so are the moments of pleasure, comradeship and pure joy. These two authors have put into a public and coherent form a body of intense private emotion which will be recognized at once as superbly true by all children with like tastes. It is this truth of youthful enjoyment which can so easily be missed, or distorted, in stories of this kind by adults.

Few schoolgirls would have the capacity to put their dreams so finely into words. These books are manufactured from the unexaggerated stuff of real life. They are not derivative, even though the well-worn scenes of gymkhana and camp are used. Their freshness can be seen if they are compared with SANDAL ASH, a family adventure story written by Patricia Ann Cox when she was sixteen. Beginning with a lifelike presentation of children in a village, engaged in a war of bows and arrows and ambushes, this pleasing tale soon edges off into a sub-plot of burglars and midnight activities which reflects wishful reading rather than wishful thinking.

To read the Oxus stories, adults must accept a certain amateurishness. This does not matter in the drawings, which have the feel of young and energetic busyness. It does not matter much in the style, though this is prolix. Nothing has been left out because, to the authors, all details have the same importance. There is none of Ransome's careful selection of detail. The conversations go on and on, very entertaining, absolutely real, but, again, full of irrelevant shoots which an adult writer would not leave unpruned.

This is adventure as girls would write it, superbly conceived, with moments of touching truth beyond the scope of an adult writer, and with a mixture of serious and comic which is inimitable. An adult writer, indeed, would be foolish to try anything like this description of the first night at the holiday farm:

> 'Fun!' Bridget stood on the bed in her excitement. 'We shall have that all right; but this isn't a place for fun only. It's a place for travel, discovery, adventure. How do we know that there are not hundreds of hidden valleys, dozens of unscaleable peaks, heaps of unrideable rides; all waiting to be found, climbed, and accomplished by us? Oh, we shall have fun here all right—but more as well, much more.'
>
> After which spirited speech she added a hasty good night and, seizing her sponge-bag, barged back into her room.
> Katharine Hull and Pamela Whitlock. THE FAR-DISTANT OXUS (Collins, 1960. First published, 1937) p. 17.

This kind of style, supported by goodwill and talent in equal proportions, is irresistible, but it is also apt to be long-winded, and I think any children must find these stories long and at times difficult to follow. The hunt for Maurice, for instance, in OXUS IN SUMMER, must be read in one enthusiastic sitting if it is not to be muddling.

All this serves to emphasize the sad but salutary fact that, on the whole, it is better for adults to write children's books—not so much because of superior powers of expression as because of a more experienced and objective sense of form.

CROWNS, a story outside the Oxus sequence, and written later, has a far more mature construction, but has retained the intensely romantic, personal feeling of the earlier adventures. This is the tale of a dream world, imagined by four children who are rapt away in spirit as they crouch hidden in an attic during a London party. In the kingdom they rule together, each finds the deepest desire fulfilled. Charlotte, who is a masterful child, explores over the frontier and narrowly escapes death; indeed, one of her servants is killed, and there is no boggling at the horror of the moment. Andrew, whose temperament is solitary, goes into the marshlands to live with shepherds; Eliza enjoys peacocks and silken cushions at the palace; and Rob, the real ruler among them, indulges a love of power and exposes the Chancellor's plots against them.

The source of this vividly imagined world lies, presumably, in some unusually stimulating history lesson or a vivid textbook. There is throughout the book an intense fusing of intellectual and emotional life, sometimes offered almost as the raw material of a story, as in this description of the dwarfs' tapestry:

Eliza gazed at the yards already worked, hanging along the walls. Here was the beginning of time, the age of ice, the plains and hills in long cream-white stretches of snow, the frozen glacier in grey-white, mauve-white silk. Here were flames of scarlet and yellow fire spiking across the ice. Here were the plains and hills, and the river, melted into life; a team of oxen were at plough, shepherds were driving a flock across the hills, sailors lugging up nets of fish. Here were miniatures of the town and the market-place. Here the ragged range of mountains which could be seen from the palace when the weather was especially clear, and here last of all was the building of the new palace, boulders being rolled up the cliff by gangs of workmen as ants roll barley seeds.

Katharine Hull and Pamela Whitlock. CROWNS (Cape, 1947) p. 118.

The whole of this fascinating tale reads as though one of the children in THE AMULET had taken the pen from Edith Nesbit's hand; the authors have looked back unerringly from their older stance and have seen the wonderful kingdom, still, as girls would see it.

The most difficult task for a young person writing *con amore* is to find universal utterance for private thoughts; and if this is what she wants to do, she is allying herself to all those adult writers, from Ransome downwards, who have enclosed children firmly in their own world. A different kind of selectiveness is needed in those family stories which present children as they fit into a larger world. One of the most striking stories published in 1960 was THE GREAT GALE by Hester Burton, a story based on the East Anglian floods of 1953. A boy and a girl, children of the local doctor, are the central figures, but they are there definitely as members of a community, not as the little hero and heroine. They belong to Reedsmere. They know and love the old couple, Jim and Hepzie, whose cottage is so dangerously near the sea; they are used to the trenchant remarks of Canon Crowfoot; they understand the village hierarchy and its routine. All this stands them in good stead when they find themselves alone in their house when the floods begin. Their actions thereafter are brave and resourceful; they are also well-organized. We have an eye on the children right through the story. We sympathize with Mary when her best friend from the post-office is in danger. We watch Mark sizing up the situation at the Hall, where the villagers have collected. But the children never take our attention away from the whole picture, the picture of a village in difficulties. There is nothing portentous about this book but, indirectly, it shows individuals living in a community and depending on one another, and it is a welcome change from the innumerable stories in which children seem to drift on the fringe of real life.

Another story with a sober realism of its own is Elizabeth Grove's WINTERCUT, about a canal family held up for repairs at a lock-side. Sal and Joe, the younger children, make friends with Don Landreth and stay at his home, the lock-house, and from here the children set out into the winter hills to prospect an old canal route. The Landreth parents enter into the spirit of the expedition, but in a sensible, partial way, and the feeling of home comforts side by side with enterprise is most attractive. If the sincere picture of the Landreth home gives depth to the story, so does the description of the narrow boat, and the summing-up of the canal dweller's outlook by Sal, as she prepares to set off once more:

Drawing by William Stobbs for Elizabeth Grove's WINTERCUT (Cape)

The water in the dipper was icy on her skin. When she had washed, she went to the closed cupboard ... and brought out a long bundle which she laid out on the side-bed. Pushing the little folding table back again against its shelves, she started to take off her shabby dungarees. 'Uhuh,' she said to the woollen frock and the stockings which Mrs Landreth had lent her and which were hanging over the stove ... 'Ta very much, but not my rig.'
Elizabeth Grove. WINTERCUT (Cape, 1957) p. 187.

Two worlds have met, their inhabitants have made some impression on each other, and they have parted. The simplicity of the theme, echoed by the fine, strong style and the equally strong drawings, make this a book in a thousand.

Unique among writers for children is William Mayne, who gives to his wildest treasure-hunts a background of balanced and complete

Drawing by Christopher Brooker for William Mayne's
THE ROLLING SEASON (O.U.P).

family life. THE THUMBSTICK, with its hunt over the Yorkshire dales for an old religious emblem, always comes circling back to the farm, to the rapid, idiosyncratic, absolutely authentic talk of a family—of Mrs Bargate, humorous and sensible, of John, with his flurries of enthusiasm and his moods of despair, of that splendid, trenchant centenarian, Great Aunt Airey. THE ROLLING SEASON roams up and down dried-up Wiltshire hills and in and out of two houses, and the finding of water to save the hamlet, the gang of toughs poling down the muddy canals, the brassy sky and the dry grass, the casual chatter, all make up a wonderfully real whole. I know no recent children's stories more *actual* than William Mayne's, whether he is writing about a school or a village or a small town; and perhaps he is a little difficult for children to appreciate just for this reason, because he utterly ignores any compromise, any of the formulas which endear more popular writers to children. But the child who plunges into his stories, forgetting fashion, listening to the dry, crisp dialogue, and seeing in his mind's eye the scenes so minutely and economically visualized, has found a companion for life, no less.

Now Ransome does not give us a *round* study of family life, as Mayne does, for he is committed to the children's point of view; but they have among themselves very clear and changeable relationships, though their relations with grown-ups are static. If you want to read a shrewd account of child behaviour, look at WINTER HOLIDAY, where the Blacketts and Walkers cautiously approach Dorothea and Dick, newcomers to the district. See how the two strangers stand aloof, envying the solidarity of the little group, and see how each individual learns to get used to a change of friends. It is a wonderful piece of social management. And what child with imagination does not warm to Titty Walker, with her shrinking from noise and heartiness, her burning courage in a crisis? In PIGEON POST Titty finds she is a natural dowser. Terrified at first, she faces her responsibility (for their holiday plans depend on finding water in the hills). She goes away alone, screwing herself up to test her gift; and when she has found water, her first impulse is to boast about it. Every stage of her feelings is beautifully described, but within the action of the story, and at the same time we see how this incident affects the other children. To Nancy Blackett the new-found spring is a challenge: 'Barbecued billygoats!' she exclaims, 'If it's there, we'll get it out all right if we have to dig through to Australia', and you can hear the ring in her voice. But to Dorothea, a budding author, there is more to it than this:

'I'm going to put it in a story . . . Different, of course. I'm making you a boy, and you do that business with the stick all by yourself and you've got a spade with you and you start digging. It's at night, and the moon rises through the clouds, and all of a sudden you've dug deep enough and the water comes spouting up into the moonlight . . .'
'Go on,' said Titty. 'What happened next?'
'I'm not quite sure yet,' said Dorothea.
Arthur Ransome. PIGEON POST (Cape, 1936) p. 162.

There are children who find Ransome's books tedious because they are not interested in sailing, camping or skating, but there are few who will not change their minds if they have the patience to look beyond the technical details to the characters. They will find, in the end, that Ransome's stories last them longer than the similar tales of Kitty Barne or Lois Lamplugh or Tyler Whittle. I enjoy stories by these writers enormously. I like the free air the children breathe, their rousing conversations, their ingenuity; but I can never remember which is which—not even if I look at the illustrations; and in fact the unmistakable, squarish faces of William Stobbs's children (appearing in stories by the three writers I have just mentioned) give me an odd feeling that I am meeting the same boys and girls over and over again. Stobbs is a magnificent illustrator, and few people can create atmosphere as he can in an historical story, but his portraits interrupt the imagination as it rolls together known faces, impressions and dreams, so that eventually a character in a book takes on the semblance of a real person—but a different person to each reader. Harold Jones, who has illustrated several of M. E. Atkinson's family stories, has clearly a good idea what her characters are like, but he subordinates this knowledge to his ideas of design, and the result is a collaboration of artist and writer from which each gains.

An author must find time to establish his characters, no matter how much else he has to do. His details may date his story, but this will hardly matter if his characters are interesting. Who can now read E. V. Lucas's pioneer tale, THE SLOWCOACH? It has dated badly, not because the Avories go off in a horse-drawn van, leaving behind them a house run by four servants, but because the characters are not interesting enough to keep your attention from these period details. Nor are they any better in Lucy Bellhouse's story of twenty-five years later, THE CARAVAN CHILDREN, which is dedicated 'To all Nurses, Maid-servants, and Governesses who with such care and devotion look after and love other people's children'. And Barbara Willard's boys and girls who take the road with an unorthodox grown-up in SNAIL AND THE PENNITHORNES are going to suffer the same fate, long before it is old-fashioned to tow caravans behind cars.

But now look at a twenty-year-old camping story by a writer who is, above all, a creator of character. The plot of E. H. Young's CARAVAN ISLAND is far from original. Cicely and Stephen, who go to Skye with their young Aunt Judy, are furious because at the last minute two younger cousins, Laura and Hugh, are added to the party. Nothing out of the way happens in this camp, but everything that does happen seems memorable, because the children and their aunt are established as individuals right from the start. When Laura is lost in the hills, it is not only the hunt for her that makes you want to read on, it is also the fact that Aunt Judy, who believes that children should be resourceful, now wonders guiltily whether she has left them alone too much. When the bull gets out, it is not only the dramatic incident that matters, but Stephen's view of it, his plan to get a good audience for his untruthful version:

. . . he was wondering what would be the best time to tell the story of the bull. Tonight, perhaps, when they were sitting round the fire in the twilight; it would seem more terrifying then, when every shadow could be mistaken for the animal and every sound might herald his approach.

E. H. Young. CARAVAN ISLAND (Black, 1940) pp. 196-7.

The small adventures of the children are no more exciting than the ebb and flow of their feelings, their cross-alliances, the wearing away of hostility between the two families, the drawing-out of Cicely and the suppressing of Stephen, and a hundred and one little points subtly conveyed.

When we are reading stories about families, we must have some idea how the children regard each other. Personality will not do unless it is live, changeable personality. I would almost suggest that a family story without a quarrel was not worth reading—not because of the dramatic value of a quarrel, but because it is natural for children to be constantly rubbing corners off each other. E. Nesbit's Bastables live in the memory, never out of date, because they are children as we all know them, quarrelling, disagreeing, arguing, taking sides; they know each other in the way members of a family do, and at the same time they are always discovering new things about each other. Elizabeth Enright's New York Melendys, Gillian Avery's Victorian Smiths and Squerryes, and the riotous Cares children drawn by E. C. Spykman—all these have the hall-mark of the real *family*. This is the kind of thing which really happens in families:

> Theodore, who was thirteen and had red hair, green eyes and freckles, would do anything when he was in a temper, especially if someone had managed to hit him squarely in the neck with a mud-pie. Jane had decided to run and her neat new sneakers had carried her like wings. She had escaped into the house and upstairs where she had packed a few clothes, and by jumping into the soft loam of the geranium bed while Ted was banging at her locked door, had got off across the fields. Her intention had been to climb up to the middle of the old maple at the lower end of the barn field, unpack, and set up housekeeping in a place of peace and quiet, where in the cool shelter she could concentrate on hating Theodore. It had seemed a good idea . . . But now she was on her way home, because it had not worked. Living in a tree was quite impractical. Nothing would stay where you put it.
>
> E. C. Spykman. A LEMON AND A STAR (Macmillan, 1956) p. 2.

M. E. Atkinson's CRUSOE ISLAND stands out among many similar tales because of its family relationships. The opening chapter, with five children cooped up by rain and snarling at each other, is gloriously real, and so is the aunt who admits to herself that, fond as she is of her young relations, she would far rather be by herself. And (not to insist too much on the sharpness of quarrels) how valuable is the constant shift of loyalties in PATTERSON'S TRACK, an excellent story by Eleanor Spence about three Sydney children, on a back-country visit, trekking through the bush with local friends. The story is memorable for its plot, which rests on the unravelling of a piece of local history, but still more on the behaviour of the children during their exacting journey. At the end of it, town-bred Barry has thought twice about the yokels and his sister has questioned his authority for the first time; none of the children is quite the same as before. These are cheerful, extroverted children; there is no dreary musing over emotions. All the same, you can watch the family pattern of town and country children changing and re-forming. This is a splendid study of character in action.

For girls, character-drawing is always an essential part of fiction. Schoolboys demand more fact and less feeling, and, for them, stories based on a sport offer a specially suitable version of the family story, where they can see how people behave almost without noticing it. The method is not essentially different from the method that produced LITTLE WOMEN or the stories of the Melendys, but the emphasis is different. For instance, in Hugh de Selincourt's agreeable tale of village cricket, THE SATURDAY MATCH, the real point of the story is the delicate development of the relationship between father and son, between brother and sister, but every conversation, every nuance of expression relates to the match. In the same way, Clare Huchet Bishop's unusually good story, THE BIG LOOP, depends both on her vivid account of the Tour de France and on her portrait of young Andre and his efforts to triumph over poverty and inexperience and make himself worthy of his famous cyclist father. Robert Bateman, in YOUNG CRICKETER, YOUNG CLIMBER and YOUNG FOOTBALLER, combines technical detail (used dramatically) and a view of how character is tested in very ordinary situations.

Stories like this have, among other things, helped to widen the social background of children's stories. The dominant adults in Bateman's stories do not belong to the professional classes. They are a police inspector, a small farmer, a clerk and so on. Up to twenty years ago, children's books were keyed to the middle-classes, where most of their readers were to be found, and the rare stories about working-class or lower middle-class families suffered from an inevitable self-consciousness.

If you go back to the children's books of the last century, of course, you will find class-distinctions taken for granted. In Mrs Molesworth's story, THE RECTORY CHILDREN, Mrs Vane, the vicar's wife, is at first doubtful whether she should allow her young daughter to make friends with Celestina, whose father keeps a stationer's shop. But Celestina is well-behaved and intelligent,

Bridget needs a companion in her lessons, and the problem is solved frankly and with no loss of dignity on either side.

It is when writers begin to feel guilty about class that trouble sets in. You get the curious sentimentality for instance, of Alice Hegan Rice, whose stories of fifty years ago, MRS WIGGS OF THE CABBAGE PATCH and LOVEY MARY, turn humble characters into something foolishly music-hall in behaviour. This was still a danger at a much later date. Eve Garnett's stories about the Ruggles family are warm-hearted and sincere, but until she has really written herself in and is completely at ease with them, there is a facetious note, a note of apology and condescension; the Dustman and the Cleaner are put into inverted commas as well as into capital letters. There is some fine writing in THE FAMILY FROM ONE END STREET but there is also this note:

> In spite of a wife and seven children (not to speak of Ideas) Mr. Ruggles was a very contented sort of man. When the wind was in the East and blew bits of dirt from his dustbins and cart into his eyes and mouth he spat and swore a bit, but it was soon over. So long as he had his job and his family were well and happy, and he could smoke his pipe and work in his garden, see his mates at the Working Men's Club once or twice a week, dream about his Pig, and have a good Blow Out on Bank Holidays, he wanted nothing more.
>
> Eve Garnett. THE FAMILY FROM ONE END STREET (Penguin 1942. First published, 1937) p. 120.

It is a relief to turn to FURTHER ADVENTURES OF THE FAMILY FROM ONE END STREET, which perhaps owes its more relaxed tone to the climate of the 'forties and 'fifties. Here the author is thinking about children first and foremost, and in this enchanting picture of town children coming to terms with the country there is not a breath of condescension. Without Eve Garnett, probably, we should not have had MAGNOLIA BUILDINGS, a recent story by Elizabeth Stucley with the same loosely constructed plot, the same setting in a London working-class flat. The Berners family recalls the Ruggles at every turn. Mum is a cleaner; Gloria at fourteen thinks in terms of nail varnish and glamour, as Eve Garnett's Lily did; like Kate, Doreen hankers after education. But in style and presentation there is all the difference. Elizabeth Stucley may have had to learn about the kind of life the Berners lived, but she writes about them as people she knows, not as members of one class.

If they are left to themselves, children probably will not notice the point of class in a story, unless someone suggests that they should. It is a mistake to assume, as some critics do, that Secondary Modern children in the country, for instance, want to read about Secondary Modern children in the country. A book like GRIFF AND TOMMY by John Griffiths, with its entertaining picture of a family in a mining village, or Christine Price's DAVID AND THE MOUNTAIN, with its picture of a Welsh shepherd boy, do not address themselves to any particular set of children; they stand on their own merits as honest pictures of a particular environment. A BOX FOR BENNY, Leila Berg's touching story of a boy in the Jewish quarter of Manchester, is already established as a minor classic because it describes with grace and humour and precision a particular small boy belonging to a particular class and race—describes him as an individual, with his own problem. This is a book for children of all ages and all backgrounds.

The sensible author lets his young heroes and heroines take the problems of class, such as they are, in their stride. Mrs Molesworth knew what she was doing when she made Biddy disregard the difference between her own home and Celestina's (though she was aware of it), and, allowing for the social changes of the last half-century, that is just what James Reeves is doing, for instance, in MULBRIDGE MANOR, when he describes a group of children playing on the common. They know quite well that Anne is poor, that her background is not the same as theirs, but the only difference it makes to them, and to old Miss Matilda at the Manor, is that Anne can't get away often to help to find the missing will because her mother needs her at home.

In MINNOW ON THE SAY, by Philippa Pearce, one of the best children's books of recent years, young David, whose father is a bus driver, realizes his home life is different from Adam's. He sees the difference in practical terms. Adam lives in a large old house on the river, not in a council house, he has his meals at different times, and he does not always have enough to eat. It is for David's mother to work out how she can offer Miss Codling a cake without hurting her pride, for Mrs Moss realizes the intangible differences which David and Adam can happily ignore. This exquisite story has innumerable threads in its rich canvas—the pervasive presence of the river, every ripple exactly described; the treasure hunt, with its intricate and unexpected ending; the sure handling of a child's joy in living, which Ardizzone echoes in his drawings. But one of the most interesting threads is the sensible, subtle treatment of class difference; the contrasting, by implication, of the Moss household, with its safe, small prosperity, and the old house where Miss Codling fights to preserve her standards.

It might surprise those who think Britain is clinging to her class distinctions in defiance of the rest of Europe, to find in a Swedish story an extremely interesting use of this very subject to produce a dramatic plot. Harry Kullman, in THE SECRET JOURNEY, makes it the cornerstone of his tale of young David, who lives in a well-to-do part of Stockholm. David's father warns him against the other end of the town, where, he says, the children are nothing but savages. David, left alone for the day and feeling bored, decides to prove this to himself. He takes a bus ride to a factory district, gets involved in a gang fight, and after some uneasy moments, becomes the friend and ally of Dumpy and Skinny and their uninhibited lieutenant Rose-Marie. David is intrigued by the contrast between their life and his:

> He noticed to his surprise that their life seemed much more lively, and much less patterned than his own. They had no piano lessons, no dancing classes, and their father never took them for an evening stroll. Nor could he really understand whether they were rich or poor. One moment he thought they must be tremendously rich (Dad bought an accordion last year—although an uncle has it now), and in the next moment Skinny explained, giggling:
> 'We'll have to make the best of living here while we can, ha-ha, because we haven't paid the rent this month.'
> Harry Kullman. THE SECRET JOURNEY. Translated by Evelyn Ramsden (University of London Press, 1959) p. 121.

The urchins, in turn, regard with misgiving David's collar and tie, his accent and his apparent timidity. But prejudice dies a natural death. The children retire to a room where there is a gramophone. They put on a record and David teaches the little girl to dance, while the boys look on admiringly. That moment, when they agree to differ, is memorable for its honesty. Geoffrey Trease makes the same point in THE MAYTHORN STORY, where a boy from a back street in a Welsh town goes out for a day on the hills and meets Sandra, who is staying with a snobbish grandmother. There is perception in the story of Mike's friendship with Sandra, his visit to her home (where her grandmother deliberately tries to upset the girl by showing up his manners), and his unfortunate entanglement with the affairs of Shirley next door.

There have been a good many stories in the last few years about children of different backgrounds learning to get on together. For a time the theme may well become hackneyed, but gradually it will be treated with less conscious purpose. Already the tone seems to be easier; for example, in Ann Thwaite's story of London grammar-school girls, THE HOUSE IN TURNER SQUARE, which combines antiquarian research and personalities most skilfully. Books like this are still, not surprisingly, written from a middle-class point of view, but here is an author who is not disconcerted by this. Joanna Shepherd, the librarian's daughter, and Audrey Pitt, who lives in a council flat, are slow to make friends. Audrey is afraid of her friend's posh house and Joanna of Audrey's bluff manner. Their approach to each other is helped by their mutual interest in the Georgian houses and their history, and by the matter-of-fact attitude of their parents. Common sense and a warm interest in people have given this book a quality lacking in many others of its kind.

What writers like this have done is to bring their stories nearer to the world of grown-ups, not by giving grown-ups a more prominent part in the story, but by giving a child's view of adult problems. They have contributed to that reality which can exist in a family story even when it has an improbable plot; whereas a story where every scratch on the door, every honeycomb on the bedspread is exactly described, lacking the active participation of the author and his characters, may have nothing to offer to the lively-minded young reader. A family story must be about people. Without people— alive, variable, interesting—no matter what superlatives may be quoted on the back flap of the book, the dust-jacket is likely to remain unblemished and untorn by the fingers of enthusiastic readers.

Reading List

Family stories

*Atkinson, M. E. AUGUST ADVENTURE. *Bodley Head* 1936. Illustrated by Harold Jones.

*Atkinson, M. E. CRUSOE ISLAND. *Bodley Head* 1941. Illustrated by Harold Jones.

*Avery, Gillian. THE WARDEN'S NIECE 1957, TRESPASSERS AT CHARLECOTE 1958, illustrated by Dick Hart. JAMES WITHOUT THOMAS 1959, THE ELEPHANT WAR 1960, illustrated by John Verney. *Collins.*

*Badcock, J. C. THE TRUANTS. *Hutchinson* 1953. Illustrated by Margaret Wetherbee.

Baker, Margaret J. ACORNS AND AERIALS 1956, THE BRIGHT HIGH FLYER 1957. *Brockhampton.* Illustrated by Terence Freeman. Domestic adventures for eight and upwards, with good use of village background and sharp observation of character in action.

Ballantyne, Joan. HOLIDAY TRENCH. *Nelson* 1959. Illustrated by Edward Ardizzone. Children on holiday trying to keep cars from spoiling their beach: full of authentic talk and behaviour of children.

Barne, Kitty. DUSTY'S WINDMILL. *Dent* 1949. Illustrated by Marcia Lane-Foster. Charming story of troubles and adventures in a Sussex family business: exceptionally well-described background.

*Barrett, Anne. THE JOURNEY OF JOHNNY REW. *Collins* 1954.

*Bateman, Robert. YOUNG FOOTBALLER 1958, YOUNG RUNNER 1958, YOUNG CRICKETER 1959, YOUNG CLIMBER 1959, YOUNG JOCKEY 1960. *Constable.*

Beddington, Roy. THE PIGEON AND THE BOY. *Bles* 1957. North Country industrial town; a boy learns how to rear and train racing pigeons.

*Bellhouse, Lucy. THE CARAVAN CHILDREN. *Harrap* 1935. Illustrated by Barbara Moray Williams.

*Berg. Leila. A BOX FOR BENNY. *Brockhampton* 1958. Illustrated by Jillian Willett.

*Bishop, Clare Huchet. THE BIG LOOP (1955 U.S.A.). *Dent* 1958. Illustrated by Carl Fontseré.

Boden, Hilda. MARLOWS AT NEWGALE 1956, MARLOWS DIG FOR TREASURE 1958, MARLOWS IN DANGER 1959, MARLOWS AT CASTLE CLIFF 1960. *Brockhampton.* Illustrated by Lilian Buchanan. Unexacting domestic adventures intended for children of eight and upwards: good, easy characterization and dialogue: setting mainly Pembrokeshire.

Boucher, Alan. THE RUNAWAYS. *Nelson* 1959. Illustrated by Margery Gill. Practical and exciting tale of three children hiding from unwelcome aunt in New Forest.

*Burton, Hester. THE GREAT GALE. *O.U.P.* 1960. Illustrated by Joan Kiddell-Monroe.

*Chauncy, Nan. THEY FOUND A CAVE. *O.U.P.* (1949) 1958. Illustrated by Margaret Horder.

Chauncy, Nan. TIGER IN THE BUSH 1957, illustrated by Margaret Horder. DEVIL'S HILL 1958, illustrated by Geraldine Spence. *O.U.P.* Tales of the Lorennys in their remote Tasmanian home: wild life and daily adventures, from the angle of a small boy.

*Coatsworth, Elizabeth. ALICE-ALL-BY-HERSELF (1938 U.S.A.). *Harrap* 1959. Illustrated by Marguerite De Angeli.

*Cox, Patricia Ann. SANDAL ASH. Harrap 1950.

Eager, Edward. HALF MAGIC 1954, MAGIC OR NOT ? 1959. *Macmillan.* Illustrated by N. M. Bodecker. American family tales with freakish humour and some sharp drawing of personality.

*Enright, Elizabeth. THIMBLE SUMMER (1938 U.S.A.). *Penguin* (Puffin Story Books) 1955. THE SEA IS ALL AROUND (1940 U.S.A.). *Heinemann* 1959. Illustrated by the author.

*Enright, Elizabeth. THE SATURDAYS (1941 U.S.A.) 1955, THE FOUR-STOREY MISTAKE (1942 U.S.A.) 1955, THEN THERE WERE FIVE (1944 U.S.A.) 1956, SPIDERWEB FOR TWO (1951 U.S.A.) 1956, *Heinemann.* Illustrated by the author.

*Enright, Elizabeth. GONE-AWAY LAKE (1957 U.S.A.). *Heinemann* 1959. Illustrated by Beth and Joe Krush.

Estes, Eleanor. THE MOFFATTS (U.S.A. 1941) 1959, THE MIDDLE MOFFATT (1942 U.S.A.) 1960, RUFUS M. (1943 U.S.A.) 1960. *Bodley Head.* Illustrated by Louis Slobodkin. Lively tales of American small town of Cranbury between the wars, and the everyday exploits of average but highly amusing children.

Estes, Eleanor. GINGER PYE. *Harcourt*, New York 1951. PINKY PYE (1958 U.S.A.). *Constable* 1959. Illustrated by Edward Ardizzone. A family and their cat and dog: whimsical literary flavour and an endearing humour, setting Cranbury and New York Bay.

Fennimore, Stephen. BUSH HOLIDAY. *Heinemann* 1948. *Penguin* (Puffin Story Books) 1958. Illustrated by Sheila Hawkins. English boy getting used to Australian backblocks; very natural.

*Fischer, Marjorie. STREET FAIR (1935 U.S.A.). *Routledge* 1936.

*Garnett, Eve. THE FAMILY FROM ONE END STREET. *Muller* 1937. *Penguin* (Puffin Story Books) 1942. Illustrated by the author.

*Garnett, Eve. FURTHER ADVENTURES OF THE FAMILY FROM ONE END STREET. *Heinemann* 1956. Illustrated by the author.

*Graham, Eleanor. THE CHILDREN WHO LIVED IN A BARN. *Routledge* 1938. *Penguin* (Puffin Story Books) 1955 (revised edition).

*Griffiths, John. GRIFF AND TOMMY. *Dent* 1956. Illustrated by Antony Lake.

*Grove, Elizabeth. WINTERCUT. *Cape* 1957. Illustrated by William Stobbs.

*Hull, Katharine and Whitlock, Pamela. THE FAR-DISTANT OXUS. *Cape* 1937. *Collins* 1960 (slightly abridged). ESCAPE TO PERSIA 1938, OXUS IN SUMMER 1939, CROWNS 1947. *Cape*. Illustrated by Pamela Whitlock.

Kaeser, H. J. MIMFF (1937 Sweden) 1939, translated by Kathleen Williamson. MIMFF IN CHARGE 1949, MIMFF TAKES OVER 1954, translated by David Ascoli. MIMFF-ROBINSON 1958, translated by Ruth Michaelis-Jena and Arthur Ratcliff. *O.U.P.* Illustrated by Edward Ardizzone. Enchanting stories about a small boy and his adventures, at home in Denmark, at school or camping on a Swedish island.

Kästner, Erich. LOTTIE AND LISA (1949 Germany). *Cape* 1950. Translated by Cyrus Brooks. Illustrated by Walter Trier. Two girls at holiday school discover they are identical twins, and succeed in reconciling their divorced parents. Light-hearted but with sound sense and principles.

'Kim'. THE BOYS OF PUHAWAI. *U.L.P.* 1960. Illustrated by Dennis Turner. Two Maoris and an Irish boy, their everyday adventures in and around a New Zealand dairy farm: told from boys' point of view.

*Kullman, Harry. THE SECRET JOURNEY (1953 Sweden). *U.L.P.* 1959. Translated by Evelyn Ramsden. Illustrated by Claes Bäckström.

*Lamplugh, Lois. NINE BRIGHT SHINERS 1955, THE PIGEONGRAM PUZZLE 1955, VAGABOND'S CASTLE 1957, ROCKETS IN THE DUNES 1958. *Cape*. Illustrated by William Stobbs.

Lavrin, Nora and Thorp, Molly. THE HOP DOG. *O.U.P.* 1952. Illustrated by Nora Lavrin. East-enders hop-picking in Kent. Level-headed study of a variety of men, women and children.

Lloyd, Marjorie. FELL FARM HOLIDAY 1951, FELL FARM FOR CHRISTMAS 1954, FELL FARM CAMPERS 1960. *Penguin* (Puffin Story Books). Illustrated by the author. The five Brownes and their domestic and holiday adventures in the Lake District: gay and readable.

Lockhart, David. THE HOUSE THAT MAC BUILT. *Dent* 1960. Illustrated by Geraldine Spence. Easy, convincing tale of children building a look-out house.

Love, Margaret. AN EXPLORER FOR AN AUNT. *Blackie* 1960. Illustrated by Susan Einzig. Gang of cousins in Cornish house instructed in enjoying adventure by unorthodox aunt: good fun, excellent studies of children sorting out their differences.

*Lucas, E. V. THE SLOWCOACH (1910). *Edward Arnold* 1955. Illustrated by M. V. Whielhouse.

Masefield, Judith. LARKING AT CHRISTMAS 1953, APRIL FOOLS 1954. *Collins*. Illustrated by Shirley Hughes. Boy and girl in manor house, acting plays, arranging circus in the village: distinguished by gusto, inventiveness, and natural dialogue.

*Mayne, William. THE THUMBSTICK 1959, illustrated by Tessa Theobald. THE ROLLING SEASON 1960, illustrated by Christopher Brooker. *O.U.P.*

Michael, Manfred. TIMPETILL (1937 Switzerland). *O.U.P.* 1951. Translated by R. P. Aston. Illustrated by Richard Kennedy. Children of a German-Swiss village run it for a week in parents' absence: neat and interesting story, with plenty of good characterization.

*Molesworth, Mrs M. L. THE RECTORY CHILDREN. *Macmillan* 1889.

*Parker, Richard. MORE SNAKES THAN LADDERS. *Brockhampton* 1960. Illustrated by Jillian Willett.

*Pearce, A. Philippa. MINNOW ON THE SAY. *O.U.P.* 1955. Illustrated by Edward Ardizzone.

Pertwee, Roland. THE ISLANDERS 1950, ROUGH WATER 1951. *O.U.P.* Illustrated by Ernest Shepard. Three boys on river island in Devon, fending for themselves and dealing with a crook and an unpleasant relation.

*Price, Christine. DAVID AND THE MOUNTAIN. *Bodley Head* 1959. Illustrated by the author.

Pullein-Thompson, Diana. THE SECRET DOG. *Collins* 1959. Illustrated by Geraldine Spence. Cockney and Jamaican boy fight for the right to keep a mongrel they rescue from river: good London working-class background.

Pullein-Thompson, Diana. THE BOY AND THE DONKEY. *Collins* 1958. Illustrated by Shirley Hughes. London working-class streets and a boy training a ragman's donkey for the Donkey Derby.

Pye, Virginia. RED-LETTER HOLIDAY. *Faber* 1940. Illustrated by Gwen Raverat. One of the earliest holiday adventure tales, about Kensington middle-class children fending for themselves in a Cornish cottage.

*Ransome, Arthur. SWALLOWS AND AMAZONS, 1930. SWALLOWDALE 1931. *Cape*. Both republished with Ransome's illustrations 1938.

*Ransome, Arthur. PETER DUCK 1932, WINTER HOLIDAY 1933, COOT CLUB 1934, PIGEON POST 1936, WE DIDN'T MEAN TO GO TO SEA 1937, SECRET

WATER 1939, THE BIG SIX 1940, MISSEE LEE 1941, THE PICTS AND THE MARTYRS 1943, GREAT NORTHERN? 1947. *Cape.* Illustrated by the author.

Redlich, Monica. JAM TOMORROW. *Nelson* 1937. Children of absent-minded Rector housekeeping when help walks out: good impression of ordinary family on its mettle.

*Reeves, James. MULBRIDGE MANOR. *Heinemann* 1958. Illustrated by Geraldine Spence.

*Rice, Alice Hegan. MRS WIGGS OF THE CABBAGE PATCH (1901 U.S.A.) 1902, LOVEY MARY (1903 U.S.A.) 1903. *Hodder & Stoughton.*

*Selincourt, Hugh de. THE SATURDAY MATCH. *Dent* 1937.

Seredy, Kate. THE OPEN GATE (1943 U.S.A.). *Harrap* 1947. Illustrated by the author. American family moving from New York and settling on a farm: homely encounters with neighbours, the seasons and a new way of life.

Sheppard-Jones, Elizabeth. THE SEARCH FOR MARY. *Nelson* 1960. Illustrated by Jane Paton. Adopted child runs away, two children follow clues across England to Wales: natural and convincing.

Sindall, Marjorie A. MATEY. *Macmillan* 1960. Illustrated by Sheila Rose. Girl and her father moving from Battersea slum to caravan in the country: fine characterization.

Sindall, Marjorie A. THE BUDDS OF PARAGON ROW. *Heinemann* 1954. Illustrated by Vera Jarman. Working-class widow with a clever daughter and a son led into bad ways: sincere and touching, with plenty of humour.

*Spence, Eleanor. PATTERSON'S TRACK. *Angus & Robertson* 1959. Illustrated by Alison Forbes.

Spence, Eleanor. THE SUMMER IN BETWEEN. *O.U.P.* 1959. Illustrated by Marcia Lane-Foster. Girls in Australian township during long holiday: friendships, projects and adventures.

Spence, Eleanor. LILLIPILLY HILL. *O.U.P.* 1960. Illustrated by Susan Einzig. Australia in the 1890's: English family settling in township and learning new social pattern.

*Spykman, E. C. A LEMON AND A STAR (1955 U.S.A.) 1956, illustrated by Prudence Seward. THE WILD ANGEL (1956 U.S.A.) 1957. *Macmillan.*

Street, Dorothea. THE DOG-LEG GARDEN. *O.U.P.* 1951. Illustrated by Evelyn Cooke. Doctor's family playing in rented garden, learning about gardening and people.

*Stucley, Elizabeth. MAGNOLIA BUILDINGS. *Bodley Head* 1960. Illustrated by Dick Hart.

Theobald, Tessa. A SHADOW ON THE SEA. *O.U.P.* 1957. Illustrated by the author. Straightforward tale of four children looking after themselves.

*Thwaite, Ann. THE HOUSE IN TURNER SQUARE. *Constable* 1960. Illustrated by Robin Jacques.

*Trease, Geoffrey. THE MAYTHORN STORY. *Heinemann* 1960. Illustrated by Robert Hodgson.

Urmston, Mary. THE FIVE BRIGHT KEYS. *Doubleday,* New York 1946. American family settling in the country track down their keys and so meet neighbours who become friends.

Wayne, Jennifer. CLEMENCE AND GINGER. *Heinemann* 1960. Illustrated by Patricia Humphreys. Friendship between middle-class girl and a rackety boy of poor family who helps her in money-making plans.

Weaver, Stella. SISTERS AND BROTHERS. *Collins* 1960. Family relationships tackled with honesty: a family makes adjustments when a foreign orphan is brought to live with them.

Weir, Rosemary. THE SECRET JOURNEY. *Parrish* 1957. Children making their way from Cornwall to Windsor in a tilt-cart: good details of housekeeping, routes, etc.

Weir, Rosemary. THE HUNT FOR HARRY. *Parrish* 1960. Intellectual family moves to poor London district, becomes involved in muddled affairs of a coloured man and his child. Cross-country travelling, clues and chance-met people all brilliantly described.

*Whittle, Tyler. SPADES AND FEATHERS 1955, illustrated by Raymond Sheppard. THE RUNNERS OF ORFORD 1956, CASTLE LIZARD 1957, illustrated by William Stobbs. *Cape.*

Whittle, Tyler. THE BULLHEAD. *Dent* 1958. Illustrated by Geraldine Spence. Lively story of family navigating sea-going barge to East Coast.

*Willard, Barbara. SNAIL AND THE PENNITHORNES 1957, SNAIL AND THE PENNITHORNES NEXT TIME 1958, SNAIL AND THE PENNITHORNES AND THE PRINCESS 1960. *Epworth.* Illustrated by Geoffrey Fletcher.

Willard, Barbara. THE HOUSE WITH ROOTS. *Constable* 1959. Illustrated by Robert Hodgson. Family threatened with eviction because of new road: lively story about real personalities.

Willard, Barbara. EIGHT FOR A SECRET. *Constable* 1960. Illustrated by Lewis Hart. Village, newly enlarged by factories and housing-estate: good study of clash of children from different backgrounds, with adventure on a lake and an island.

Woodberry, Joan. RAFFERTY TAKES TO FISHING 1959, FLOODTIDE FOR RAFFERTY 1960. *Parrish.* Illustrated by the author. Domestic adventures of a small boy in an Australian coastal town. The atmosphere is cheerful and authentic.

Wright, Alison. THE BLAKES. *Dent* 1952. Illustrated by Sheila Macgregor. Factory-worker looking for a job buys a bus and takes his family across country: real and lively, but with an unconvincing happy end.

*Young, E. H. CARAVAN ISLAND. *Black* 1940. Illustrated by H. J. Haley.

Drawing by Edward Ardizzone for Philippa Pearce's MINNOW ON THE SAY (O.U.P.)

Chapter 15 | *Growing Up*

It is, after all, a fair test of a book, whether it still has its dust-jacket on or not—unless it is a second or third copy bought for a family of obsessive readers. A reviewer wrote recently:

> In the bad old Victorian days children's books made (we are told now) not nearly enough concessions to their diminutive readers. Their authors crammed them with instruction and moral uplift. They used an uncompromising, polysyllabic, adult vocabulary. They bombarded the youthful mind with raw, if not unadulterated, heroic legend. They were not what is today known as 'entertainment', or anywhere near; and the denizens of the nursery undistracted by TV or the Pleasure Principle, read and re-read them till they fell to bits.
> Ulysses in Modern Dress. *The Times Literary Supplement*, 20 May, 1960.

Why do children still read LITTLE WOMEN? What does Louisa Alcott give them still which they do not always find in contemporary stories? Could it be that her gently humorous tales are nearer to reality than the more up-to-date versions children take, mint-new, from the library shelf?

From their first junior books onwards, children should be able to find something of what people and places are really like. The writer who studies his public too closely may well leave out, on some misguided principle, a good deal of adult comment that children really need. It is only too easy to underestimate the understanding of the young. What we give them must be strong and honest. Victorian story-books are criticized for their repressions and omissions. We would do well to ask whether writers of today give children any more of the truth, or indeed as much.

How many family stories there are in which the plot centres round poverty: how few in which you can really *smell* that poverty. LITTLE WOMEN has a permanent place on the bookshelves of the young because of its sterling honesty. The author herself described the book as 'Not a bit sensational, but simple and true, for we really lived most of it, and if it succeeds, that will be the reason for it.' Whoever doubted, when reading about the scorched breadth in Jo March's evening dress, that these girls were poor? And it is the same with every issue that touches the Marches. Love, social adventure, jobs, friction among themselves, illness and death—the author looks at everything squarely. Brought up in a liberal family, where children were treated as sensible individuals, it never occurred to her that her young readers would expect anything else.

Ethel Turner, whose children's stories (especially SEVEN LITTLE AUSTRALIANS and THE FAMILY AT MISRULE) have been in print continuously for nearly seventy years, has the same forthright attitude to her material. These two splendid writers did not put death-bed scenes into their stories out of custom or morbid interest, but because death was part of the life they were writing about. It happened. Beth got ill, Judy Woolcot was hurt, and for once there was no happy ending. Their brothers and sisters faced the loss, some with complaint, some quietly, some only partly realizing it, but they all faced the fact of death, and there is no reason why young readers today should not do the same when a story demands it.

This is not to suggest that every story for older boys and girls should include a death-bed scene. Any scene that arises will be the better for being played straight. In LION AT LARGE, Richard Parker describes a dangerous situation and makes sure that it does impress the readers as being really dangerous. In the middle of the night a primary schoolboy wakes and sees from his window a lion standing by the gate. It is hardly surprising that he is not believed when he tells this story next morning, for he hardly believes it himself. All the same, he and his ally Ingrid, a farmer's daughter, do find the lion, hiding in a hollow tree. Together they plot and plan, buy food, think up excuses for being absent from school. At first the lion, hungry and wounded, seems friendly enough; but this is a wild beast, even if it does come from a circus. Barry has wonderful dreams of walking back to the village with a docile lion at his heels, but things do not happen like this. The children are in real, frighten-

Drawing by Paul Hogarth for Richard Parker's LION AT LARGE
(Brockhampton). Emphasizes the author's description of real danger

ing peril before rescue comes, and the author hides none of it from
his readers (who will be, incidentally, between eight and ten).

The problem of realism is more complicated, naturally, when we
come to books for older children, between thirteen and fifteen.
What is the writer to give them? How is he to make sure that they
still want to read what he writes? How is he to satisfy their craving
for experience without hustling them away from the last tentative
years of childhood? They must, now, have books that will tax and
stimulate them. If they can still cheerfully read adventure stories,
and most of them can, they will get more out of these if they show
some grasp of moral as well as physical danger and development.
In THE MAN FROM DEVIL'S ISLAND, Arthur Calder Marshall
has used a theme which could have been treated in a romantic,
unreal fashion. The setting is the island of Trinidad. A prisoner has
escaped from a French penal settlement. Three children in their
early teens find him on the beach, in a distressed condition, and deter-
mine to help him. What begins as an exciting adventure ends by being
a serious, even a bitter experience. Gradually the children realize
how many issues depend on their action. They see dimly the neces-
sities of the law. Through the reaction of their parents, they begin
to understand how little in real life is clear-cut. Their gay deter-

Drawing by Keith Vaughan for P. H. Newby's THE SPIRIT OF JEM (John Lehmann)

mination to do good flags and diminishes under pressure from the external world which they have blithely ignored. This is certainly not a moral story. No lesson is preached to interrupt the action. Excellent as this adventure story is, however, no child can finish it without having second thoughts about his own niche in the adult world.

A later story, THE FAIR TO MIDDLING, is still more exacting. Here the children of an orphanage are taken to a fair through the kindness of Lady Charity Armstrong, their gracious patron. Behind the familiar coconut-shies and merry-go-rounds are booths with less obvious attractions. Devils and angels, in human guise, wrestle, as it were, for the souls of the orphans and their preceptors; their wares are at once actual and symbolic. A boy who is going blind, and an ugly, unwanted schoolmistress who loves him, wander together through the blare of catchpenny tunes and hear together the glorious music of the soul which the boy now knows he can create.

Two nasty children suffer a prolonged sojourn in a very modern hell. Lady Charity herself wanders hysterically though a maze with the Superintendent, both seeking lost youth and innocence.

There is a story here, as well as a hidden meaning, and a compelling story it is. The simple force of allegory can be found too in a Kafkaesque tale by P. H. Newby, THE SPIRIT OF JEM, limpid in style and alarming in its implications. It is a mature story, with bold, uncompromising illustrations. The devil walks here, as he walks through Mr Calder Marshall's fair. He walks now in the shape of Jem, a boy who can make people forget their identity. Ostensibly, he is saving them from a mysterious enemy whom only he knows: really, he is destroying their individuality. The boy who tells the tale is at first deceived by Jem. When he realizes that this is, in fact, the enemy of freedom, he tries desperately to get support from his fellowmen, and to save Mr Bowler, who, playing the pipe which stands for grace and hope, has been imprisoned by Jem. Anti-war, anti-fascist, anti-totalitarian, a sermon for the freedom of man's mind—all these things, and, besides, a story which moves forward quickly, smoothly and with a grand simplicity.

Books like this are not for every child. But if some find allegory puzzling and even tedious, they still appreciate the truth about human nature, in the most straightforward family tale. There is no reason why such stories should not be outspoken about what people are like. Writers need not pretend that parents are always kind and tolerant, always interested in what their children are doing: their readers know otherwise. We can only hope that those writers who prefer to forget the acuteness of children about grown-ups will put up their pens for lack of readers; and, with family stories for older children growing tougher, more aware of life, more adult all the time, I believe this is what will happen, if parents will help by accumulating or suggesting books like this, contemporary or classic. Harvey Darton was justified, perhaps, in calling THE WIDE, WIDE WORLD 'that astonishingly lachrymose work,' but, putting up their umbrellas against Ellen's tears, children of today still learn from her relations with bitter Miss Fortune, as they learn from THE SECRET GARDEN, with its hints of deep unhappiness. These are not depressing stories, they are expandable. They open a window on the world, through which children will see more and more each time they read; and they do still read these books.

Let us hold fast by the writer of today who gives our children expandable stories, stories which draw them forward into knowledge of people. By Ruth Adam, for instance, because, in A STEPMOTHER FOR SUSAN OF ST BRIDE'S, she puts into a rather sensational story about a hospital sister some uncompromising, shrewd scenes where a prospective stepmother and a girl come to grips with each other. By William Mayne, who in UNDERGROUND ALLEY describes another kind of stepmother whose insensitive behaviour does more harm than direct cruelty. The truth of the following passage is sifted through the personality of a schoolgirl:

> The affair of the exchanged socks was the first thing to meet her at home. Gwen had looked for them to sew tapes on when Patty was out, and there was a battle of words and opinions about it. It stopped when Daddy came up from the cellar for his tea, but the matter was not settled at all, and Gwen said she would take the grey socks back and change them again. After tea Patty disposed of the argument by sewing tapes on both pairs and putting one pair on. Gwen found out too soon, and was very angry. Patty went down into the cellar, taking the alarm clock to remind. her of the time, and fastened herself away.
>
> She calmed her rage by stirring paint and listening to Daddy sawing and chiselling next door at his secret construction.
>
> 'I've got my secret, Daddy's got his, and Gwen's got the baby,' she thought. 'Why can't she manage that and leave me as we were?'
>
> William Mayne. UNDERGROUND ALLEY (Oxford University Press, 1958) p. 78-9.

Adult relationships must make their appearance in books for young people in the right way, to the extent that they would notice them in their own lives. It is no use thrusting a complex story of human relations on a schoolgirl, disguised as an adventure story. In THE SPARROW CHILD, by Meriol Trevor, the quest for a lost chalice is mingled with a complicated love-affair, past and renewed, between young Philip's relations. A girl of twelve might become interested in the adventure but would probably be confused by the hints at an ancient issue between Barny and Carey; an older girl would find the love-story precious, and irritating in its vagueness. A better proportion is achieved in TAWNY BRUSH, a story by Peggy

Cannam about a Gloucestershire farm where Mrs Blake, whose husband had left her ten years before, is battling, with the help of her four sons, to keep the place and the family going. There is much to attract a girl in this book—the glowing picture of the country, the precise account of how Lexy tames a fox-cub, the candid comment and affection between the girl and her mother and brothers, and, above all, the picture of Mrs Blake, lonely, often bad-tempered, facing the difficult task of adjustment when her husband comes back.

Books like this are a necessary corrective to the sickly, unreal view of life and love thrust at schoolgirls in the pages of magazines designed for them, and the 'junior novels' which form a growing side of children's publishing are, too often, gentle, rosy and unreal also. If these so-called novels are intended for twelve-year-olds, the writers would do better to confine themselves to adventure and slip romance in as the sideline it normally is at this age; as Elisabeth Kyle does in CAROLINE HOUSE, or Kathrene Pinkerton in her stories about the Bairds and Randolphs in Alaska, or as Geoffrey Trease does in his undergraduate story, THE GATES OF BANNER-DALE. Trease, indeed, was among the first writers of family stories to allow a place for the moments when boy and girl comradeship becomes something deeper. His earlier stories about Bannerdale show Bill and Penny talking with a rough jocularity that hides a delicate awareness of each other. Relationships of this kind will appear more and more now that such stories cast about more widely for their subjects and settings, and we must watch for those writers who can treat boy and girl love sensibly as well as sensitively; for we do not want to jump from the determinedly sexless note of the past to an unattractive sensationalism. A recent story by Catherine Storr, MARIANNE AND MARK, brings out interesting points about this change. The author contrasts Alice and Josie, two fifteen-year-old girls in Brighton, with their jobs and their boy friends, and Marianne, who has grown to an unaware fourteen in an intellectual home and feels she is missing something. The comfortable friendship she establishes with Mark, after a disastrous mistake over Alan and his motor-bike, rounds off a story that is very shrewd about young people and has an agreeable distinction in style and treatment.

If a young love affair is the subject of a story, it must be treated with this kind of shrewdness and without evasion. A younger sister could learn much and achieve a better understanding of her elders if she reads Maureen Daly's SEVENTEENTH SUMMER, with its delicate but frank picture of an American small town and a girl working through her first love affair. Angeline Morrow belongs to a comfortable middle-class home and is disconcerted as well as flattered when Jack Duluth, who works in her father's bakery, begins to take her out. There is an anthropological exactness in the descriptions of drug-store and dance-hall, and of the stylized behaviour of young people who like to think themselves grown-up. Above all, Angeline's feelings, her fear and excitement and the inconvenient warnings of her fastidious mind, are convincingly described. When Jack first visits her house she is strung up; his spoon clicking on his teeth, as he eats ice-cream, becomes a symbol of all the mannerisms she has been trying not to mind:

I saw my mother raise her eyebrow just a little. Just a little, as if a quick thought had passed through her mind, and my heart shrank up into a tight ball of loathing till I felt that my whole inside would rattle around like a hard, brown peanut in a shell. In my mouth was a bitter taste as if I had been sucking a penny and I couldn't even raise my eyes to look at anyone.
Maureen Daly. SEVENTEENTH SUMMER (Hollis & Carter, 1947) pp. 158-9.

We could do with more novels of this kind in England, and though we would not now echo exactly the definition of girls' literature offered by a critic in 1888*—'while it advances beyond the nursery, it stops short of the full blaze of the drawing-room', there is a lot of sense in the view. Mrs Molesworth's novels, which date from that period, give many shrewd comments on the behaviour of young people which are still interesting today, and there are later romances, like Gene Stratton Porter's A GIRL OF THE LIMBERLOST, which fill the gap between school and adult reading. Lush and exaggerated as this story seems now, it is no superficial romance, but a candid, at times a cruel study of a repressed woman taking out her loneliness and disappointment on her daughter, and of that

*Edward Salmon. JUVENILE LITERATURE AS IT IS. H. J. Drake, 1888, pp. 221-2.

daughter meeting romance eagerly because of what she has learned from her mother's failure.

Elnora is not a schoolgirl, of course. She is working her way through college, earning her right to independence. Stories for children commonly ignore or minimize the importance of jobs. Does it really matter, in most family stories, what father does for a living? We are told this merely as a way of defining the status of the family. 'Daddy is a doctor', you read, or 'Father is in the Treasury', or 'Dad is a clerk at the Town Hall'; even, occasionally, 'Dad is on night-shift at the factory.' But though the head of the family may sometimes be described as coming home tired, his children show little interest in his work. More often than not the writer seems to have chosen it to keep him occupied while his children proceed with their adventures.

As for these children, they need not always be on holiday from school; and indeed, with the widening of the social content of children's stories, more and more of them have young heroes and heroines who are working, and who find adventure in and through their jobs, rather than outside them.

One of the most readable books of this kind is Lois Lamplugh's THE SIXPENNY RUNNER, a good-luck tale and none the worse for it. Leaving her middle-class children whose adventures in NINE BRIGHT SHINERS and ROCKETS ON THE DUNES were so vigorously told, Miss Lamplugh has turned her attention to their friends the Allens, who live in a converted railway-carriage on the dunes. Ned, the oldest boy, has maturity thrust upon him when his father has an accident and has to give up his groundsman's job. The boy leaves school at fifteen, goes to work with a greyhound-breeder, and studies for G.C.E. in his spare time. An attractive setting and a bit of fairy-tale (Ned is given a runt pup to bring up and she turns out to be a brilliant racer) make this an engaging tale for a twelve-year-old, but there is plenty to interest an older child. Ned works hard and the author takes care that we appreciate this, that we know how often he doubts whether this exhausting night-work is worth the trouble. The problems of a working-class schoolboy have been tackled honestly within the framework of a first-class story.

This is the real strength of Richard Armstrong's splendid yarns, the tales of Merchant Navy apprentices and also SABOTAGE AT THE FORGE and THE WHINSTONE DRIFT, where boys working in a

foundry and an iron-working come upon adventures which rise out
of their jobs and which their training helps them to tackle. The
author has explained the serious purpose of his stories:

> I wanted as far as possible to forearm the boy at the beginning of
> adolescence—not ramming a weapon into his hand willy-nilly, but
> showing him the size and shape of it and where it lies in such a
> way that he would take it up without realizing he was doing so and
> find himself using it when he needed to.
>
> So in the book (he is writing of SEA CHANGE here), I try to give
> him a factual picture of life as it comes at a boy in the Merchant
> Service, to make him familiar with the tools and instruments used
> there and show him how they fit into the general scheme of things.
> I bring him into contact with the kind of people he would meet
> and outline some of the problems and emotional conflicts he
> would have to face, the difficulties and the possibilities such a life
> would hold for him. And finally, I try, whether this is ultimately
> the line of activity he chooses to follow or not, to make him aware
> through it of his own power, his value as a human being; to give
> him confidence in himself, in the richness of life in the real world
> and his capacity for living it.
>
> Richard Armstrong, in CHOSEN FOR CHILDREN. Edited by
> Marcus Crouch. (Library Association, 1957) pp. 52–3.

This is a fine aim, and Richard Armstrong has fulfilled this while
giving his readers thrilling yarns and a sympathetic gallery of heroes
in the process of growing-up but still retaining the angular contours
of boyhood. There is no reason why stories should not be purposive
in this way so long as they still keep the hall-mark of the author's
personality in style and narrative.

The 'career-novel' which has become so popular in recent years
does not stand up well in comparison, but it is only fair to judge this
type of book by its own standards. It is necessarily a compromise
between the junior novel and the handbook. So that the information
about careers may be as complete as possible, the hero or heroine is
pushed up the ladder or through the mill with unnatural speed.
It is usually, in fact, up the ladder, for no author can get far if his
hero stays in the outer office; but sometimes the load of experience
is shared between two friends or two rivals. In JANET CARR,

JOURNALIST, Josephine Kamm takes the reader into the office of a woman's magazine, where two girls fresh from secretarial school are drafted, one into the fashion department and one into features. Within the limited pattern of the career novel, the temperaments of these two are effectively contrasted, and their rivalry animates a very thorough account of the routine of a magazine.

Although the formula for this kind of book leaves little room for establishing character, it is character, all the same, that really counts. More than one writer has drawn an efficient picture of life at a riding-school. In RENNIE GOES RIDING, Monica Edwards goes further. She presents as her heroine a girl suffering from the effects of wartime bombing, a girl who seems unsuitable for a job that is tough physically and perhaps tedious to the intelligence. Rennie's career is far from easy, and her disappointments and moments of despair are very real to the reader because she is so real a person; horse-obsessives, reading the book for its subject, will find they have got an unexpected pleasure from the interplay of character.

I particularly enjoyed Duncan Taylor's BOB IN LOCAL GOVERNMENT for the same reason. An unpromising title, and Bob is a very ordinary boy, but the author finds adventure in the tastelessly-decorated local office, where an unpleasant senior clerk torments tenants and underlings with his ruthless interpretation of the official code. Information in plenty can be dug out of this story, but it is a fine study of character, too, of the perils of work in close association with an uncongenial personality.

No career novel, of course, gives a full picture of real life. Sex is presented as romance, and only incidentally. Virtue inevitably triumphs. It must be stressed that these are properly books for school-children, not for anyone much over the age of fourteen. They serve as an introduction to adult life, not as a complete version of it.

Not that any work of fiction attempts to provide this, but in so far as it must be attempted, many stories for school-children make a more honest attempt than a great many adult novels. All the same, young people must plunge into adult fiction, from twelve or so onwards, and must do this unafraid and unchecked. We can advise and suggest, but we should not select or censor. The glitter of the forbidden is potent for young people. We must trust them, rather, to choose, as they should have been choosing all along, the books which are most valuable to them. They will form their taste after trial and error and in no other way.

The most valuable quality a child can have, in his reading life, is curiosity. Easily squashed, it is as easily encouraged by the provision of books varied in style and content. If our children can advance into the world of adult fiction with an intense curiosity about human relations, about the position of man in the world, about the technique of writing, they will not go far wrong. If they have grown up with good will towards reading as a necessity of life and one of its major pleasures, they will confirm what they have long unconsciously known, that 'all books are children's books.'

Reading List

*Adam, Ruth. A STEPMOTHER FOR SUSAN OF ST BRIDE'S. *Hulton* (Girl Novel) 1958.

*Alcott, Louisa. LITTLE WOMEN (1868). *Dent* (Children's Illustrated Classics) 1948. Illustrated by S. Van Abbé. *Penguin* (Puffin Story Books) 1953.

Alcott, Louisa. LITTLE WOMEN GOOD WIVES (1871). *Collins* 1954.

Alcott, Louisa. JO'S BOYS (1886). *Blackie* (1939) 1949.

Alcott, Louisa. LITTLE MEN (1871). *Blackie* (1937) 1949.

*Armstrong, Richard. SABOTAGE AT THE FORGE 1946, illustrated by L. P. Lufton. THE WHINSTONE DRIFT 1951, illustrated by M. A. Charlton. *Dent*.

*Burnett, Mrs Hodgson. THE SECRET GARDEN (1911). *Heinemann* (New Windmill Series) 1950. *Penguin* (Puffin Story Books) 1951.

Byers, Irene. TIM OF TAMBERLEY FOREST. *Max Parrish*, 1954. Agreeably written story of a boy learning forestry.

*Cannam, Peggy. TAWNY BRUSH. *Lutterworth* 1957. Illustrated by Sheila Rose.

*Daly, Maureen. SEVENTEENTH SUMMER (1942 U.S.A.). *Hollis & Carter* 1947.

Furlong, Agnes. ELIZABETH LEAVES SCHOOL. *Harrap* 1956. North Country town; secondary school girl goes to work in big store and makes a success of it. Very natural story.

Hogarth, Grace Allen. AS A MAY MORNING. *Hamish Hamilton* 1958. Girl and her first adult emotions: sincere and attractive.

Knight, Captain F. FAMILY ON THE TIDE. *Macmillan* 1956. Illustrated by Geoffrey Whittam. Girl growing up and realizing complexity of other people.

*Kyle, Elisabeth. CAROLINE HOUSE. (see Chap.13).

*Lamplugh, Lois. THE SIXPENNY RUNNER. *Cape* 1960. Illustrated by William Stobbs.

*Marshall, Arthur Calder. THE MAN FROM DEVIL'S ISLAND 1958, THE FAIR TO MIDDLING 1959. *Hart-Davis.*

*Mayne, William. UNDERGROUND ALLEY. *O.U.P.* 1958. Illustrated by Marcia Lane-Foster.

Meader, Stephen. BLUEBERRY MOUNTAIN. *Bell* 1960. Illustrated by Edward Shenton. Two boys selling berries by roadside, starting their own plantation. Technical details and characters equally good.

*Newby, P. H. THE SPIRIT OF JEM. *John Lehmann* 1947. Illustrated by Keith Vaughan.

Norris, Phyllis. MEET THE KILBURYS. *Nelson* 1947. Girls helping their mother to start a hostel for a day school: domestic tale full of good sense and shrewdness.

*Parker, Richard. LION AT LARGE. *Brockhampton* 1959. Illustrated by Paul Hogarth.

*Pinkerton, Kathrene. HIDDEN HARBOUR (1951 U.S.A.) 1954, SECOND MEETING (1956 U.S.A.) 1956, THE SECRET RIVER (1958 U.S.A.) 1958. *Bodley Head.*

*Porter, Gene Stratton. A GIRL OF THE LIMBERLOST (1909 U.S.A.). *Hodder & Stoughton* 1912. Abridged edition, *Brockhampton* 1959. Intelligently edited.

Raymond, Margaret. A BEND IN THE ROAD. *Longmans* 1934. Welsh steel-worker in American town, troubles of his daughter in her search for independence.

*Storr, Catherine. MARIANNE AND MARK. *Faber* 1960.

*Trease, Geoffrey. NO BOATS ON BANNERMERE 1949, UNDER BLACK BANNER 1951, BLACK BANNER PLAYERS 1952, BLACK BANNER ABROAD 1954, THE GATES OF BANNERDALE 1956. *Heinemann.* Illustrated by Richard Kennedy.

*Trevor, Meriol. THE SPARROW CHILD. *Collins* 1958. Illustrated by Martin Thomas.

*Turner, Ethel. SEVEN LITTLE AUSTRALIANS (1894) 1949, THE FAMILY AT MISRULE 1895. *Blackie.*

*Wetherell, Elizabeth. THE WIDE, WIDE WORLD (1851 U.S.A.) 1852. *U.L.P.* 1950. Edited and illustrated by Joyce Lankester Brisley.

Career novels

Allan, Mabel Esther. HERE WE GO ROUND. *Heinemann* 1954. Girl helping in nursery school while waiting for training college: characters exceptionally interesting, a touching story.

Denniston, Robin. THE YOUNG MUSICIANS. *Chatto & Windus* 1955. Lively story of College of Music, with good characters and plenty of variety.

*Edwards, Monica. RENNIE GOES RIDING. *Bodley Head* 1956.

Edwards, Monica. JOAN GOES FARMING. *Bodley Head* 1954.
Excellent characters and an interesting outline of practical training.

*Kamm, Josephine. JANET CARR, JOURNALIST. *Bodley Head* 1953.

Mack, Angela. CONTINUITY GIRL. *Chatto & Windus* 1958. Lively tale with plenty of hard fact.

Meynell, Laurence. POLICEMAN IN THE FAMILY. *O.U.P.* 1953. Illustrated by Neville Dear. Takes a recruit through training school and practical training up to his first beat: interesting and extremely readable.

Meynell, Laurence. THE YOUNG ARCHITECT. *O.U.P.* 1958. Illustrated by David Knight. A particularly good combination of fact and convincing fiction: Colin Winter goes from small Bucks town to a London college.

Summers, D. O. KEN JONES, ELECTRICAL ENGINEER. *Chatto & Windus* 1959. Straight-forward story of two boys climbing the ladder, one by university training, the other through apprenticeship. Extremely interesting.

*Taylor, Duncan. BOB IN LOCAL GOVERNMENT. *Chatto & Windus* 1958.

Wilson, Granville. JONATHAN ENTERS JOURNALISM. *Chatto & Windus* 1956.
Boy on provincial newspaper: good picture of small town and its doings.

TITLES
Authors
Illustrators

Forest, Antonia, 179–80, 192, 263, 267
FOREST FIGHTERS, THE, 248
FOREST OF BOLAND LIGHT RAILWAY, THE, 114
Forester, C. S., 150, 207, 244, 245
Fortescue, Hon. J. W. (Sir John Fortescue), 54–6, 66
Fortnum, Peggy, 34, 48, 71, 80, 95, 96, 130, 168, 267
FORTY-TWO STORIES (Hans Andersen), 72, 94
Foster, Marcia Lane, 194, 195, 290, 294, 309
FOUR MYSTERIES SOLVED BY NORMAN AND HENRY BONES, 268
FOUR PLUS BUNKLE, 96
FOUR TO FOURTEEN, 10, 18
FOUR-STOREY MISTAKE, THE, 291
FOX IN THE ISLAND, THE, 123, 129
FOXY-BOY, 151
Françoise, 20, 33
Freeman, Barbara, 94
Freeman, T. R. (Terence), 129, 131, 150, 193, 196, 268, 290
FRENCH LEGENDS, 96
FRENCHMAN'S SECRET, 194
FRIDAY'S TUNNEL, 263, 268
Friers, Rowland, 151
FROZEN PLANET, THE, 221
Fry, Rosalie, 47
Fuller, Roy, 210–12, 221
Furlong, Agnes, 308
FURTHER ADVENTURES OF NILS, THE, 114–5
FURTHER ADVENTURES OF THE FAMILY FROM ONE END STREET, THE, 286, 292
FURY, SON OF THE WILDS, 59, 65
FUTURE TOOK US, THE, 131

GABRIEL CHURCH-KITTEN, 66
GABRIEL CHURCH-KITTEN AND THE MOTHS, 66
Gàg, Wanda, 22, 33
Galdone, Paul, 65, 66
GALLOPING HOOFS, 65
Gannett, Ruth, 47
Garland, Henrietta, 32
Garland, Rosemary, 45, 49
Garner, Alan, 94
Garnett, Eve, 286, 292
Garnett, David, 250
Garnett, Henry, 242, 245
Garrard, Phyllis, 192
GATES OF BANNERDALE, THE, 303, 309
GAUNTLET, THE, 117, 126, 131
GAZE AT THE MOON, 183, 184, 194
Gekiere, Madeline, 21, 32

GENTLE FALCON, THE, 246
Gernat, Mary, 195
Gervis, Ruth, 195, 196, 268
Giguere, George, 223
Gill, Margery, 130, 245, 268, 291
GINGER PYE, 291
GIRL OF THE LIMBERLOST, A, 304–5, 309
GLASS SLIPPER, THE, 75, 94
Gleit, Maria, 268
Godden Rumer, 21, 33, 37, 47, 51, 66
GOLDEN HEN, THE, 96
GOLDEN IMPALA, THE, 151
GOLDEN KINGDOM, THE, 208, 221
GOLDEN LAND, A, 96
GOLDEN MONKEY, THE, 214, 222
GOLDEN OCEAN, THE, 240, 247
GOLDEN PAVEMENTS, 195
GOLDEN SHORE, THE, 126, 130
GOLDEN STALLION'S REVENGE, THE, 223
GOLDEN STALLION TO THE RESCUE, THE, 223
Goldsmith, Beatrice, 248
GONE-AWAY LAKE, 291
GOOD LUCK TO THE RIDER, 195
GOOD WIVES (see LITTLE WOMEN GOOD WIVES)
Goodall, J. S., 222
Gordon, Anne, 194
Gorsline, Douglas, 249
Gough, Philip, 96
GRAEME AND THE DRAGON, 78, 95
Graham, Eleanor, 273, 292
Grahame, Kenneth, 15, 17, 19, 52, 63–4, 68, 69
Gramatky, Hardy, 41, 47
GRANNIE'S WONDERFUL CHAIR, 78–9, 94
GRASS ROPE, A, 140–1, 151, 175
Graves, Ralph, 250
Graves, Richard, 221
Graves, Robert, 250
Gray, Elizabeth Janet, 245
Gray, Reginald, 222
GREAT GALE, THE, 278, 291
GREAT GEPPY, THE, 157, 169
GREAT IRON CHEST, THE, 74
GREAT NORTHERN? 294
Green, Peter, 64
Green, Roger Lancelyn, 10, 18, 95, 115, 226, 245
Greenall, Frances, 209, 221
Greene, Graham, 14, 19, 33
GREEN-COATED BOY, THE, 114
Greenaway, Kate, 21, 24, 33, 36
Grey, Zane, 197, 220, 223
GREY ADVENTURER, THE, 235, 248

DATE

"RESERVE"
Child Lit
DEC 15 '67
"RESERVE"
Child lit
"RESERVE"
Teaching
W.shop
JAN 30 1970
Jan 30
/5 Jan
4-26-71
Jan 9
10-13-73

GAYLORD